JAMES
CORDEN

May I Have Your Attention, Please?

THE AUTOBIOGRAPHY

JAMES
CORDEN

Mary I Have Your Attention, Please?

THE AUTOBIOGRAPHY

791. 45028

C
CENTURY · LONDON

Published by Century 2011

2 4 6 8 10 9 7 5 3 1

First published in Great Britain in 2011 by
Century
Random House, 20 Vauxhall Bridge Road,
London SW1V 2SA

www.randomhouse.co.uk

Addresses for companies within The Random House Group Limited
can be found at: www.randomhouse.co.uk

The Random House Group Limited Reg. No. 954009

A CIP catalogue record for this book
is available from the British Library

ISBN 9781846059353

The Random House Group Limited supports The Forest Stewardship Council (FSC®), the
leading international forest certification organisation. Our books carrying the FSC label are
printed on FSC® certified paper. FSC is the only forest certification scheme endorsed by
the leading environmental organisations, including Greenpeace. Our paper procurement
policy can be found at www.randomhouse.co.uk/environment

Typeset in ITC Giovanni by Palimpsest Book Production Ltd,
Falkirk, Stirlingshire

Printed and bound in Great Britain by
Clays Ltd, St Ives plc

This is for all the people who have helped and supported me along the way, whoever you may be. Truly, thank you.

INTRODUCTION

I've always thought that the first few lines of any book would be the hardest to write. Where do I start? How do I begin to tell you, someone I don't know, someone I've more than likely never met, about my life? My life? My story. How do I do this? I'm only thirty-two and, if I'm being completely honest, at least two of those thirty-two years were spent playing PlayStation and eating Crunchy Nut cornflakes. I could try and be clever and start in the middle and jump back and forth in time. Like *The Social Network*. Though that jumped between various courtrooms and depositions to Harvard University and the creation of a website that changed the way we socially interact. Mine would jump from my parents' front room to my bedroom and all that would have happened in between is I'd have grabbed a bag of Quavers.

I've just realised you may not have actually purchased this book and are doing what I do when buying a book and reading the first page to see if you like it. I'm guessing so far you're not overly impressed. If this is the case, let me start by saying that you look and indeed smell incredible today. Are those new shoes? No? New-ish? Well, they're a triumph. They really suit you. I tell you what, don't look now but, as you're reading this, everyone around you in the shop is checking you out and saying how hot you are. Seriously. There's something about you holding this book that really brings out the best in you. Now I come to mention it, you look slimmer holding this book.

The truth is, my head's a little all over the place today. Yesterday was Tuesday 22 March, and it's a day that will be etched in my memory for as long as I live. It was the day I became a father. My son weighed in at seven pounds eight ounces and it's by far the most amazing thing that's ever happened to me. He's a day old and so far seems like a good bloke, but as yet we don't know what to call him. He came a week early, and although that's brilliant, this was supposed to be my big week for writing this book. For really getting stuck in. So, with a heavy heart, I've left him and his mother sleeping peacefully at the hospital. There he lay, nestled in his mother's arms, his head pressed to her chest, and as I looked back at him, I wondered what he might remember as his earliest memory.

I remember mine clearly. I was four years old and it was so definitive it would shape the rest of my life. In a few days' time my family will be coming home from the hospital and a new phase of life will begin. A new chapter: experiences I can't even begin to contemplate. It feels like the right time to take stock of my old life, and that first memory feels like the right place to begin.

I have two sisters: Andrea, who is three years older than me, and Ruth, who is four years younger. My mum, Margaret, is a social worker and my dad, Malcolm, used to be a musician in the Royal Air Force, but is now a Christian book salesman. I know, it's not the most straightforward career path from being exceptionally good at saxophone, clarinet, flute and drums, and travelling the world with the Air Force to then suddenly selling the Bible and Christian worship CDs to little shops in the southeast. But the Church and Christianity were always a big part of my life growing up, even before Dad changed jobs. I say the Church, but to be more precise it was the Salvation Army. And it's here, at the Salvation Army in High Wycombe, where my first memory takes place.

It was my younger sister Ruth's christening. Our family were very involved in all aspects of church life. Mum was in the Songsters (basically, the choir), Dad played in the brass band (basically the . . . well, brass band) and both wore the Salvation Army uniform. A hideous black suit that looked a bit like a policeman's uniform. It was a Sunday morning service and the Salvation Army officer (basically the vicar or priest) had been talking for a couple of minutes when he asked our whole family to join him on the platform. I walked up holding Mum's hand and approached the altar where he was speaking. Dad handed Ruth over to the vicar and as a family we formed a semicircle round him. Except, because of the configuration of the altar and where we were standing, it meant I couldn't see Ruth being blessed at all. So the vicar grabbed a chair and said, 'Come on, James, come and stand on here so you can see.' I crawled up onto my knees and then up onto my feet, so that I was standing; and what I saw then, at that moment, changed something inside me for ever.

This may sound incredibly dramatic and hard for you to believe, for a memory to be this vivid or important at such a young age, but I promise you. I remember this as if it was yesterday. I stood on that chair and looked out towards the congregation and saw row after row of people staring back at me. There were probably about forty or fifty people in the congregation that day, but to my four-year-old self it looked like a sea of millions. The whole point of me being on that chair was to see Ruth being blessed and the Devil being renounced from her soul; but from the moment I saw people looking at me, I don't think I once looked at Ruth or what was happening on the platform. Because, in my eyes, this was no longer a platform. This was a stage.

I started to pull faces and dance my arms around and a ripple of 'ooh's and 'aah's from the people watching turned into giggles, and giggles turned into laughs as I bent over and looked back at them through my legs. The longer I carried on, the more people were looking at me instead of watching the christening take place. Even the people on the platform were giggling, as I was by now pretending to sing into a microphone. I don't know what happened to my insides up there, but they changed forever. This felt good. Really good. As the blessing came to an end, the vicar welcomed Ruth into the church and then turned to me, ruffled my hair and said, 'And thank you, young James. Quite the little performer.' Dad handed Ruth to Mum and tried to hold my hand as he replied to the vicar, 'Ha! Quite the little show-off more like.' The congregation started to laugh again, which I took as a signal to raise my hands triumphantly in the air and jump off the chair like it was a climbing frame, ignoring my dad's help. I landed on my feet to a healthy round of applause. As I stood there, looking out on the clapping audience, I realised – even at the age of four! – that this was the greatest feeling I had ever had. I walked down the steps back to my seat between Mum and Dad, smiling the biggest smile. It felt incredible. My whole body was tingling.

What was that? What just happened? I thought to myself. And as I sat down between Mum and Dad, staring at the back of the person in front of me, I instantly became bored. I'd had a fix of something incredible, and, in a flash, it was gone. From invincible to normal in a few seconds. In my head it became simple: if people are looking at me, and only me, it feels amazing. And that was that. From that moment forward, every day became a quest to be noticed. To have the attention of people. Of you.

INTRODUCTION TAKE 2

O K, phew. One chapter down. Does what I just wrote count as a chapter? It does, doesn't it? Hang on, should my chapters have titles? Isn't that what these sorts of books do? Title each chapter with something either profound or witty? I fear mine will be neither.

Hang on, let me ring Jack the publisher and ask him if the chapters should have names. Wait there . . .

. . . Answerphone. 'Hi, you've reached Jack . . .' Why do people say that on answerphone messages? 'Hi you've reached . . .' Clearly I haven't. The very reason you're recording this message is because I haven't reached you. I didn't leave a voice-mail. I'm hoping Jack will see a missed call from me and call straight back. He will, won't he?

I'm worried about this book.

What should I say or not say? What if you don't believe a word I've said? I'm only thinking this because I've read autobiographies before and found myself saying that. So far, everything I've told you happened actually did happen. The attention-seeking stuff at the christening, that's completely true. Even though I was only four years old, from that moment I knew exactly what I wanted to do. I wanted to entertain people, to act, sing, dance; everything and anything that would mean people would look at me and smile.

Teachers would say this to my mum and dad at parents' evenings and repeat it in my end-of-term report. The end-of-term report – always a horrible day for me in our house because I would spend most of the term coming home from school and lying to my parents about my academic achievements.

'How was your day at school, son?' Dad would ask.

'Oh, it was amazing, Dad. Mrs Aitkinson says I might get moved up a year because my maths work is so advanced,' or something equally preposterous would be my reply.

'Really?' Dad would say, astonished.

'Oh yeah, all the teachers have said that since the last parents' evening you went to, when they told you about how disruptive I'd been and you came home, shouted at me and threatened to send me to boarding school if I didn't improve, I've been much better and, get this, probably the best in my class.'

Dad would ruffle my hair, tell me how proud he was and let me have a Club biscuit or a Trio from the biscuit barrel. I would carry on with these lies all term, mostly because I saw how happy they made my dad. It felt silly to come home and say, 'Oh, Dad, I'm a nightmare. I know. I'm only ten, but I'm shit at school.'

All my lies would've been fine had it not been for the end-of-term report, and the horrible, gut-clenching truth it brought. At our school, everyone used to be given their reports ten minutes before the end of term. They'd be sealed in an envelope and would remain that way until your parents opened them at home.

Now, I'm going to let you in on a secret here, something I have never, ever confessed as long as I've been alive: I once – prepare yourselves – stole my own end-of-term report.

God, that feels good. To get that off my chest. I've been living this lie for twenty-two years. I stole it and I've been keeping this dirty secret for that whole time. How did I do it? you ask. OK, I'll tell you.

If this book was a film, this bit would be like *Ocean's Eleven* where you see exactly how the heist had taken place. If you can try and imagine that kind of music, y'no, a funky mix of brass and heavy bass. Except not in Vegas. No. In the Park County Middle School in a small, sleepy village outside High Wycombe.

I was ten years old and it was the last day of term. Everyone seemed in a good mood because we were breaking up for Easter. Normally a good thing, two weeks off school. Well, two weeks and two days, to be precise, as we had some teacher-training days stuck on the end. (Ah, teacher-training days – hands down the best phrase you'll ever hear at school. Well, that and frozen pipes. Both amount to the same thing: days off. Though frozen pipes edge it because they meant you'd probably get to go sledging instead of going to school. One year, at my secondary upper, our whole heating system got shut down because two pipes got smashed on the exact same day that three of the hardest fifth years had bought new sledges. An incredible coincidence? Sorry, I digress, let's get back to *Ocean's Eleven*, High Wycombe-style.) So I'm standing in the playground, a lone figure, my chubby frame stood stock-still in amongst the games of football and hopscotch off to my left and right. Everywhere I look, kids are having fun. Apart from me. In my eyes was fear: fear because this was school report day; extreme fear because the last school report day my dad shouted at me like never before. He shouted so much it made my mum cry.

He'd lost it because, at just ten years old, teachers were writing me off. Not completely – there were glimmers of hope – but on the whole they said I was too disruptive, too attention-seeking; basically, too much to teach. I knew I'd been a bit better this term, but I also knew I'd not been good enough.

The last parents' evening had been so bad that late one night I woke up to hear the unfamiliar sound of my parents arguing.

I walked out of my room and sat on the stairs in our humble semidetached, listening to Mum and Dad argue about me. It was a truly horrible thing to hear. Dad was repeatedly telling Mum that I'd fallen in with the wrong crowd of boys, that all the teachers said I was a bright kid, but that I was too lazy and needed a kick up the backside. In reply, Mum was saying that I was only ten and that I was a good kid, not a bully or an angry child, that this was a phase and it would pass. Their voices got louder and louder, the anger in both of them driving their opinions of what to do with this good-for-nothing child of theirs further and further apart.

It got so heated, with Mum's defence of me becoming ever more forceful, that in a real outburst, my dad said, 'Sometimes I wish I was your son. You can see the bad in me all the time, but never in him!'

Mum didn't say anything; she just tried to take in what Dad had said. Did she only see the bad in Dad? What was he saying about them, and their marriage? I sat on the stairs, hiding behind the coats on the banister, knowing that this argument was all my fault. My parents, the two people who I loved more than anything in the world, the people who I owed everything to, were arguing and being driven apart by me. I stayed on the stairs as Mum and Dad reached the silent part of the row. They were still arguing, make no mistake about that, but they were doing that silent arguing where you pretend to do something like tidy up the newspapers or take the tea and coffee cups out to the kitchen, but actually you've just put the argument on pause. (And whilst we're on pause, I should say that my parents rarely ever argued. That's why this was even more harrowing.)

After a while, Dad started to speak up, this time more measured. He said he was worried. Worried that if they, as parents, didn't act now, I could be a lost cause; that I needed a stricter routine to get the best out of me. And slowly but surely the volume of their voices began to rise.

'He's not a bad kid, Malcolm!' Mum shouted.

'Not yet! But if he carries on the way he's going, he will be!' Dad screamed back.

'What do you want to do then, Malc? Tell me. What's the answer?' Mum was sitting down on the sofa with her head in her hands. Dad went to the kitchen and returned with a brochure for an all-boys boarding school about ninety miles away from where we lived. Dad was a musician in the Royal Air Force, so he could send me to boarding school free of charge.

'I've looked into this and I think it might be the best option.' He handed it to Mum, who had a brief look and burst into tears.

'How could you even consider sending James to boarding school? Separate him from his sisters! How could we do that?' Mum said, aghast at the prospect.

Dad explained that he'd only picked up a prospectus, that nothing was fixed as yet, and that Mum should calm down. Then came Mum's final word, which encapsulated what had been festering for weeks and been on display for the last hour. She stood up, looked at Dad and, cool as ice, said, 'If you ever mention sending James to live away from us again, I will leave you. I will. I will pack my bags and take the three kids with me. I will not allow you to split up this family.' And with that, she left the room.

I couldn't sleep that night. I lay on my bed, staring at the ceiling, wondering how I'd caused such a mess. I wasn't that bad, was I? Or maybe I was. It was around this time I started to tell the aforementioned 'I'm the ideal pupil' lies to Dad. Yeah, that's right. Rather than actually improve at school, I chose to lie about it instead. I did try, honestly I did – hand on heart. I tried to be better at school, but showing off and being the class clown was like a drug to me. And an addictive drug at that.

Every day I'd walk to school and have a pep talk with myself about how I had to remember how much I'd upset my parents and just concentrate on my schoolwork. That would last about two hours and then I'd get bored and want to make the class laugh again. For precisely this reason, I knew that whatever was written in that school report wasn't going to be good. It might have been better than it had been last term, but it wouldn't be good enough. I couldn't bear the thought of upsetting Mum and Dad again, and the fact that I had been lying was only going to make it worse. Maybe my lying would be the final straw and Mum would agree with Dad and send me away to boarding school. There was only one thing for it: I had to get to that school report before they did.

So there I was, back in the middle of the playground, my heart beating, my brow covered in a sheen of sweat. (OK, I'm making this far more dramatic, but it's sort of true.) How was I going to do this? All of the school reports had to be signed by Mr Cox, the headmaster. He would read what the teachers had written and then write his final comments. Thinking fast, I walked off the playground and headed in the direction of his office.

Now, as a pupil, you couldn't get close to Mr Cox's office without a teacher or dinner lady asking what you were doing. What could I say? I needed an excuse, but nothing came to mind. I walked past the school hall, past the canteen and, before I knew it, there I was, outside his office. Mrs Quarterman the school secretary/nurse came over and said, 'Are you OK, James?'

What should I say? Think of an excuse, quick.

'Yes, thanks, miss.' Nice.

As she stood up to come over to me, I caught a glimpse of what could only be, could it, please God . . . yes! Behind her, on her desk, piles and piles of school reports. The motherload.

'Who are you looking for?' she asked.

'You, miss.' I blurted out. What did I say that for? Why the hell would I need to see Mrs Quarterman?

'Why? What's wrong?' she said innocently.

Think, man, think. Say something, anything!

'I've hurt my knee, miss.' There, that was that. It was the first thing that came to mind. I'd gone with the knee: a brave choice, though not completely stupid. Knees are funny things, especially on a growing kid, and I was almost certain Mrs Quarterman wasn't qualified enough to dismiss any of my symptoms.

'Well, come in and sit down.' I immediately fashioned a limp, and took a slight intake of breath whenever I put my weight on my right leg. 'Where does it hurt?' she asked as she began bending my knee slowly up and down. Now, the trick to faking any kind of injury is, whatever the nurse tries the first two times, whether that be prodding or pressing or bending, you have to say it's fine.

'Does that hurt?' he or she will ask, to which you say, 'No, not particularly.'

'What about if I do this? Any pain?' they'll ask, trying their second technique.

'No, not really,' you reply, seemingly as mystified by it as they are, and then – and this is the crucial part – whatever they try next, you yell in pain. It works every single time. Without question. Most people faking illness or injury have the whole thing worked out and think you have to be in extreme pain everywhere. That's the sign of a faker. A pro like me waits and makes his move at the right time.

'Aaarrgghhh!' I yelled, as Mrs Quarterman pressed her thumb against the back of my knee.

'Ooh, James, what have you done?'

'I don't know, miss. It just suddenly started really hurting.' She looked and tweaked and bent and prodded some more, and whenever she ventured near the back of my knee, I closed my eyes and winced a little. I didn't yell again. (Never yell twice, you don't want it to seem too severe. It's just got to be severe enough to make her think of possible remedies.)

'Have you got PE today?' she asked me.

'No, not today, miss,' I said in a standard unwell-type voice, though quite why my knee hurting would affect my voice is beyond me.

'OK, well, I think you're going to be OK. You've probably just pulled a muscle. Would it help if we put a Tubigrip on it?' I sat staring deep into Mrs Quarterman's eyes. I must have looked like a puppy that's about to be put down.

'If you think it'll help, miss.'

She stood up and headed towards the kitchen area, round the corner from where we were sitting. 'Janice, where are the Tubigrips?' she called out.

Out of my line of sight, Janice replied, 'Ooh, they're either under the sink or in the green locker next to the coat hooks.' And so, turning her back to me, Mrs Quarterman wandered round the corner towards the sink, leaving the reports unguarded.

This was it. My only chance. Now or never. I leapt up and started leafing through the reports. I presumed they'd be in alphabetical order, so mine would be near the top in the Cs, but no, dammit, they were in class blocks. My eyes were darting over other pupils' names; my brain registering information quicker than it ever had before; my fingers flicking faster and faster. But where was my report?

'They're not above the sink, Jan,' Mrs Quarterman shouted.

'Must be in the locker then,' Janice replied.

Time was running out. The names and reports kept coming thick and fast. Alan Wayman, Matthew Stopp – I was getting closer, surely: both of these guys were in my class . . .

'Found it!' shouted Mrs Quarterman. 'You're right, Jan, all the bandages are in the locker.'

Shit! She was on her way back. Mrs Quarterman shut the locker door and I could hear her footsteps getting nearer. I scrambled through a couple more reports, knowing that if I didn't see it, then that was it. I'd have failed my mission. Then suddenly, like a shaft of light in a dark tunnel, there it was. My name: James Corden.

I grabbed it and in one swift move shoved it down the back of my trousers. And there it stayed, nestled between my underpants and grey polyester slacks as Mrs Quarterman rolled the Tubigrip over my knee, until the bell rang for afternoon break.

I ran out past the playground and into the spinney, the small copse of trees between the school and the street I grew up on. Once I got myself a safe distance away from the school, I grabbed the report from my trousers and began digging a hole with my bare hands, so quickly that to anyone passing by I would have looked like a deranged psychopath burying the evidence. Remember, this was break time, so I only had ten minutes to hide the report.

Once I'd finished digging, my nails crusted brown and my knees all dirtied up, I threw it into the hole and covered it with mud and dry leaves and anything else to make it disappear. I pegged it back into the playground, put my muddy hands in my pockets and slowly started limping (just in case Mrs Q was watching me, y'no?) into the toilets next to the canteen. There, I got busy scrubbing my hands, rubbing them hard, as if I was trying to wash away the lie.

As the muddy water swirled down the sink, I was overcome by a huge pang of guilt. What had I done? Who was I? I looked in the mirror, my guilt-ridden face staring back at me, feeling like Bruce Willis in *Die Hard* – I'm not joking, I was honestly this dramatic as a ten-year-old – and I knew what I had to do.

I got back to class and stayed there, much quieter than usual, until about ten minutes from the end of the last lesson, when Janice came into the classroom with the pile of school reports from Mr Cox's office. There were twenty-five kids in our class, but I – and only I – knew that Janice was holding twenty-four reports.

Mrs Aitkinson took the reports and started walking in amongst us, handing them out. 'These envelopes are sealed and they shall remain sealed until one of your parents opens them, understood?' The class replied with a murmured 'Yes, miss.'

She walked past me three times. Back and forth, looking

down each time she passed. I was so nervous that I started to sweat. I knew that the only way I'd get away with it was by saying and doing absolutely nothing. I had to just ride this one out.

'James,' Mrs Aitkinson started, looking straight at me, 'I don't seem to have a report for you. Wait here.' She left the classroom, and I did nothing. Just sat stock-still, trying to keep myself together. One slipped word here could land me in more trouble than I'd ever known. A couple of minutes later, she came back into the classroom and checked over her desk, then left again. What was going on? Did they suspect anything? Did they know?

I could see the top of her head out of the window talking to Janice. A couple more minutes, then they both came into the classroom and looked on the floor, once more checking the desk, lifting things up and putting them back down, only to lift them up and put them down again. Then Mrs Quarterman came back into the class and the three of them had a private conversation by the blackboard.

By now, my palms were sweaty and my breath was getting shorter. All I was trying to do was look calm. I can't imagine I was succeeding. The clock was ticking nearer to 3.20 p.m.: home time.

Mrs Quarterman and Janice left the classroom, leaving Mrs Aitkinson to continue picking things up and hunting around on the floor. She asked the whole class to check the floor for a brown envelope, like the ones our reports were in. Then, just as the clock ticked past 3.18 p.m., in walks Mr Cox. The big dog.

He had a quiet word with Mrs Aitkinson, accompanied by a lot of head shaking and sighing. Then he turned to me and said, 'James.' I felt my whole face go red, felt my school tie strangle my neck. 'Are your mum or dad collecting you from school today?'

I tried to speak but no words would come. I coughed, cleared my throat and tried again. 'Er, no sir, I walk home. I only live over the road,' I said in as breezy a manner as I could muster.

'Right, well, we have a slight problem with your report. You'll have to get yours when we come back after Easter. I'll notify your parents and apologise to them.'

Whoa, whoa, whoa. Wait. Was that it? No great inquest? No putting me on the stand? No examination and cross-examination of my whereabouts? No looking through my bag? Nothing? That was all he had? Nothing? Weird.

Three twenty p.m. came, the school bell rang and that was that; I walked out of the school gates like Tim Robbins in *The Shawshank Redemption*. Well, sort of – I was wearing my own shoes. (I was also guilty as hell, but you know what I mean.)

As I walked in through the back door of our house, Mr Cox was leaving a message on our answerphone, saying there had been a mishap with my report and he'd get to the bottom of it over the break. I was completely in the clear. By the time the Easter holidays were over, Mum and Dad had forgotten all about my school report. When we returned in the new term, Mr Cox issued me with a brand-new report, which, as I'm sure you can guess, never saw the light of day. I put it in my bag, and when I got home I stuffed it behind the boiler in our airing cupboard. My parents have never seen it. Well . . . until now. Because here, in all its glory, is the very school report that was hidden in our house for eighteen years until I moved out.

Everything I was like as a ten-year-old is here in this very book. Mum and Dad, I'm so sorry I kept it from you, and I'm truly sorry I was the reason for so many of your rows. You were and are the most wonderful parents I could ever ask for. So loving and caring and you only ever put the three of us (me and my two sisters) first. I am so proud to be your son and love you both very, very much. I'm sorry I hid this from you.

CLASS ..... 3 B

SUBJECT	REMARKS
ENGLISH	James tends to be rather too easy-going in his attitude to English work, he is careless with grammar, spelling and comprehension work and his Test stories are far too brief and tend to be somewhat silly showing a lack of effort. His spoken vocabulary is better than his understanding and comprehension skills.
Grade D-	
READING	James reads very well with a lot of expression and he has quite a good vocabulary.
MATHS	James has not covered enough material and as a result he has had disappointing test results. He has made an effort at times but son loses this enthusiasm. He does find a lot of the work difficult, but if he paid more attention to instructions and advice and set his work out more carefully he would have fewer problems.
March Test Grade D+	
ART & CRAFT	James tends to rush his art but he can produce some good work.
P.E. & GAMES	James enjoys sports and is a keen competitor.
SCIENCE	This work is capable of some good work but there is not always enough care or detail.
SOCIAL STUDIES	James is capable of some good work but much work is left unfinished. His individual topics show a lazy attitude to the work.

GENERAL REMARKS:- James' biggest problem remains his lazy attitude to work. He does not put in enough effort into his work and so has not made enough progress, particularly in maths. He is capable of producing a lot more work than he does, despite the fact that he does find much of the work difficult. Unless his attitude changes he will continue to fall behind. He must start to pay more attention to his school work, and less to his clowning and showing off. He does read very well and shows an aptitude for dramatic activities.

Class Teacher's Signature ....

All the above I have to conclude.

I am not sure I would wish to change James' unique attitude to everyday situations — his greatest asset is his humour, his home dishonity and musical ability but he should try to achieve a little more with success.

"normal school success"

Headmaster's Remarks ....

.... Parent Signature

Parent's Signature

OK, Jack the publisher just called back and said I don't have to have chapter titles, but that it is advised. So I've decided not to have titles as such. More kind of chapter profiles, with some lifestyle suggestions to make the book more enjoyable. Or perhaps just bearable! I shall recommend a soundtrack for each chapter, a snack and a movie choice. Though I accept that reading a book and watching a film are probably mutually exclusive. But it's your call. Try them together or separately; it's totally up to you.

CHAPTER 1

BEST MUSICAL ACCOMPANIMENT:
'Silent Night'

BEST FILM TO WATCH ALONGSIDE:
Nativity

BEST ENJOYED WITH:
a warm mince pie

I was born on 22 August 1978. My full name is James Kimberley Corden. It's OK, you can go ahead and laugh. Kimberley. I mean, seriously. It's basically a family tradition. I know nothing more than that. My dad is called Malcolm Kimberley Corden, his dad has the middle name of Kimberley and his dad had it. And on it goes. It was a horrible name to have at school. Awful. When you're at school, anything that sets you apart, whether it be a name, an accent or even your hair colour, is an invitation for ridicule. It's always been the case that the first son in our family will carry the middle name Kimberley. At the moment, as it stands, I don't know whether my one-day-old son will have it too. My dad would love it and it would, I'm sure, mean the world to my grandad. But can I really subject my son to the same name-calling that I suffered? Who knows? We've not got a first name for him yet.

We lived for the majority of our family life in a small village called Hazlemere, just outside the town of High Wycombe. My parents still live there and, whenever I go back, every street corner is full of different memories. I say 'street' corner – it was hardly the ghetto, more like one big housing estate with a small parade of shops, a doctor's surgery, a vet's and a chip shop. It was a wonderful place to grow up.

It's only now I realise how painfully ordinary High Wycombe is as a town. It's grey, plain and its big selling point is that it has a chair museum. Before we moved to Hazlemere we lived on Walton Drive, which is a bit nearer Wycombe town centre, and before that we briefly lived on a military base in Uxbridge. If Walton Drive sounds familiar to you in any way at all, it may be because some terrorists were arrested during a raid there a couple of years ago; they'd been planning on bringing down various aeroplanes around the world. Literally two doors down from our old house.

My mum has a habit of adding personal drama to situations simply because we may have been somewhere once. 'Can you believe it?' she said at the time. 'Terrorists, two doors down from our house.'

'But it's not our house, is it, Marg?' Dad corrected. 'It was, twenty-seven years ago. That's quite a lot of time that's passed since we lived there.'

'Still,' Mum said. 'Makes you think, doesn't it?'

I never realised the sacrifices Mum and Dad made for us growing up. Dad played saxophone in the RAF band and so he and his young family were allowed to live for free on the military base. Pretty much all of the other musicians in the Force lived there, but Dad's never been one to follow the crowd. He decided quite early on that he didn't want us growing up on the base and then stuck to it adamantly. He wanted us to experience different people from different backgrounds, instead of living in what I think he saw as the very insular, blinkered and barricaded life on a Royal Air Force base.

Living off base meant finding the money to buy their own house, so Mum and Dad scrimped and saved to try and make it work. Dad worked all over the shop, teaching clarinet and saxophone to local kids in the back rooms of our house or at local schools. But when it came to the crunch and they needed to find money for a deposit, there still wasn't enough there. So Dad sold the one thing he owned of value – his beloved saxophone. It meant he would have to use one of the ones in the band room, which he hated doing. But he did it, for us.

Mum told me a few years ago that when we moved a second time, from Walton Drive to Hazlemere, when my little sister Ruth was born, they looked at their finances and realised they had £25 a week more going out of their account than they had coming in. When you're young, you don't really take these things on board – it's just life as you know it.

We would holiday in a borrowed caravan at a farm in Devon. Sounds quite romantic, doesn't it? A Devon farm. Conjures up images of something out of *Lark Rise to Candleford*. The farmer, with his big bushy beard, wandering around aimlessly, chewing on a piece of corn. The farmer's wife, filling the air with the scent of her freshly baked bread as she waves the free-range geese out of the back door of the thatched cottage. Well, I can officially tell you that the farm we holidayed at was nothing like this. The nicest and most polite way I can describe it to you is that it was, frankly, a shit hole. A half-brick, half-corrugated-iron building set in the middle of a muddy wasteland, with a nine-by-five-foot concrete swimming pool that was filled with cold hose water. How's about that for romantic?

One year we went, there was another family camping on the site. Dad got talking with the dad of the other family and it turned out that they weren't on holiday as such; they were living on the site. For ever. I keep expecting them to turn up on a Channel 4 documentary when the daughter gets married.

But however much I'm doing it down, I have to say that I remember those family holidays so fondly. Sitting in the caravan playing cards while the rain poured down outside, swimming in the ice-cold pool, cycling around the muddy countryside – believe it or not, they were happy times. I guess we were a fairly ordinary family, though I'm not sure 'ordinary' actually exists when it comes to families. No family is ordinary. But when it's your own and it's the only one you know, everything feels very natural, like life couldn't be lived any other way. I grew up thinking that nothing we did as a family was particularly different; it's only now that I realise quite how different it was.

You see, every single Sunday we would wake up, put on uniforms, go to church in Wycombe town centre and march through the streets playing brass instruments. I know. And I thought this was completely normal. We didn't do it for our own amusement; we were all fully signed-up members of the Salvation Army. Mum grew up in a Salvation Army family, and when she met Dad and they fell in love, Dad found God and joined the Army too.

The Salvation Army is a wonderful yet complicated organisation. First and foremost it's a church, but it's also a charity that helps many people in need around the world. The whole uniform-wearing thing came about because its founder, a man called William Booth, wanted it to stand out from other churches and look and feel like a new movement.

So that's what we'd do, as a family, every Sunday. Mum and Dad made it clear that we had to go until we were sixteen and then we could make our own choices. I have both great affection and also contempt for our time as Salvationists. I made some of my best friends there at various music and drama weeks in the school holidays; three guys in particular: Jason, Anthony and Gavin. So close were the friendships I formed then that they still remain a big part of my life today, and one of the afore-mentioned three would go on to have a title role in a television programme I'd write many years later. I wonder if you can guess which one?

So, in many respects, I have a lot to thank the Army for, and all of the important things I learnt whilst in Sunday school or in various worship groups have been beneficial to me in one way or another as I grew up. However, it's only now, with hindsight, that I can look back and recognise that some of the people who were part of our church were hypocrites and fakes. So many of the people within that building every Sunday, praying and playing in the brass band, were pretty much some of the least Christian people I've ever met.

Going to church every week certainly doesn't make you a Christian, in the same way that *not* going to church every week doesn't stop you being a Christian. All I'm saying is, religion and the Church couldn't be more different. A religion is about faith, a hunch if you like. Whereas the Church is both formed by and made up of people – and when people get involved in organising anything, they will make mistakes. If those people happen to be idiots, as many were at the Salvation Army in High Wycombe, you end up with a mess of a place masquerading as something it most definitely isn't. It's a bit like FIFA.

Sundays were a nightmare: three services – morning, after-noon and evening – with a rushed roast dinner and a march in between. I vividly remember the frantic journeys back and forth into town with Dad picking up various old ladies who needed a lift to get to the afternoon and evening services. It was the complete opposite of the Commodores song 'Easy'. But, I suppose, it was a big part of what brought our family together and what made it such a close-knit group.

I've always been incredibly grateful for the loving and supportive family I grew up in. We were and are still incredibly close. In many ways I feel closer to my two sisters now than I ever have. Andrea, being the eldest, was the responsible one, and often put in charge of looking after me and our younger sister Ruth whilst Mum and Dad were at work. She's now a terrific mum looking after two children of her own, Joel and Ellen, who I'm sure are easier to look after than Rudi and I were. (Who's Rudi? I hear you ask. OK, this could be confusing, so we might as well get it out of the way now. Her whole life my little sister Ruth has rarely been referred to as Ruth. In fact, I imagine the last time she was officially called Ruth was on the platform during her christening. On the whole she's called Rudi, and that's how I'll refer to her in the book. It's what we call her the most, but over the past few years she's been named: Muller, Rudi-Muller, Reeyads, the Vamulle, Gbronehead, Sabina, Gbronio . . . There are plenty more but I figure you get the point.)

I'd like to say now that Andrea and Rudi are without question two of the best people I've ever met. They are funny, bright, caring and incredibly supportive. In many ways I would go so far as to say that when it comes to performing, whether it be acting or singing or anything else (but maybe not dancing), they are probably more gifted than I am and ever will be. Andrea has an incredible singing voice and Rudi is one of the funniest people you could ever have round a dinner table. But I guess what sets me and them apart is desire.

I have this need – a burning ambition – to be in the spotlight, whereas with Andrea and Rudi it's something they can take or leave. For me, growing up, it was as vital as oxygen. Many hours of many days were spent dreaming of stardom; ridiculous things like taking the final bow on the West End stage or writing my life story at a crazily young age like thirty-two! Andrea and Ruth didn't need it. They have enjoyed the limelight at different times, but it's not something they crave.

I've often wondered why it is that I do what I do. Why I have this lust for people to pay me attention? And why they, two very talented people in their own right, are happy without it? The strange thing is that pretty much every aspect of fame has changed since I was a kid. When I was young, saying you wanted to be famous wasn't what it is now. These days, fame is seen as a dirty word, and the world seems fuller than ever of people who are famous for doing nothing.

That wasn't what I was dreaming of. My dream was always to be an actor, and I knew that if I ever did become famous, it would be because I'd done something memorable – played a part so well that people would talk about it, and want to talk to others about it. Fame was a by-product of having done something.

Ever since Rudi's christening, I had been first in line to put myself forward for any kind of chance to perform in front of an audience. The first one that really sticks out comes when I was seven years old. It was the Christmas of 1985, and my Sunday school was casting the nativity play. I, of course, wanted to play Joseph. Joseph is the part you want in the nativity. No doubt about it. He's front and centre for the whole ten-minute production. It takes a seven-year-old actor of great skill and deep emotional truth to really convince the audience that he's a middle-aged man taking his pregnant wife to Bethlehem for the census.

But I wasn't chosen to play Joseph. No. Matthew Peddle was chosen to play Joseph. As you can imagine, this was a kick in the teeth for me as a young, up-and-coming seven-year-old, but I did understand why Hazel, the casting director/Sunday school teacher chose Matthew. He was ten – three years older than me – and I couldn't argue with the fact that Joseph himself was probably older than both of us, so going with the older boy seemed fair. I stepped aside, and immediately set my sights on the next best part.

The only problem was, I didn't know what the other best parts in the nativity were. I knew about the shepherds, the three wise men and a few animals, but I knew I needed more info if I was going to beat my two main rivals: Spencer Wells and Barry Dobson. They would also be sniffing around the best parts and, like Matthew, were older than me too. Maybe we could be the three wise men? Hmmmm, I didn't mind being a wise man, but I knew if it was between me, Spencer and Barry, I would be the least important wise man. You know, the one carrying a box of Terry's All Gold chocolates with the words 'Terry's' and 'All' scribbled out with a black felt tip. I'd take a wise man, but it wasn't ideal. But it's better than being a shepherd, definitely. You don't want to be a shepherd. No way. That's the last thing you want. If you're a shepherd, you're basically set-dressing: a seven-year-old boy wearing an old dressing gown, a tea towel on your head, holding – if you're lucky – a toy lamb and a big stick. I had my limits. How could I find out for sure what the best parts were in the nativity? Where else would a seven-year-old turn? His mum.

So, travelling home from Sunday school with Mum, I put the question to her:

'Mum, in the nativity, who was there in the stable?'

Mum thought for a while and then said, 'Well, you've got Joseph and Mary, baby Jesus, the three wise men, the shepherds . . .' She went on and told me about the characters I already knew.

'But what about other people? Was there no one else there?' I asked.

'I'm not sure, James. Why do you want to know so much?' I couldn't tell her. She might think it was silly to want a part so desperately. We drove in silence for a while before Mum turned to me and said, 'If you think about the Christmas carols, they'll tell you all the people involved.'

I pondered this for a second. *Yes!* She was absolutely right. The Christmas carols! That's how I'd find out what the best parts were. I started singing 'Once in Royal David's City' in my head, but there aren't many characters there of any real note. 'O Little Town of Bethlehem' isn't so much about the characters, it's more about the – you guessed it – little town of Bethlehem. Then I happened upon the perfect song, 'Silent Night'. I started reciting the lyrics in my head. And then it happened . . . Bang! I knew the part I wanted to play, a part I could call and make my own. Not some guy holding gold or frankincense; a real part; a character who was there throughout, who would, if I played my cards right, steal the show. I kept the name of the character secret all week. I couldn't wait to see Spencer's or Barry's face when I pulled this peach of a role out of the bag.

Sunday came around and, after the first part of the Sunday morning church service had taken place, us sixteen or seventeen kids made our way to Sunday school in the junior hall. Once there, we sat around in a circle on the floor and our teacher, Hazel, led us in prayers. I pressed my palms together, shut my eyes but, instead of following what was being said, made my own silent prayer that no one else would steal the part I had my heart set on.

'Amen,' went the chorus of young and unbroken voices. Hazel, or Auntie Hazel as we called her, for reasons I've never been quite certain of, started to speak. 'OK, listen up kids, everyone? Everyone, please? Simmer down. From now on and for the next three weeks we're going to rehearse the nativity for the carol concert. We've got a list here of who is going to play who. Matthew Peddle, you will be Joseph, Hayley Dobson will be Mary—'

Before she could get any further with the list I raised my hand and shouted out, 'Erm, Auntie Hazel, I already know which part I'd like to play.' Silence fell in the room. I looked over at Spencer and Barry and gave them a knowing smile.

'OK James, we did have you down as innkeeper number one . . .' Innkeeper number one?! INNKEEPER NUMBER *ONE*??!! He's not even the best of the innkeepers. If you're gonna play an innkeeper, you want to be innkeeper number three. The one who has no room at the inn but takes pity on Mary and Joseph and gives them the stable to sleep in. Innkeeper number one is the worst of the innkeepers – he literally doesn't give a shit. He's happy his rooms are full and, as far as he's concerned, Mary and Joseph should've booked online if they wanted a room (and while we're on the subject, it is sort of ridiculous that with his uncon-summated wife pregnant, Joseph didn't try and book anywhere for the pair of them to stay).

Auntie Hazel continued, 'We have already worked out who's playing who, James. It's not—'

I interrupted Auntie Hazel and rose to my feet, pleading with her. 'I know which part I'd like to play, though. I've been thinking about it all week.'

'OK, James, which part would you like to play?' Hazel said with a sigh.

I took a pace forward and said in the most confident voice I could find, 'I'd like to play Round John Virgin.'

'Who?' said Auntie Hazel.

'Round John Virgin. That's the part I'd like to play.' Spencer Wells started to snigger, as did a couple of the other kids.

'I'm sorry, James, I have absolutely no idea what you're talking about.'

I could feel the heat turn up in the room, the sniggers begin to build into full-on giggles.

'You know, from "Silent Night"?' I then made the huge mistake of trying to sing in front of everyone.

'"Silent night, holy night. All is calm, all is bright . . ."' Then to emphasise who my character was I said the man's name extra loud. '"**ROUND JOHN VIRGIN**, mother and child. Holy infant so tender and mild . . ."' But it was too late. I couldn't sing any more because my voice couldn't be heard over the laughter. Even the adults were trying to contain themselves. I felt so embarrassed; I just wanted the ground to eat me up. The correct lyric is of course 'Round yon virgin, mother and child'. I'd got so excited because I'd thought the character of Round John Virgin was so central to the plot, he would spend most of the play standing in front of Joseph.

Once the room had calmed down, I was told I would be playing innkeeper number one. Which I did to the best of my ability. I really did. I shook my head in that doorway like my life depended on it. But not even Matthew Peddle's Joseph got the praise that day. No, the star of the show was a three-year-old shepherd called Jeanette who managed to upstage everyone by blurting out that she needed a wee just as the wise men arrived. Perfect improvisation if you ask me.

My experience at the nativity play only made me more desperate to get up in front of people and perform and, as I turned eight, I wondered when my next chance would come. Luckily, I didn't have to wait long, and my next appearance on stage was about to change everything.

CHAPTER 2

BEST MUSICAL ACCOMPANIMENT:
'Do-Re-Mi' by Rodgers and Hammerstein

BEST FILM TO WATCH ALONGSIDE:
Three Men and a Little Lady

BEST ENJOYED WITH:
a tasty bus ticket

For the first time ever, our headmaster Mr Cox decided that the Park County Middle School was to put on a summer concert. Children from each year would showcase various talents, and each class would perform a song or dance number too. Our class went for a song called 'I Wear a Red Sombrero'. It's one hell of a tune – I'm still waiting for it to pop up on *The X Factor* – but, for the performance, I was put on the back row in a poncho and sombrero, and stood in between Richard Cleeves and my oldest friend, Richard Shed. (He's still a friend now is Sheddy and the table I am sitting at this very moment in my kitchen was made and designed by him.) As much fun as it was doing the song, and it was a lot of fun:

> *I wear a red sombrero.*
> *It is a big sombrero.*
> *I only wear it*
> *Because the sunshine*
> *Gets in my eyes and I cannot seeeeeeeee at all . . .*

I wanted to be able to do something on my own. Luckily, one of my teachers came to the rescue and told me that I'd be reciting a poem called 'Nibble-Nibble, Munch-Munch'. It was an incredible poem. I mean, it's not up there with Auden or anything, but for an eight-year-old at a school summer concert it was the best possible thing to be reading. It was all about a guy on a bus who is so hungry that he eats his bus ticket. Throughout the poem he would eat the ticket at various points and then, when finally the bus conductor comes round, he gets thrown off the bus for not having a ticket:

> *Nibble-nibble, munch-munch, nibble-nibble munch.*
> *Nibble-nibble, munch-munch, a bus ticket for lunch . . .*

I loved performing it. It was both fun and funny – always a good mix – and for that one beautiful night in the school hall, it brought the house down. The reaction was so good that the next day, one of the mums who lived over the road from us, Sonia, suggested to Dad that he try and get me in to the Jackie Palmer Stage School. It was an after-school dance and drama club with an affiliated professional agency that would send kids to auditions.

We already knew all of this because Sonia's daughter had been going there for a while. Her name was Laura Sadler. I knew Laura really well; she was two years younger than me but she was the star pupil at Jackie Palmer's. She had been going to the school for what seemed like ages and kept on turning up on television, so to someone like me who was dreaming of making it, she was an amazing person to have around.

She was always working. One minute she'd be in a fish fingers advert, the next she'd be in *Children's Ward* or *Inspector Morse*. She went on to make films with Julie Walters and play a regular in *Holby City* until, tragically, she passed away in 2003 at the horribly young age of twenty-two. She fell from a balcony in the early hours of the morning and never recovered. It became a big story at the time and dominated a lot of the front pages, with much of the accompanying speculation being completely unfounded. What I felt was never focused on enough at the time was what an incredible actress she was. There is not a doubt in my mind that if Laura was still with us today, she would be lighting up stages and screens all over the world. She was the sweetest, kindest soul, and growing up over the road from her, and being able to watch someone who was working in so many wonderful and varied things, made me believe that all my dreams were possible. She gave me hope that extraordinary things *could* happen to people from our ordinary little town. Without Laura or her wonderful mother, Sonia, I wonder if my life would've panned out the way it has. Sonia putting a word in with the board at Jackie Palmer's had a massive effect in terms of what I'm doing now and as I've become more successful in the last few years, I've often thought about Laura. In some small way a part of me has always thought that maybe I was doing it for both of us.

Andrea, Rudi and I all joined Jackie Palmer's at the same time. I was nine years old and stayed there until I was seventeen, whereas Rudi and Andrea didn't last past the first two terms. The afternoon tap classes, filled with pushy mums and screaming stage-school brats, weren't for them. They weren't really for me, either, and to be completely honest I didn't make many friends for a long time; but I didn't mind – I just loved being in those drama classes.

Auditions became a fact of life; getting a part in a show was the reason I was there, after all. It's what Laura did all the time and she'd got dozens of jobs. I got so into it that I reached the point where I would be auditioning for something every week, sometimes three or four times a week. It was Dad who always took me along to them. But although Laura and lots of the other kids at the stage school were getting jobs, no matter how many auditions I went to, no matter how hard I tried, I just couldn't seem to make the breakthrough.

My dad actually remembers that time better than I do. I was a young kid and none of it has really stuck in my memory, probably because I didn't want it to. But for Dad, to have to watch his son being turned down again and again and again must have affected and wounded him far more deeply than it did me.

There was one particular audition at the Sadler's Wells theatre he talks about, where I was going for the part of one of the von Trapp children in *The Sound of Music*. I was twelve then, but I've always looked younger than I am and I was going for a much younger part. Theatre directors often like older kids who look young because they're more mature and can take direction a bit more easily. A group of about seventy kids had been called back for a second audition and it was a very big deal for me because Christopher Cazenove (the puffed-up English guy in *Three Men and a Little Lady*) was playing Captain von Trapp. I loved *Three Men and a Little Lady*. Who didn't? Rudi and I used to watch it all the time. That and *Grease* were our favourites. So for me, the thought of playing alongside him on stage as one of his children was really exciting.

The kids were split into pools of ten, with two boys or girls from each pool being selected to play one of the children in alternate performances. The director kicked it off by having us sing 'Do-Re-Mi'. We would start together, then he would point at one of us, everyone else would stop and that child would carry on by themselves. He pointed to me just as we hit the line 'Sew, a needle pulling thread . . .' and I went for it, I sang my heart out. To this day, I wonder if anyone has sung that line with more determination.

While I was in there singing, Dad was with the other parents outside, waiting. And he hated it; he couldn't stand the way everyone would go on and on about their skiing holidays or how they couldn't get all their stuff into their estate car so they'd had to buy a bigger one.

They were living in such a different world to ours. With me going to Jackie Palmer's twice a week, the financial strain on Mum and Dad was massive, so he didn't have a huge amount of time for small estates and too much snow and all the other crap the other parents were moaning about. Taking me to one side in between auditions, he said, 'Look, James, if it's OK with you, I'm going to wait in the car. It's just outside the stage door, though, so I'm not far away, all right?'

'Yeah,' I said. 'That's fine, Dad. But are you OK?'

'Yes, I'm great, mate,' he said, smiling. 'It's just that . . .' He looked past my shoulder to a couple of mums and rolled his eyes as one of them proudly announced that her darling Anastasia was down to the last two for some advert for paint stripper.

'Fair enough,' I said, and told him I'd see him afterwards.

This was *The Sound of Music* and, standing there in the dusty corridor, nervously waiting around to be called, I couldn't help but dream about playing to a packed theatre, listening to the applause, taking the bow at the finale. I'd been singing these songs all day, getting myself psyched up, and as far as I was concerned there was nothing else in the entire world at that moment except *the part*.

Decision time came, and while the director and his assistants deliberated, I stood outside the rehearsal room on my own. With my throat dry from hitting the high notes, I was trying to shove a straw through the hole in a Capri-Sun sachet that Dad had bought me while he was waiting down in the car chewing his nails. For three years we'd been doing this, audition after audition, part after part. I'd never been selected.

I made it through every single cut that day. At the end of every audition round, they would call out the names of the kids who could leave; if you were asked to stay, you were still in with a chance of landing the part. It got to a point when there were just three of us left. Three boys and two parts.

Finishing my Capri-Sun, I walked back into the room, shaking like a leaf. We all lined up – thirteen of us, ten girls and us three boys – and the casting director started reading out the names of the unlucky ones who hadn't made it. It was the girls' turn first and, as the names came, it was hard not to feel sorry for the ones sloping off the stage; a couple of them burst into tears. After about four or five names, she hadn't yet got to the boys and I was amazed to be still standing there, fingers crossed behind my back, hoping. And then it came, the words I'd been longing not to hear: 'and James Corden. Thank you very much, everyone, you've been great.'

My shoulders sank and once again the cloud of disappointment descended. Meanwhile, the two boys who had been chosen were leaping around and punching the air as if they'd just lost their virginity. Their mums had run in from where they were listening at the door and were hugging them, all whooping and yelping, while I just ambled out of the rehearsal room. Dad was at the bottom of the stairs waiting for me, and I remember walking down feeling the weight of it all once again. I didn't burst into tears or anything; there was no great drama. I just felt disappointed. I could hear the cacophony of noise still coming from the room above, the director's voice lifting above it all. 'We start in three weeks,' he was saying. 'We're going to have the best time. It's really going to be just amazing.'

As we got in the car, Dad sat there with the engine switched off for a moment and then, finally, looked round at me. 'James,' he said with a sigh, 'try not to worry about it. What will be, will be – that's the way life is. You've just got to learn from it like all the others. You did so well to get to this stage, you . . .' His voice just petered away. We'd had these chats before. He'd tried to pick me up after previous letdowns but, today, there was something in his tone that I hadn't heard before: a sort of weariness and resignation.

'Why don't you just knock it on the head?' he suggested. 'I don't mean stop going to the lessons or anything, but these auditions. I'm so fed up of seeing you this disappointed all the time. You don't even have to go to Jackie Palmer's any more if you don't want. There's all sorts of stuff you can do: amateur dramatics, local youth theatre. Why don't you just knock the auditions on the head and call it a day?'

For a long moment I continued to stare out of the windscreen. And then I shook my head. 'I can't do that, Dad,' I said. 'It's what I've got to do.'

Being a professional actor is all about rejection. Rejection is – ultimately – what separates a professional from an amateur. If you're an amateur actor taking part in your local theatre company, what you're doing isn't that different from rehearsing and performing in a professional show. Sure, the sets may be bigger and the tickets more expensive, but the detail and effort you put in to playing your part isn't all that different to what anyone in the West End does. The real difference is that some of those people in the West End have been rejected hundreds of times before getting there. I realised quite early on that I wasn't going to be one of those people who are handed everything at the first ask.

I don't really remember that conversation with Dad. He reminded me of it when I told him I'd be writing about that part of my life. I wonder if he remembers it so well because it was at that moment he realised how serious I was about making it. How, no matter what happened, I wasn't going to give up.

Driving home back down the A40 that evening, I would forget about *The Sound of Music* and start to daydream once more of the other ways I could perform. And it was around that time that I came to learn a lesson that's kind of been with me ever since. If it wasn't going to happen for me through auditioning or other people looking out for me, then I was going to have to go out and make it happen myself, in whatever way I could. So, over the next two years, I got myself on television (well, my voice at least), got my first job and decided a new career path was the way to get myself noticed. I was going to form my first band.

CHAPTER 3

BEST MUSICAL ACCOMPANIMENT:
'Pray' by Take That

BEST FILM TO WATCH ALONGSIDE:
Almost Famous

BEST ENJOYED WITH:
large popcorn

I was thirteen now and, after the complete non-shock of failing my 12+, I had joined Holmer Green Upper School. It was the school my sister Andrea went to, and she was two years above me. It was a pretty ordinary school about a mile, or a fifteen-minute walk, from our house. Most of my friends from middle school came along with me, so it didn't feel that different. The good news was that there were lots of new girls, and girls had recently become much more interesting to me.

It felt as if, having broken up for the summer holidays, by the end of those six weeks, everything I cared about had changed. It was as though girls suddenly came into focus. They'd always been there – sort of blurred out by Panini stickers or games of headers and volleys – but now, as I entered upper school, they were all I could see. They were amazing. Girls like Nina Woods or Beth Goody or Claire Wyatt, all of them became the objects of my desire. (I wasn't picky.) I took down my West Ham posters and replaced them with pictures of Elle Macpherson or Cindy Crawford. From now on, life was all about getting girls.

The only problem is, if you look like me, girls don't really feel the same way. I didn't seem to have the same effect on them as they had on me. This was distressing, to say the least. Even though I so desperately wanted to be, I was never going to be the guy that girls fought over. I have honestly lost count of the number of times I've heard the phrase 'I like you, but as a friend.' So I needed to find a way to make myself more attractive to girls. I realised quite quickly that being funny was something girls warmed to; they liked being around someone who would make them laugh, but most of my jokes would have me as the butt and, as much as this worked (I had a couple of snogs and fumbles here and there), it wasn't going to push me into stud mode, and it was stud mode that I was after.

One day I was walking through the assembly hall when I saw a guy from the year above playing the piano. He was brilliant. His name was Matt Lanchester, but he was known to some of the school as 'Database'. This was on account of him being a bit of a computer whizz-kid. I stood at the other end of the hall and listened as he played the most beautiful music, gobsmacked by how good he was. I walked nearer to where he was sitting and, as I did, a plan dawned on me, a perfect plan to secure stud credentials – we could form a band! I didn't know it at the time, but I had happened across one of life's great truths: it doesn't matter what you look like, if you're in a band, girls will always fancy you.

I asked Matt what he was playing and he told me it was Queen. (I later found out that Matt is *the* biggest Queen fan on earth, a true super-fan, and so it was Queen who would form the bedrock of our new band's back catalogue.) I then asked Matt whether he was up for the challenge of being the first multi-platinum-selling band Holmer Green Upper had ever produced and, kind of weirded out, he said, 'Why not?' So, with the two of us on board, we set about finding our other members.

Matt told me about a friend of his called Richard Morris who played drums. We spoke to him and he was in. So we had Matt on keyboards, Richard on drums and me on vocals. Now I know what you're thinking. What we need now – especially if we're going to do Queen songs – is a lead guitar and bass. I mean, definitely a bass. You really can't form a band without a bass, can you? Well, you can, and we did. We recruited one other member of the band and that was Paul Chalwin, who would also be on vocals. Yeah, that's right. We were the first ever two-vocalist, keyboard and drum combo. And let me tell you this: we loved it.

Every lunch hour would be spent rehearsing. It was great; we thought 'we' were great. Before long we imagined record companies knocking on our door and so we decided we'd better come up with a name for the band. We took this very seriously. This name was going to be on album sleeves and tour posters, possibly around the world, and so it had to send out the right message. Before long we decided on a name.

We called ourselves . . .

Wait for it . . .

TWICE SHY.

BOOM! Yeah, big time. It was, we thought, the perfect name for a band. It was seamless because, as Paul pointed out, 'We'll call the first album *Once Bitten*.' That sealed it. We were Twice Shy and the whole world was about to hear about us.

Except you didn't. I mean, you are now, but I doubt whether this book is even reaching the whole world. More than likely it'll be you, my mum and a friend of hers from work. Probably Linda. She likes autobiographies apparently.

No, after a couple of lunchtime concerts and one set at the school fete, Twice Shy broke up. It wasn't so much due to musical differences, as to me realising that I still wasn't getting the attention of girls. And, let's remember, this was a major factor in me wanting to be a pop star. No, I realised that even if Twice Shy did attract the attention of females around the world, it would be the sort of ladies who spend a lot of their lives going to watch Savage Garden or Meat Loaf – both very good artists, but I think you know what I'm saying. If this was really going to take off, and make me an irresistible stud, it needed to be sexy, it needed to be cool, it needed to be . . . a boy band.

For as long as I can remember, I've loved Take That. *Love* them. I'm not one of these Johnny-come-lately types who got on board since 'Patience' or 'Greatest Day'. No, I was there at the very start. They were the first band I ever really got into. I thought, and still very much do think, that they were brilliant. I used to watch their live concerts all the time and daydream about what it must be like to have that many people screaming and shouting for you, calling out your name. Most days when I'd come home from school I'd push the sofas and coffee tables in our lounge up against the walls, create my own stage and pretend to be a member of Take That. Sometimes I'd be Robbie, other times Mark, Jason or Howard, but mostly I'd be Gary. I studied them so much that I knew every single moment of every single routine. I still know a couple of the routines even now. I know this because I showed them to Take That themselves.

Three years ago when we were filming the third series of *Gavin & Stacey* in Cardiff, Take That were playing at the Millennium Stadium on their Circus tour. Joanna Page, who played Stacey, and I got tickets, and were incredibly excited at the prospect of seeing them live. This would be the fifteenth time I'd seen them, but it had been a few years since I'd last been to one of their gigs. We got to the stadium and were sitting in our seats waiting for the concert to start when a lady came over and tapped me on the shoulder and asked if we could follow her. We stood up and made our way out of the arena and ended up walking through a maze of corridors backstage. Jo turned to me and said, 'James, where are we going?'

'I think we might be about to meet Take That,' I whispered back quietly, not wanting to jinx it. Jo did a sort of silent squeal and then pulled herself together. Before long, sure enough, we were there, standing outside Take That's dressing room. The door opened and Gary was right in front of me.

'Hiya James,' he said in his soft northern lilt, 'come in.' And so Jo and I followed him into the room. I was doing my absolute best to try and hold it together. Mark, Jason and Howard came over and we talked about the tour and how it was all going, and then I did it. I had to. I blurted out, 'This is the fifteenth time I'll have seen you. Everyone at school used to take the piss out of me for liking you, but I'm so happy you're back together.' They all laughed and thanked me for my support. And then I went one step further: 'I can dance the first twenty minutes of the *Live in Berlin* video.'

Jason cracked up. 'You can't? What? Even now? I can't remember what songs we did at the opening of the Berlin show.' I'm proud to say that I took this as an invitation to show Take That exactly what they couldn't remember.

'It was "You Are the One",' I said. And then, right there in the dressing room, before they were about to play to 75,000 people, I did the dance. For about thirty seconds. Howard couldn't believe it, Mark was laughing and, when I finished, Jason said he now remembered it and had forgotten what a complex routine it was. I guess, if I was cool, I should now say how embarrassed I am that I did this. But I'm not cool. I loved it! They are such warm, kind and generous guys that they didn't make me feel a fool.

Just as we were being ushered out of the room, Gary leant in and said words that even now make me happy to remember. He said, 'Do you mind if we get a photo?' I smiled wide and said, 'It would make my day.' And so me and Take That had a photo together. It was great.

Now, I don't know if this is true, but I'm pretty sure it is, but it was only when Robbie saw that photo that he decided to rejoin the band. I think he recognised that there could be a new fifth member to take his place. I've asked him about it countless times since, but he denies all knowledge of the photo and says that the band have never talked about meeting us that day in Cardiff. Yeah, right. I think all five of us felt it that day and know it to be true even now – that if it hadn't worked so incredibly well with Rob, then I definitely would've been asked to join Take That. Just stating facts.

Joking aside, I've been lucky enough to meet all five members of the band privately over the last few years and I've managed to keep my cool a lot better than I did that day in Cardiff. They are, to a man, incredibly lovely. Just this morning Rob sent me an email with a quote from Abraham Lincoln wishing me luck for a play I'm about to start. I even saw Howard in Nando's a few months ago. And I'd just like to take this moment to say a massive thank you to each of them for always being so nice to me. They'll never know how much it's meant.

So where was I? That's right – forming my own version of Take That. Putting together a boy band became my major ambition. I was still going to auditions fairly regularly and still not getting any acting work, but it didn't matter because I'd started to think that fate was telling me to be the next Gary Barlow.

I knew I had to form the band with way more precision than I had with Twice Shy. I had to surround myself with the right guys to make sure we could actually become a global phenomenon. What I needed were people who could sing and dance and who, most of all, were good-looking. And where could I find two such guys? I knew exactly where: the Jackie Palmer Stage School. James Wilson and Tom Goodridge were, and still very much are, two incredibly good-looking guys. They were good singers and fantastic dancers, and they could both do back flips. They were perfect. I was determined that we'd be a five-piece just like my favourite group, so I went to my two oldest friends, Gavin and Jason from the Salvation Army. Jason was a brilliant singer and Gavin was small and cute, with some pretty cool moves of his own. So, between the five of us, I really felt we had something.

We would rehearse every week in the junior hall at the Salvation Army (the scene of my Round John Virgin embarrassment). We started out doing cover versions, a lot of Take That, obviously, but we'd throw in some other huge hits to mix it up a little. I'm talking classics like 'Deep' by East 17, 'Bodyshakin'' by 911 and 'I've Got a Little Something for You' by MN8. (I never really understood why MN8 were bragging about how little the something was that they were offering potential girlfriends.) We started trying to form a fan base and would play in schools or at local discos. We got the routines incredibly tight, to the point where I truly believed we were going to make it. There wasn't a doubt in my mind. Once again, we had to decide on a name for the band. Gavin was gunning for Full Frontal but he was outvoted when we heard James Wilson's genius suggestion: Insatiable. We would tell everyone who'd listen that we were going to be huge; that the reason we were called Insatiable is ''cos you just can't get enough of us'. I'm literally cringing while I type this.

I was the youngest in the band, but I was also the one who cared the most and most wanted to make us a success. Doing cover versions was fun, but I knew we needed original songs if we were going to get noticed. I went back to Matt Lanchester, the keyboardist from Twice Shy, and asked if he'd like to write songs with me for Insatiable. If he went for it, I promised him that he'd be on the cusp of making millions; everyone knew that all the money was in writing songs. Once again, he got on board. From then on, weekends became about either rehearsing with the band or writing songs with Matt. We wrote a total of three songs together: the floor-filler 'Girl, Are You Ready?'; the smoochy love ballad 'Lover'; and the summer-time sing-a-long 'I Miss My Time with You.' With those three hit records, I knew we had what it took to make it. But, just to be sure, we also worked out a Take That medley that incorporated all of their biggest songs into one, which we knew would go down a storm live. Looking back on it now, I wonder if the songs were strong enough lyrically. Lyrics were my part of the deal and I'll hold my hands up and say I'm no Bernie Taupin. At the time, however, I thought these songs were better than anything anyone had ever heard. You be the judge.

GIRL, ARE YOU READY?

It was all done in a sort of chant. I remember saying to Matt at the time that we needed a huge hit like PJ and Duncan's 'Let's Get Ready to Rumble'. The chorus went like this:

> *Girl, are you ready?*
> *Just tell me when ya ready.*
> *Girl, are you ready?*
> *I ain't gonna rush you.*
> *Girl, get ready.*
> *It's about to get steady*
> *Girl, are you ready?*
> *I ain't gonna rush you.*

LOVER

'Lover' was a killer of a ballad. I remember thinking we should release it at Christmas, with a black-and-white video and some jingling bells in the background. These are the lyrics that, in my head, would change music for ever:

> *Lover, lover, do you see?*
> *Lover, you and me*
> *We are dying.*
> *Lover, lover, can't you see?*

Hold me close
And stop the crying.

And the chorus went:

Don't hide what you want me to see
'Cos I can be everything that you want me to be.
Together we'll make it,
Together we'll stand
The test of time
Hand in hand.
(We can make it hand in hand.)

After reading those lyrics it probably won't come as a shock to hear that after a year and a half, the band broke up. It never really happened officially; there was no public announcement, which is why you're only hearing about it now. I was so disappointed. I had honestly believed that, when the day came that Insatiable finally broke up, after the millions of record sales and the record-breaking tours, ChildLine would have to set up a special call centre to deal with the traumatised, distraught girls all over the world. Instead, we broke up after six gigs, one of which was at James Wilson's sister's wedding, while another was at Gavin's family barbecue. So, not really gigs at all – more like favours to us. It wasn't how I'd pictured it panning out.

The strange thing is that my being a fan of Take That, and my interest in all things boy band, has stood me in good stead to do lots of things since. Later on, you'll read about how my first lead on television was in a fake documentary about a boy band called Boyz Unlimited, in which I played a character called Gareth, the fat one who wrote the songs. And in the last year I've co-produced an ITV special on the group JLS and, for Comic Relief, along with Alan Carr, John Bishop, Catherine Tate and David Walliams, I was part of Fake That, the ultimate Take That tribute band. Actually, it was during the recording of that video, when I was standing on a stage, sharing a microphone with Gary and singing one of his songs, that I really became grateful that Insatiable had never worked out. Deep down, I'd never wanted to be in a boy band – it was more an extension of my impossible dream of being in Take That. And, for a brief moment there, I guess I sort of was.

So neither of my bands had worked out and I still wasn't getting any of the auditions I was going for. In fact, I wasn't auditioning much at all at this point. I was almost fifteen and school was getting incredibly boring, so much so that I started bunking off. It was so easy: I would head off out the door to school, leaving the house and saying my goodbyes to Mum and Dad, walk up the road, get to the top and hide between a bush and a tree on the corner. Then I'd sit there and watch as Mum left in her car, followed by Dad a few minutes later. I'd wait a good five minutes and then head back home. And that's what I'd do. Once I was back, I'd lie around the house, watch TV, play computer games: anything to pass the time – often, if I'm being honest, close to nothing. Back then, I could waste three hours just staring at a rug – not even the whole rug, just a particular corner. When Mum and Dad got home, I'd tell them various untruths about my day and spend the evening forging a letter from one of them telling my teacher I had a sore throat and, that was that, I was home and dry. Well, almost . . .

For it was on one such bunked-off day when, unbeknown to anyone, I made my first television appearance. I was sitting, or rather laid out, on our sofa watching *This Morning with Richard and Judy* – a staple watch for any child off school – and eating my third bowl of Coco Pops, when the agony aunt Denise came on and said that today's phone-in would be all about bullying. She went on to say, 'Do you know someone who is being bullied? Are you worried your child might be in danger? Are you a bully and don't know how to stop? Are you being bullied and need help? If so, call this number . . .'

Without even thinking about it, I put down the Coco Pops, went into the kitchen, picked up the phone and dialled the number she had just read out. I didn't get through at first, but then, still not thinking, I redialled over and over again, until I finally got through. What was I doing? What was I thinking – or not thinking? I have absolutely no idea. Within minutes I was telling the researcher on the other end of the line about how I was being bullied, and that my parents thought I was at school but I couldn't go in for fear of being beaten up again. I told her my name was Chris and she said someone would call back if I was going to be on the show. And that was that. I put the phone down and went back to the sofa and the Coco Pops. I don't know what possessed me; I suppose it must've been my aching desire to be on TV. Never in a million years did I think I'd get on the show. There must be thousands of people calling in, I thought to myself. There's no way.

I was just about to lift the bowl to my mouth to slurp down the chocolatey milk when the phone rang. I picked it up and it was the researcher I'd spoken to. She asked me some more questions, to which I gave confident answers, every single one of them a lie. And then she said, 'OK, Chris, I'm gonna pass you over to Denise, who'd just like to talk to you before we go on air.' What? Exsqueeze me? Baking powder? Put me on air?! Talk to Denise?! What the hell was happening?!

Before I could hang up, I heard a new voice say, 'Hiya, is that Chris?' It was Denise, with her lovely, calming Geordie accent.

'Yes, this is Chris. Hi Denise,' I answered nervously. We spoke about the atrocities that were happening to me at the school I attended in High Wycombe. How I was too terrified to speak out. How my parents didn't even know that I wasn't at school today. (See? I wasn't completely lying.) And then Denise told me to stay on the line because, in less than five minutes, I would be the first caller on air.

I sat there, the phone pressed to my ear, trying to get my head together, Someone would come on every now and then to check on me. 'Are you still there, Chris?'

'Yep, yep. Chris is still here.'

I was starting to get nervous now. Live-television nervous. I had to remember what Denise had told me, that I should just speak calmly and clearly. Thank God for Denise. She knew exactly how hard it was for me to call in with everything I was going through . . . Maybe it was the only way I could handle what was about to happen, but I genuinely started to feel as though I was the victim of bullying. I was waiting on the phone and kept being counted down. 'One minute till we're back on air . . . forty-five seconds . . . thirty seconds . . . ten . . .'

And then down the phone I could hear the famous *This Morning* theme music and Richard Madeley welcoming everyone back. Then he turned the discussion over to today's phone-in. There I was, standing in the kitchen, wearing just my school shirt, my pants and socks, about to tell a massive lie on national TV. After Denise and Richard had introduced the bit, Richard said, 'Well, let's go to our first caller, and it's Chris from High Wycombe. Hi Chris.'

I paused briefly, took a short breath and said, in a small, shy voice, 'Hi Richard, hi Denise.' And that was that. We were off.

'Chris, you called in to tell us you were being bullied,' Richard said.

'Yes,' I replied. 'I am.'

'How old are you?'

'Fourteen.'

'And you stayed away from school today because of what's happening to you?'

'Yes,' I said. 'My mum and dad don't know I'm here. But I can't face going into school any more.'

'Can you tell me what's been happening?' Denise asked.

'I'm being bullied. Picked on all the time, you know, by the other boys. I'm bigger than them, fatter. They call me names all the time because of it. Last term one of the kids broke my arm, but I told my teachers I'd slipped over.'

And so it went on, my best performance to date, and I couldn't even hear it because the TV was in the other room. Denise talked to me for a while, advising me about what to do and being very sympathetic, then Richard told me that he really respected me for coming on. 'I think you've been very brave, very brave indeed,' he said, 'but I also think you need to talk to your parents about this. You need to talk to them about what's happening to you, Chris. And you need to do it soon.'

'Thank you,' I said. 'Yes, you're right. Thank you, Richard. Thank you very much.'

'I'm sure they'll be able to help, and perhaps there's something they can do about the school, I don't know. But it's very important that you speak to them as soon as you possibly can. Don't store this up, Chris: it won't help. You really have to talk about it.'

'Thank you, Richard,' I said. 'I will. I will speak to Mum and Dad.'

And then I was off the air. I put the phone down and just stared at it. That was weird, I thought to myself. Was I just on TV? I then smiled to myself, one of the wryest smiles I've ever had on my face. If I was Ferris Bueller, I would've looked down the camera and winked. However, if I *was* Ferris Bueller, I would never have done what I did next. I was so swept up in my new television status as Chris the bullied teenager that when the phone started to ring again, I just presumed that it was *This Morning* calling me back for some reason. Maybe it was Denise thanking me for calling. Or, better still, maybe Richard Madeley was so impressed with Chris that he thought he should be a regular feature on the show. So I picked up the phone, waiting for good news, only to hear, 'What on earth are you doing at home? Why aren't you at school? And why the hell has Auntie Marilyn just heard you on the television saying you've broken your arm?'

It was my mum. I didn't even think. It's the number one rule: if you're bunking off, you never, ever pick up the phone. Rule number two should be: don't call live television phone-ins and pretend to be someone else while talking in your own voice. But how many people would that apply to?

To this day I have no idea why I did it. Why I felt the need to carry on with such a lie. When Mum got home, she told Dad and he went mad. Not a little bit cross: a proper, full-on, red-in-the-face, Malcolm Corden rage. It's never nice being on the end of one of them.

Recently, Richard Madeley very kindly agreed to be in the latest Smithy sketch for Comic Relief, and he was absolutely great. But all the time we were filming together, I had this huge urge to tell him what I'd done all those years ago. How this wasn't actually the first time we'd spoken. But alas, the opportunity never arose. Even if it had, I wouldn't have had any idea how to tell him. God knows where you start with something like that.

To be honest, though, I mostly feel embarrassed by it. I was sent to my room that night without any dinner. And though I felt bad, and it was never nice when Dad shouted, deep down I was pleased that people knew. I'd been on television and, even though it was wrong, and even though I'd been lying the whole time, I wanted the whole world to know. The truth is, I loved it.

CHAPTER 4

BEST MUSICAL ACCOMPANIMENT:
'School's Out' by Alice Cooper

BEST FILM TO WATCH ALONGSIDE:
Ferris Bueller's Day Off

BEST ENJOYED WITH:
two hours of detention

The only time I ever really enjoyed school was when we were doing the school play. It's a time I look back on with fondness. We would rehearse every Tuesday and Thursday after school and, as the show got nearer, we would start doing evening rehearsals, until suddenly it got to a point where school didn't feel like school any more – it was a theatre.

I loved the nerves and excitement that buzzed around the place. The very same geography and history classrooms that were boring and dull in the day suddenly became dressing rooms or makeshift costume storage units full of life and purpose. The whole place changed, and if you had one of the leading parts, you would, without question, start to get treated differently. By teachers and pupils alike. You'd get let off the odd homework task as you had 'lines to learn', and everyone would constantly ask you about the play and want to know how you were feeling. All in all, for that week when the play was happening, you were seen as special. I loved it – every aspect of it – and I'm sure it won't come as a shock to hear that when there was a play on, I never bunked off.

We'd often do musicals and I was lucky enough to have a good part for most of the shows. One year, when we did *Zigger Zagger*, a musical about football hooligans, there was a review of our show in the *Bucks Free Press*. It was the first time I'd ever been mentioned in a newspaper of any kind and I remember what it said to this day, word for word:

'James Corden excels as the sergeant major. This lad is a natural and I feel sure he has a future in the acting profession.'

I couldn't believe it. I cut it out of the paper and stuck it on my bedroom wall. I would read it every night before I went to sleep and every morning when I got up. Here's the thing, though – and I've literally only learnt this in the last two years – the only thing worse than a bad review is believing a good review. If only I'd listened to our drama teacher, Mrs Roberts, when she told me not to let it go to my head. But it was too late for that. I walked around school like I was De Niro or something. So embarrassing. It was because of this behaviour and my appalling record of attendance that when the next year's school play came around, Mrs Roberts called me to the school hall to have a serious chat over lunch. She started by telling me that the show we were going to put on that year was called *Dazzle*, and that it was a musical set on a spaceship. She then informed me that she wanted me to play the lead, the captain of the ship.

When she told me, though, she looked at me in that particular Mrs Roberts way. 'James,' she said, 'don't get too carried away with this because there are some serious conditions. I've talked to other teachers and I have to tell you most of them think I'm making a mistake. You're so disruptive, so utterly disinterested in almost all your other lessons, they—'

'I'm not that bad,' I protested.

'Yes,' she said, 'actually you are.' She pointed a finger at me. 'I'm sticking my neck out for you here and I promise, if you step out of line in any lesson with any teacher between now and the school play, not only will I take the part away from you, you won't be in it at all.'

She didn't have to say any more. The play was all I lived for and, once warned, I didn't so much as breathe in a lesson without permission. I was the model student really. I even let Mr Hopkins have some peace in European Studies. And that's saying something because Mr Hopkins was my nemesis. A strange man, to say the least, who was probably better suited to lecturing at a university than teaching in school. You see, he didn't so much teach as stand at the front of the class and pontificate endlessly in a monotone. But there's plenty to come on him. Best to give it a proper lead-in, so I'll tell you how I ended up in his class.

As you probably know, it's the fourth year at upper school where you have to make the choices about what to do for your GCSEs. At Holmer Green we had to pick three options to take as well as Maths, English, Science and a language. I made my choices immediately: Drama, of course, Music and Home Economics. I wanted to be as creative as possible, so these seemed like the right subjects to choose. Suddenly things had changed; for the first time I had made my own choices and I felt really energised at the thought of spending large chunks of the day creating things, instead of being told to sit down, be quiet and listen.

Unfortunately, however, my enthusiasm didn't last long. No sooner were my options on paper than I was called to see Mr Graham, our head of year. I don't remember a huge amount about Mr Graham other than he had this sort of half-beard – not quite full growth and not quite a goatee. I do remember he was inconsistent, though. That's got to make for the trickiest kind of teacher, doesn't it? When you're that age all you want from a teacher is to know where you stand. If they're grumpy, they're grumpy; as a pupil you know they're grumpy and if you so much as look at them the wrong way you'll be met by grumpiness.

You can deal with that. Then you have the other, 'cooler' teachers, the ones who are daring enough to show they have a sense of humour, and so long as you don't step too far out of line, will treat you with the same amount of respect you're prepared to show them.

I'm not saying that Mr Graham was bad at teaching – actually, I remember him being really good in the classroom; it's just that you never quite knew where you stood with him. One day he would be fun and almost revel in the rolling of his eyes when you were a bit cheeky. Then the next day he'd have you marched down the staff corridor for doing the smallest thing wrong. It was all very confusing.

So, a few days after I'd submitted my GCSE choices, I was summoned to his office. As I trudged down the corridor, I was hoping that today the side of the bed he'd got out of was so lovely that he'd decided I should direct the school play and that's what this meeting was about. I waited in the staff corridor, leaning against the wall, looking on as the passing teachers glared and tutted at me.

'I'm here for a meeting. I haven't been naughty!' I wanted to shout. But that wasn't an option. If you so much as breathed too loudly in the staff corridor you were immediately shushed by Miss Ventress, the school nurse/secretary.

Finally the waiting was over and I was called in. I sat down and took a good look at Mr Graham, trying to read him. He seemed in a good enough mood, I supposed. When I say good, I mean he didn't glare at me the moment I opened the door. He told me to sit down and our conversation went something like this.

'James,' he said, 'I've been looking at your GCSE options and I'm rather concerned.'

'Really, sir. Why?'

'Drama, Music and Home Economics?'

'Yes.'

'Hmmm.' He arched one of his eyebrows. 'They're not exactly what you'd call serious subjects, are they?'

'Well, they are to me. I'm very serious about Drama and Music. Very serious indeed. And I think everyone in the school can see how seriously I'm taking Home Economics.'

'James, you can't do Music, Drama and Cooking as your options. I can see what you're trying to do and it won't wash. No way. What use will Music and Drama be in the outside world?'

By this point, as you can imagine, I was slightly put out. 'Well, that depends what I do, sir, doesn't it? I mean, what use is Science to a milkman? No use at all, but even if you want to be a milkman, you still have no choice but to take it. I'm going to be an actor, I—'

Mr Graham jumped right in. 'James, you're not *going* to be an actor. You'd like to be an actor.'

'Yes, but—'

'It's all very well having dreams. We all have dreams, but at some point you have to live in the real world. No, I'm afraid it's out of the question. You can't do both Music and Drama. You simply can't.'

I was wide-eyed now and could feel the heat in my cheeks. 'But—' I spluttered.

'Only three students have chosen Music as an option so we're taking it off the syllabus this year. I'm sorry, we can't have a class with only three students. It just isn't possible.'

'Oh right. Sure. I mean, God forbid that a class in this school should have fewer than forty kids to a teacher.'

(OK, I didn't say that. I wasn't that politically aware; I was only fourteen after all. What I actually said was . . .)

Truth is, I don't remember what I said. I'm not sure I said anything. I was most likely speechless. I just didn't know how this could be deemed acceptable. What if one of those three students was potentially a brilliant musician? What college or university was going to take them seriously if they didn't even have something as basic as a GCSE? I tried to imagine how I'd feel if there was no Drama course that year. I'd have been so upset that I'm pretty sure I would've asked Dad if I could move schools. I'd have left my friends and everything else behind to do Drama. Music came a close second to that, and that had just been taken away.

I was getting irritated now and Mr Graham kept telling me to calm down. But I couldn't let it rest. I didn't want to do Science. I couldn't see how I had any use for it and I wasn't the only one – none of my mates wanted to take Science either. Why were we made to do this when Music – something that would be really useful to me and that I had a real passion for – was not even being run as a course?

Mr Graham told me he hadn't been born yesterday and he knew why I had chosen Music and Home Economics. It was because they were a doss; easy subjects for someone like me to breeze through. I argued that Music would and could become a big part of my career; that one day I was going to be number one in the charts. He laughed loudly and rolled his eyes and I sat there with my face screwed up while he made a point of telling me that no matter what I said or did, it wasn't going to get me anywhere. The decision had been made and that was that. I had no choice. I had to choose something else.

I wracked my brains, trying to think of some way I could come out of this with my integrity intact. Then suddenly it came to me. I looked at Mr Graham, smiled a tad wickedly and uttered the words 'Religious Education'.

If he thought Music was an easy option, nothing comes easier than RE. You just sit around chatting about things that may or may not have happened. I felt so smug right then and I can still hear the three scoops of sarcasm in his reply. 'And why, exactly, do you want to do RE?' he asked me.

'I don't. I want to do Music. But if I can't do that, I'll do RE instead 'cos it's easiest.'

Amazingly (and this is the sort of school I went to), Mr Graham informed me that for the exact same reasons that Music wasn't being run as a GCSE, neither was RE. It was ridiculous. Three kids wanted to do Music and were told this wasn't sufficient. Only two wanted to do RE, so that was absolutely off the syllabus. I couldn't believe what I was hearing so I asked Mr Graham which subjects were available and, word for word, this was his reply: 'European Studies and Information Technology, but Mr Longman' – the IT teacher – 'has made it clear he doesn't want you in his classroom.'

So that was that, what a waste. Filling out the form, choosing my options, going to 'have a chat' with Mr Graham – the whole thing. What was the point of any of this stuff when the bottom line was I had to suffer Mr Hopkins and European Studies? Even now I can't understand why Mr Graham bothered to call me in that day. He just laughed at my dreams and proceeded to inform me what I would be studying, without any apparent regard for the things I cared about.

From that moment on, school meant nothing to me. I didn't understand school and school had made it quite clear that it didn't understand me. Being told I had to consider the history and geography of Europe every day for the next two years, all in the hope of obtaining what I saw as a pointless qualification, made me give up on the whole ethos of education.

I decided I would only focus on the subjects that mattered to me: Drama, English and, of course, Home Economics. The rest was, as far as I was concerned, free time. I stopped taking a bag to school; most days I wouldn't even have a pen. European Studies in particular became only about pulling the focus away from the teacher to where I was sitting, on my own at a single desk while everyone else was seated in rows of four. Sometimes I'd sleep, other times I'd try my hardest to be ejected from class just so I had something different to look at. It wasn't inspiring in the slightest. I used to dream of having a teacher like Robin Williams in *Dead Poets' Society*, someone who would inspire me to leap up on a desk and cry, 'O Captain, my Captain.'

The thing with actively trying not to learn anything is that it quickly becomes boring. I would try to think of more and more ways to entertain myself, and I'm sorry to say that they usually came at the expense of Mr Hopkins. One time that really sticks out is when he came up to the back of the class to look at Katie Aslett's work. He was bending over, looking over her shoulder, right in front of my desk, and suddenly, without thinking, I lifted up the lapel of his blazer with the chewed biro I had borrowed from Stuart Turner and dropped the pen into his pocket. He didn't feel a thing. He walked back to the front of the class, quite oblivious.

I waited a good five minutes until he was back in his groove, droning on about historic monuments in Bavaria or something, and then I raised my hand. Patiently I waited for him to acknowledge me. I waited and waited. He had seen me, but he knew that whatever I was going to ask would have nothing to do with the subject at hand, so he was ignoring me.

'Sir,' I said, running out of patience; now I was supporting my raised arm with my other hand wrapped around the back of my head.

'Yes James, what is it?' he replied gruffly.

'Sir, have you seen my pen?' I asked, innocently enough.

His eyes rolled towards the ceiling. 'No, I haven't.'

'Sir, are you sure you haven't seen it? It's just it was here before you came up, and now it's gone.'

Mr Hopkins looked at me, understandably confused, given that I clearly had no intention of ever writing anything down in any of his lessons. So what was I doing talking about a pen?

'No,' he said. 'I've not seen it. Look on the floor.'

At that I got down on my hands and knees and pretended to hunt for the biro. I was down there a full minute or more until, with all the mischief I could muster, I stood up and said in a voice not dissimilar to one I'd seen used in various court-room dramas, 'Sir, have you stolen my pen?'

Mr Hopkins, who was wiping the blackboard at this point, swivelled round and glared at me. 'Don't be so ridiculous, James. Why would I have stolen your pen?'

I was now standing in front of my desk. The rest of the class had stopped any work they were doing and were all looking my way. 'Sir,' I went on, 'I think you've stolen my pen. Why would you do such a thing?!'

Mr Hopkins was starting to get agitated now. He told me to stop being stupid, sit down and be quiet.

But I wasn't letting it lie.

I demanded that he empty his pockets.

He refused.

'Sir,' I said, 'if you're innocent, you'd happily empty your pockets. The fact that you won't tells me only one thing.'

The rest of the class knew I was up to something and they were joining in now; even the best-behaved students were telling him to show me that he had nothing in his pockets.

And so, under pressure from the entire class, Mr Hopkins had to give in. He was red-faced, muttering under his breath, visibly annoyed at the indignity of having to respond to my demands. With his eyes firmly fixed on me, he reached into his left pocket and froze. For a moment he just stared. Then he pulled out my half-eaten, ink-stained biro.

I slapped my forehead hard in mock surprise and let go the loudest gasp.

Half the class laughed; the others seemed stunned into silence. Before Mr Hopkins could say anything, I pointed my index finger at him and let out a cry. 'THIEF!' I shouted. 'THIEF!! Why would you do such a thing?'

You've never seen a man so angry at this point; that wasn't going to stop me, though . . .

'You've got loads of pens, sir. Why would you steal from a pupil?'

His face turned a shade of crimson that can only be described as medically unsafe and, drawing back his hand in an arc, he lobbed the blackboard cleaner right at me. It came like a bullet, so hard and fast it was little more than a blur. It missed my head by inches.

'GET OUT!!' he yelled. 'GET OUT OF MY CLASSROOM. *NOW!!*'

Mr Thomas, the teacher from next door, came rushing in. 'What the hell is going on?' he demanded. I smiled to myself as I watched Mr Hopkins trying to explain how he had come to find my pen in his pocket, and then I was marched out of the classroom and handed a week's detention.

I told everyone I was going to go to the police to report Mr Hopkins for stealing. At one point I think I even said that this was bigger than all of us, and who knows how many other teachers' pens had been ill-gotten gains.

I really had washed my hands of the whole education thing now and these types of situations would occur almost weekly. I would constantly be on detention and always be in the staff corridor, though I wasn't a nasty student. I never bullied anyone or tried to make anybody feel bad. My pranks were purely for my own amusement. I think in some strange way I viewed it as a kind of performance, an extended, real-life, real-time improv.

It was all very silly really and I'd like to take this moment to state categorically that I don't think my behaviour was cool. It was foolish, and the way I acted meant I was dismissed as nothing more than stupid, an oaf, someone who didn't care and therefore shouldn't be cared about. I wish I'd learnt my lesson at the time, that my attitude would only ever result in people thinking I was a prat but, alas, I fear this is a lesson I've only recently learnt – in the last year and a half, in fact.

There's nothing cool about not caring, or, more to the point, wanting to be seen that you don't care. People will do and say things all the time that will make you want to jack it all in, but it's the people who stick it out, who dig deep and put their heads down and persevere – these are the people who get the biggest response. I've lived most of my life acting like I don't care, wanting to seem like I'm cool or brash, and the sad truth is, I care more about how people see me than anyone I know.

When *Gavin & Stacey* became popular and I'd be invited on to various chat shows, I would act my most supremely confident and try to be the funniest or rudest version of myself, when actually, deep down, all I wanted was to be taken seriously. The same rules apply in adulthood as they did at school. There's nothing wrong with caring and there's nothing wrong with being quiet and showing that you might feel vulnerable. As I say, it's literally in the last eighteen months or so that, for the first time, I've been comfortable enough in my own skin to actually just be myself.

CHAPTER 5

BEST MUSICAL ACCOMPANIMENT:
'Theme from *Rocky*' by Bill Conti

BEST FILM TO WATCH ALONGSIDE:
Invictus

BEST ENJOYED WITH:
Lucozade Sport

Even though there were plenty of times at school when I would rather have been anywhere else, it'd be silly not to admit that there were also times that were really good fun. As I've said already, the plays were a big highlight and there was one other lesson I'll always remember very fondly: PE.

Ah yes. Physical Education. I'm sure you've already worked out that this wasn't my strongest subject. That's not to say that I didn't enjoy it – I did. I enjoyed it a lot, actually. I was just rubbish at it. And I mean totally rubbish, woeful, crap, pants, chod – whatever word you want to use, I'm pretty sure it fits. Believe me, you know you're bad at PE when you're playing mixed indoor football and even the girls are shouting at you. It's bad news.

At the start of my fifth year, aged fifteen, when the first PE lesson of the year came round, the whole year was told to go to the sports hall, the regular kind with floor markings, benches down one side and ropes tied against the wall, where we would be told about what to expect that year. We all sat on the benches, chatting away, when Mr Atkinson, the head of PE (and a teacher whom everybody liked) came in. He spent three or four minutes asking for quiet and then explained that in our final year PE was going to be a little different. They were going to split the year into different groups, and if your name was called, you were to move into one of the groups Mr Atkinson specified.

He began reading out names. 'Steven Hawes. Group A.' Steve, or Deano, as we called him, was the school's football star. He'd represented England at every junior level and was at that time a schoolboy on the books at Sheffield United.

'Lyndsey Reece. A.' Lyndsey was an incredibly gifted runner who used to run for the county or something like that. When she heard her name, she moved over to the A group with Steven.

'Andrew Frewin. A.' Frewin was a brilliant footballer and had had trials at lots of big clubs. He was one of those natural sportsmen who was good at everything.

And so the list went on. Everyone could see what was happening: they were forming an elite sports lesson for the brightest and best. It was fair enough: those guys could climb a rope in no time so you could see why the school didn't want them being held back by the rest of us. Except, and here's the thing, the rest of us wasn't the rest of us at all. Once the A team had been sorted, they moved on to the B team. This was where the majority of my friends ended up: Richard Shed, Kevin Wilkinson, Stuart Turner; all pretty classy athletes in their own way.

As more and more names were read and the benches started to thin out, I looked around the room at the people left and it suddenly dawned on me what was happening. There weren't just two groups – there was a third, as yet unmentioned group, Group C, and I was very much a part of it. I looked at the people who were left and took in the biggest bunch of misfits I've ever seen. And when I say biggest, I mean *biggest*. Group C basically consisted of anyone who was big – so that was the likes of me, Simon Phillips, Luke Smythson, Chris Briggs. Then there were all the hard-nuts, the guys everyone was scared of: Craig

Thompson, Jason McKenzie, Jez Pope and Alex Carver. And all the geeks. Every. Single. Geek.

It was a low for all of us. This was our last year of PE and we were in a group we didn't want to be in with people we didn't want to be with. We were the shit, the leftovers; Danny DeVito to everyone else's Arnold Schwarzenegger. And boy, did they know it. The girls were sniggering at us and the boys of the A and B groups were shouting out how crap we were. Mr Atkinson told everyone to stop, but even he said it with a wry smile.

Depressed and downhearted, we made our way to the changing room and as we walked in, Craig Thompson thought it would be fun to trip up as many people as possible. Alex Carver did his usual ritual of grabbing a discarded towel and whipping as many people as he could round the legs, which all the other bullies thought was hilarious.

From then on, every PE session became a game of trying to be the person who wasn't picked on. Or whipped by a towel. It's not that it even particularly hurt, it was just the embarrassment of feeling helpless whilst people attacked and laughed at you. I often became the butt of these jokes: it wasn't real, out-and-out bullying; it was more that there were very real times when I wasn't popular. I would feel it, not just in PE, but throughout my days at school. I was so often the joker that when the joke turned on me, it would feel like the whole school was ganging up against me. It would come in cycles: one minute I'd be popular and the next I'd be an outcast. I don't think this is an unfamiliar feeling at school, and I'm pretty sure that most people feel this way in their youth at one time or another, but for me, it would often feel as if it was all or nothing. I was either in with everyone or I was out.

Back to the changing room: Mr Atkinson came in after us that first morning and was met by a chorus of dissenting voices. Alex Carver piped up first. 'Sir, this is bullshit! Why are we in the pricks' group?!' Ever the charmer.

Jez Pope was next. 'Yeah, sir. Whose idea was this? Why are we in with the swots and the fatties?' The dissenting voices became louder and louder until you could barely hear yourself think. Everyone in the class was upset – mostly at the embarrassing way we thought the announcement had been handled.

Once he'd managed to calm us all down, Mr Atkinson took the towel from Alex Carver (who in the heat of the previous exchange had even tried to whip his own legs) and started to speak. He stood with his wide-legged stance, hands on hips and addressed us, like a general to his troops. 'You are not the lesser PE group of the year. You are not the misfits, the outcasts or anything else the others were calling you. You are unique; you are the trail-blazers; you are the first of your kind. You, each and every one of you, are this school's first ever rugby team.'

We all looked at him like he was mad. Our school had never played rugby, were never taught rugby and we didn't even have a rugby pitch, or posts for that matter. We played football and occasionally cricket. As the voices of dissent started up again, Mr Atkinson spoke. 'Look around you. Here in this room we have the perfect makings of an exceptional rugby team.' I checked around the room and saw Will Harvey, whose glasses had steamed up as he took a big breath of his inhaler. 'We have fearless power and strength.' Mr Atkinson pointed to the group of bullies. 'We have size' – he gestured over towards Chris Briggs, Simon Phillips and me – 'just what we need to make up a terrific front row of a scrum.' He smiled then as he turned his attention towards the small, skinny group of nerds huddled in the corner. 'And as for you lot, you've been running away from bigger boys for years. You're perfect for the backs.' Even the nerds themselves smiled at this bit. 'Believe me, boys, we can do this. Together, we can become a force at rugby. That's what our PE classes are going to be about. You've not been omitted from the other classes; you've been selected – hand-picked because I believe you have what it takes.'

I was near punching the air by the end of it. It was such an inspiring speech that I imagine even the hardest members of the group must have swelled with pride a little. I certainly felt it. I had no idea how to play rugby, but in that moment I wanted to learn. I'd played football for the first team twice and, on both occasions, let's just say that I'd been 'not very good'. So 'not very good', in fact, that when we were low on numbers for one match, Ross Birbeck was picked instead and he was in the year below me. It was shaming. But this was our chance to be a team, our chance to shine. 'Right then,' Mr Atkinson said, clapping his hands and motioning everyone to get changed, 'let's get out on that pitch and have a go!'

That would have been the perfect finish, right? All of the motley crew, jogging out onto the field with our shoulders back and heads set forward. You can imagine the slo-mo shot of it, like astronauts walking out to the rocket. Except, out of the nineteen or so boys sitting in the changing room, only five had their kit.

Mr Atkinson wasn't pleased. He turned to Craig Thompson first: 'Why haven't you got your sports kit?' he asked.

'I don't know, sir,' Thompson replied in his low monotone.

'Well, do you know where it is?'

'I don't know, sir.'

'You don't know, or you don't care?'

'I don't know, sir.'

Mr Atkinson was understandably starting to get frustrated. 'You don't know much, do you?'

Thompson looked at him straight in the eye and repeated, 'I don't know, sir.' You had to hand it to Craig Thompson some-times: he had a way with words. It's fair to say that some teachers at school were a little frightened of Craig. He was so big he was almost a caricature – like the type of bully you'd find in *Grange Hill*, the one who used to pick on Gonch because he was ginger. Craig was tall and stocky and built like a fridge. He had an electric shaver that he used to carry in his rucksack and he could often be found at the back of the class having a shave. When the teacher asked him what he thought he was doing, he replied that he hadn't had time to shave that morning. He was twelve at the time!

I remember one lunch break he just walked into the staffroom and started making himself some toast. He did it with such self-assurance that it was only when he asked Mrs Spiller where the Marmite was kept that any of the teachers even realised he was there. He was a maverick – a scary maverick. One summer's day, aged fifteen, he actually drove his dad's Vauxhall Carlton to school. Seriously. He parked it in the staff parking bays. His dad called the police to report it stolen and, minutes later, was incredibly embarrassed when his son pulled up outside as he was on the phone. He didn't just ignore the rules; it was like he was completely unaware of them.

He could be horrible if he wanted to be. Sometimes he would just walk up and say, 'Corden, you fat bastard,' then punch me in the back of the head and walk on. Once, and only once, did I challenge him. I don't remember exactly what I said, but basically I tried to level with him and say it wasn't cool of him to be doing this. While I was talking, he was blankly staring at me, and then, from nowhere, he spat the most disgusting greeny right in the middle of my tie. It was horrible. Having said that, I don't think he was aiming for my tie, so it could've been worse.

Mr Atkinson must have given some thought to the fact that some, if not most of the class would have turned up without their kit. So he decreed from that point forward that if we didn't have our kits, it would be an immediate detention, and if we forgot them twice in a row, it would be a double detention, which meant lunchtime as well as staying for an hour after school. He meant business.

With lots of us kitless, he called off practice and instead

wheeled in the big television/VHS combo to show us videos of rugby matches, pausing now and again to point out formations and various set plays. He pointed to specific players and asked different individuals to watch how and where they moved around the pitch. The fact that we were contemplating something new excited me. Though, looking round that room, I was worried about whether we could make this team happen. Chris Briggs was so interested that he was playing *Super Mario Bros* on his Game Boy, which he'd cleverly hidden in his scrunched-up jacket. He only got found because, while Mr Atkinson was explaining line-outs, he shouted out, 'Luigi, you piece of shit!' at the top of his voice. He got the first of many detentions given out over the coming weeks.

Over time, and mainly due to Mr Atkinson's passion about making us a team, we started to get swept up in the excitement. Everyone in the class had become more inquisitive, more interested in what he was trying to do, more focused. It got to the point where, during one lesson, when Mr Atkinson was showing us scrum positions, Craig Thompson asked a question. (I honestly think this may have been the first time in his school life he'd done such a thing.)

'Why have they got gaffer tape round their heads, sir?' In Craig's deep, scary voice, the words 'gaffer tape' sounded pretty ominous. Mr Atkinson wasn't fazed, though. 'Well, there's various reasons, Craig, and I'm glad you asked. The principal reason is to protect your ears when you're in the scrum. The force that these guys push with can, over time, cause damage to their ears. Another reason is that, years ago, some less sporting members of the opposing team would try to bite the ears of other players in the scrum.' The whole class winced at this news. 'That's where the saying "cauliflower ear" comes from. Because of the damage done to players' ears when there was biting. But that doesn't happen any more.' As more hands shot up to ask more questions about a sport none of us knew how to play, the bell went to signal the end of the lesson. I can safely say we all walked out of the changing rooms more worried than when we had gone in.

Over the next few weeks the rugby training continued. I can't begin to imagine what we must have looked like, trudging out onto the field. We were such a mishmash of identities, so completely disjointed, and yet, somehow, for those few hours of PE, we came together.

The training sessions were always lively. They would essentially become fights, organised fights. There's a fine line between sporting aggression and going out of your way to drop-kick the crap out of whoever had the ball and, I can assure you, most of our team hadn't found the line yet. Nedeem Jacobs was the smallest member of the team, an innocent-looking mixed-race boy who used to literally shake with nerves at the thought of doing PE, let alone playing rugby. I knew Nedeem pretty well because he used to do the lighting for the school plays and he was a really nice guy. He had the most magnificent head of hair I've ever seen on a boy his age. It would just stand up in a flat top all on its own, without any product. Completely remarkable. I looked out for him as much as I could because he got picked on a fair amount. Not because of his hair, or his race, but just because he was small.

That's the worst thing about being at school – anything that's different is seen as bad. Too tall, too fat, wrong trainers, wrong bag. It was a minefield every day. But it was often worse for Nedeem and I can barely remember ever seeing him smile. He spent most of his time at school just trying to get through the day without any scrapes. It's safe to say rugby wasn't his sport. He was petrified of every aspect of it. Sometimes he would be in tears just watching the horrific violence going on around him. He would never try to catch the ball; he'd actively move out of the way if it was flying towards him. But Nedeem wasn't alone: there were plenty of other boys who wanted nothing to do with the ball as they were so scared of messing it up, or getting crunched. And then, on the other hand, there was the group of boys using rugby to have an organised fight and looking for every opportunity to crunch people. Mr Atkinson knew it was up to him to somehow blend these two completely opposite sides, the two sections of the school that stood furthest apart: the bullies and the bullied. The training sessions became more organised. We would work long and hard on line-outs and different strategies and we slowly started to become . . . well, not a team exactly, but part of something.

What Mr Atkinson had done was teaching at its very best. He took a group of boys who were all in some way lost and gave us something to aim for, something to make our own. You could feel its effects throughout the whole school. The bullies were less inclined to bully because they had started to see the person before them instead of just another victim. This in turn made the group of normally terrified, bullied boys come out of their shell a bit more. And me, well, I just loved being picked for something sporty. I enjoyed sport so much, but in the same way that those terrible singers who audition for *The X Factor* love singing.

I'll never forget the lesson when Mr Atkinson told us not to get changed into our kit. We were all ready for practice and he walked into the changing room and simply said, 'Follow me.' Unsure of what was going on, we followed him down the Maths corridor, past the Science block and into the main assembly hall. It was here Mr Atkinson stopped and turned to address us. 'I've brought you here to show you something. Something that has been made and created especially for you. Each one of you is the reason that the school has done this. If you ever feel as if you're less important than the other pupils here, come and look at this. And remember that this team is the reason it was created. Come and take a look.'

We were all slightly confused – Craig Thompson more than usual – but before any of us could say anything, Mr Atkinson pushed open one of the fire doors and led us out onto what used to be a barren area of grass round the corner from the football pitches. All nineteen of us stopped, stared and then oohed and aahed at the sight before us. Because the land was barren no more. No, in front of us now was a full-size rugby pitch. It was brilliant, somehow beautiful, the two massive goal posts stood like iron angels casting shadows over the freshly cut pitch; its ice-white markings enticing us to run over them and give our all for Holmer Green's first ever rugby team. It was a magical moment, only slightly ruined by Alan Turpin turning to Mr Atkinson and saying slowly, 'What is it, sir?' It was at that moment we kind of realised how far we had to go. But boy, did we have momentum.

Our first match was barely two weeks away and we had started to have extra training sessions after school. But, as we found out, it's quite tricky to have a decent training session when only seven of the team remember to turn up. I remember feeling very disheartened by this, but Mr Atkinson never let his head drop. He was taking a huge risk, spending the school's money on a rugby pitch that lots of people – his colleagues included – thought was a waste of time. But he never let that message get to us. He kept on telling us that we could, and would, become the pride of the school. Amazingly, over time, this belief did slowly seep into all of us, and one day as many as nine of us turned up at after-school training. I still wasn't 100 per cent on every aspect of the game, but I did know that I was only allowed to throw the ball backwards, which was more than Alan Turpin had managed to figure out. He just couldn't for the life of him get his head around any aspect of the game. I mean, none of us could really, but with Alan . . . sometimes in training you'd look up for someone to pass to and he'd be there, trying to tie two worms together.

Despite this lack of basic knowledge, our first match day finally arrived. We were playing Sir William Ramsay Upper

School, which was based about six miles from our school. Like us they had only recently formed a team, so Mr Atkinson thought it would be good for both teams to play against each other as our standard was similarly crap.

The whole day seemed to build towards 4 p.m., to this Clash of the Titans. The bullies had a strange, serene quality: they weren't stealing anyone's lunch, or trying to throw Nedeem's bag on top of the Science block. They were quiet – a braver man than myself might even go so far as to say they were nervous. The game was all any of us could think about: our first match, the possibilities, the potential to be heroes. The start of a brand-new era in our sporting lives. (I'm saying this as if everyone felt this way. I'm sure they didn't. This was what was happening in my head, because I wanted everything to be like either *Grease* or *Dead Poets' Society*.)

The bell rang at the end of the day and I made my way to the PE block. I could hear some noises coming from the changing rooms. 'Aha!' I thought to myself. 'It must be my team mates doing some sort of Haka dance to really bring the side together.' I walked a little faster because I didn't want to miss out on any team-building experience.

Excitedly, I burst into the room, only to find Alan Turpin and Jez Pope rolling around on the floor punching the crap out of each other. Not only that, they were being cheered on by the rest of the team, and Simon Phillips was even leaning in and throwing cheap shots onto the back of whoever was nearest to him. I couldn't believe what I was seeing. I looked over at Nedeem Jacobs who was huddled in the corner, close to tears, and realised I had to stop this, for the good of the team.

'Stop! STOP!!' I shouted as I leapt into the circle, grabbing Jez Pope and yanking him off Alan. 'What are you *doing*?' I said theatrically. 'We are supposed to be a team! We can't be fighting with ourselves. We have to support each other and take our fight out there onto the pitch!' In my head uplifting, inspiring music was starting to swell – this was going to be a speech that this team would still be talking about when they were old men. This would also, I imagined, put forward a good case for me being handed the captaincy, which meant it would be me lifting the inevitable trophies we'd win at the end of the year. 'This is our first match. We should be getting in the zone. We are no longer individuals – we're a unit. And we stand side by side as we walk out onto that turf, knowing that every single one of us is ready to do what it takes to bring home a victory!' I felt incredible. I was sure the whole room was being moved to tears by my speech; that this would be a defining moment in the life of this team and they were all about to break out into a slow hand-clap that would grow into a deafening round of applause. What actually happened was Alex Carver, who was standing on the changing room benches, shouted, 'Shut up, Corden, you fat prick,' before he leapt from the bench and elbowed me in the back. I fell on top of Alan Turpin and then I heard the always terrifying shout of 'BUNDLE!' Within seconds there were seventeen boys piled on top of me and Alan.

The feeling of being close to the bottom of a bundle is without question one of the scariest experiences any young boy can go through. You can't breathe and you can't move – never a good combination. This bundle was particularly unpleasant because of the sheer size of some of the boys involved. Most bundles would feature a combination of one or two big guys, but because this was the rugby team, every single one of the school's bloaters was now on top of me. If anything, it was the pinnacle of what many bundlers had been hoping for. Not Alan Turpin, though. His face was a shade of beetroot I'd never witnessed before or since. He couldn't breathe and was trying to say something, maybe his last words. Honestly, he looked as if he was going to die. I wanted to shout to save us both, but when I opened my mouth, I couldn't speak either.

It was the voice of Mr Atkinson that finally managed to collapse the bundle. He stormed into the room and went totally mad, shouting at the top of his voice, telling us we all had to grow up. At one point, he yelled, 'Look at Alan.' I don't think he meant for the rest of the class to laugh, but what could we do? Five minutes after the bundle had collapsed, his face was still so red he looked as if he had the worst sunburn known to man.

Mr Atkinson told us that we needed to concentrate, that training was one thing, but playing in a match was another. With time ticking away towards kick-off, he talked us through the set plays, the line-outs and the scrums and spoke about the need for discipline. Finally, he told us he was proud of every single one of us and that we had it in us to win this game.

With our chests puffed out and our heads held high, we walked out of the changing rooms and took our first steps onto the pitch. I don't know what we must've looked like. The most mismatched rugby team in history? All of us completely out of shape – either huge or tiny, tough or terrified, with nothing in between. Craig Thompson looked like a man possessed, Nedeem was shaking like a leaf and Alan Turpin – still red-faced – didn't really know what was going on. We were about half as ready as we'd ever be.

The game kicked off and it soon became clear that Alan wasn't the only one without any idea. We were a shambles: running into each other, dropping balls and generally getting absolutely battered. We were 12–0 down within five minutes, and it got worse from there. As the game continued, they scored try after try after try. Inevitably our heads dropped, but Mr Atkinson was still there on the sidelines, barking orders.

The defining moment of the match came with a scrum about fifteen minutes into the first half. The front row of the scrum was Simon Phillips, Craig Thompson and me: basically the biggest boys in the school. We put our arms over each other's shoulders, leant over and pushed forwards. We were pushing back and forth for about twenty seconds and then a blood-curdling scream erupted from their side of the scrum. I can still hear it now: it was deafening. 'AAAAAaaaaRRRGH! OH MY GOD! OOOWWWWWWW!'

The referee blew his whistle and the scrum collapsed. No one had any idea what was going on until we saw the screaming player with a hand pressed to his ear. He was almost in tears and in a hell of a lot of pain. 'He was biting my ear,' he whimpered and, as he moved his hand from his ear, blood started trickling down his face.

'Who? Who was?' asked the referee.

'Him!' he said, pointing at the boy in question. We followed his finger out past Simon, past Jez Pope, past Alex Carver until there, standing in front of all of us, was Craig Thompson, his teeth covered in blood, looking like a vampire.

'So? He didn't have his ears taped up.'

He honestly thought that it was totally legit, and so he kept on arguing with the referee. Mr Atkinson, who was now on the pitch, was trying to pacify Craig, but he wasn't having it. He was getting more and more angry, literally spitting blood everywhere. 'Why did you tell us about it if it's against the rules?' When the referee raised his red card to send him off, the red mist descended and Craig shoved the referee back so hard that he fell over, which made the opposition teacher get involved. All hell broke loose and, before we knew it, the game was called off.

I trudged back towards the changing rooms, disappointed and angry. This was supposed to have been a monumental day in the school's history, and we hadn't even lasted until the second half. I didn't get changed. I just grabbed my uniform, scrunched it up inside my bag and left.

As I walked home in my muddy kit, I felt so annoyed that such a great chance had been thrown away. I felt for Mr Atkinson, who'd nearly built this bunch of misfits into a real team, only to see it crumble. I got in and told Dad what had happened. 'Don't worry,' he said, 'you'll play again. They're not gonna build that pitch and go to all that trouble for just one game. It's in the past now, All you can change is the future.'

He was right, of course, and the ever-optimistic Mr Atkinson started the next PE lesson with a full and frank run-through of the rules of rugby. The phrase 'You cannot – and I can't stress this strongly enough – punch or bite other players' was used a lot.

We played seven matches in total, over two terms, and we never even scored a single point. The whole team was a disaster. The worst was when we got beaten 177–0 by the Royal Grammar School. And that match also descended into a fight. During a line-out, Jez Pope and Chris Briggs both decided they'd had enough and just started throwing punches all over the place. We were losing so badly that I think they thought they might take some solace in at least winning a fight. Only they didn't. They got well and truly whupped, along with the rest of our hardest lads. I think a few of our team enjoyed seeing the bullies get a taste of their own medicine, even if it was in between try after try after penalty after try. It was difficult to keep any faith with the thing, to be honest. One match we played, quite a few of our team didn't turn up, so we used the other school's substitutes and Mr Atkinson filled in too.

I think word must have got out about how rubbish we were to play, because the last match we ever had was against a local young offenders' institute. Watching them get out of the minibus was quite possibly the scariest thing I've ever witnessed. They didn't have matching kit, and one of them played in his jeans. They walked onto the pitch and just stared at us.

Right before kick-off, one of them put his hand up and said, 'Hang on a minute.' He then reached inside his pocket and jogged over to the touchline where he handed Mr Atkinson ten Silk Cut and a lighter and said, 'Hang on to these, will ya, mate.' These guys were real.

The game kicked off, and for once we were the better team. Athletically they were good, but we'd obviously played in – and lost – more games than they had. We were moving the ball nicely around the pitch and matching them muscle for muscle when we needed to. It was a nasty affair at points, but no one complained because we were both playing the game in the same way. One lad punched me so hard in the stomach I fell to the ground like a dead bird, but there weren't any afters. I picked myself up and carried on.

For a long time, the game stayed at nil–nil. We'd played six matches and had never scored a point: no try; no penalty; no drop kick, no nothing. It was a sad state of affairs, but that, finally, was all about to change . . .

The ball was picked up out of the scrum and passed out left towards Greg Pearson. He passed it to Will Harvey, who, amazingly, dropped a shoulder and burst past two of their players. Then there was a succession of about seven or eight passes, each one taking us closer to the try line. Richard Dunn made an impressive darting run and, just as he was tackled, managed to get it to Rob Higgins. Higgins stepped inside but was met by a sea of opposition shirts – all different colours. At least four convicted hard-nuts were bearing down on him fast but, incredibly, for someone who didn't quite know the rules, he kicked the ball out to the right. It flew about fifteen feet in the air, over the heads of the opposition and into the arms of the only man who didn't want any part of it. Yep, you guessed it: Nedeem Jacobs. He'd caught the ball – a massive achievement in itself – and was holding it, just staring at us, his team mates.

The opposition were now all charging towards him at a real clip, and so, fearing for him, we all just shouted, 'RUN, NEDEEM! RUN!' Mr Atkinson was pointing at the try line and shouting pretty much the same. And so that's exactly what he did. Little Nedeem Jacobs started running as fast as he could, his thick head of flat-topped hair barely moving as he did what he did best, what he'd been perfecting for pretty much the past decade – running as fast as he could to get away from the bullies. And, man, was he fast. He left all but two of them for dead, his head down, focused on the try line. But the guys chasing him were quick and they were catching up with him fast.

'GO ON, NEDEEM!' shouted Jez Pope.

'COME ON, JACOBS! YOU CAN DO IT!' was the cry from Simon Phillips.

'What's going on?' said Alan Turpin.

Nedeem had now run almost half the length of the pitch and was starting to tire, when one of the biggest young offenders appeared out of nowhere, making inroads diagonally across the field. He was really gathering momentum and all we could do was watch and wait for the inevitable: he was gonna take Nedeem out. It wouldn't be a legal challenge, but it would definitely mean we wouldn't score the try.

'MAN ON NEDEEM!' shouted Mr Atkinson.

Then suddenly the boy jumped, the whole humongous force of his body intent on bringing Nedeem down. Everything dulled into slow motion. He leapt, arms stretched out to grab and rip Nedeem apart and, as he did – and I'll always remember this – Nedeem had a burst of pace, side-stepping to put himself out of the young offender's reach, which in turn meant the boy chasing behind him clattered into his team mate, ending with both of them on the floor. It left Nedeem with an open field.

Mr Atkinson was jumping up and down. 'YES, NEDEEM! GO ON!' It was the most beautiful moment. We were cheering and jumping around, none of us able to contain our excitement as Nedeem made stride after stride towards the touchline. We couldn't believe we were going to score a try. This team of misfits and outcasts was actually going to have achieved something. To win, just once: that was all we needed.

As Nedeem sprinted over the touchline, he held his arms aloft and turned and looked back at us. I had never seen Nedeem look so happy. He punched the sky and shouted, 'YEAAAHHH!' and we cheered right back at him. This was his day in the spotlight, his moment to be the hero. It was spectacular until . . . well, then he did something that neither I nor anyone else on the team that day is ever likely to forget.

Nedeem shouted out, 'YEAAAHHHH!' again, and then threw the ball on the ground like an American football player. He just tossed it on the floor. We all looked on, stunned. In rugby, the ball has to be touched onto the grass behind the try line; if it's not grounded, it's not a try. Everyone, pretty much in unison, shouted, 'NOOOOOOO!' Mr Atkinson crouched down with his head in his hands, his face a picture of disappointment and bewilderment. In that moment, Nedeem's face turned from elation to abject despair. The young offenders burst out laughing and, to cap it all, eventually went on to win 3–0.

That was it. Over the next few weeks, every one of us lost our appetite for rugby. I think even Mr Atkinson went off it too. Who could blame him?

Nedeem left the school the following term, though I think it had more to do with his family moving away than the rugby incident. On his last day he came and told me how sorry he was about the try. I told him to forget about it, that it was just a game and it didn't matter.

'I enjoyed it though,' he said quietly. 'That moment. Being in a team. It was good fun.' Looking back now, he was right. It was amazing fun while it lasted. And I hope that wherever Mr Atkinson is, whatever he's doing, he'll look back on those couple of terms and feel proud. Despite the fights and the record-breaking losses, the rugby team did exactly what he wanted it to: it brought a group of mostly lost souls together. And for a moment, just a short moment, we all believed in something. Ourselves.

CHAPTER 6

BEST MUSICAL ACCOMPANIMENT:
'Pass the Dutchie' by Musical Youth

BEST FILM TO WATCH ALONGSIDE:
Dazed and Confused

BEST ENJOYED WITH:
a bag of Wheat Crunchies, a Yorkie and a Twix

So, with the rugby season finished, school dragged on until we reached the summer term and, inevitably, exams. I don't suppose it will come as much of a shock to discover that I was completely unprepared for my GCSEs. Nor will you fall off your chair when I tell you that I had no idea about this weird 'revision' thing everyone was talking about. It was supposedly so important that we'd been given the last two weeks of the summer term to spend doing it.

I phoned Claire Alcock, who I was in love with at the time. We'd been to see Take That together and I was besotted by her. In return, she told she liked me 'as a friend' – a phrase that was becoming all too familiar.

I called her to ask her what we were supposed to do exactly for revision. She picked up the phone and, as I heard her voice, my heart skipped its usual couple of beats.

'Claire,' I said, 'they've given us this time off but I don't really know what to do with it. I mean, I'm not sure what revising is really.'

'Well, it's just looking back over your notes, James, isn't it?'

I paused for a moment and said, 'Right, right, your notes. Yeah, I knew that, of course.'

'It's not difficult,' she told me. 'Just go back over the stuff you wrote in class and it'll help you focus on the questions in the exam.'

Notes? What was she talking about? I didn't even have any books, never mind notes.

So, the weeks of precious cramming time went by and I watched a lot of Wimbledon and then all too soon there we were in the exam hall, seated at solitary desks, working on papers that were supposed to shape the rest of our lives. I remember European Studies in particular; I'd love to lay my hands on that exam paper. I remember exactly how it looked – crisp and white and sort of virginal. The idea was to fill in the answers on the pages provided; some had big chunks of white space, others much smaller. Needless to say mine remained relatively clean.

I remember writing my name, though, and also that there was space in the border next to the first question for the examiner to make their comments. I decided to address this space specifically and write the examiner a friendly note. It went something like this:

Dear Examiner,

How are you today? Very well, I hope, though I imagine a little bored? I guess that marking paper after paper must be just a tad tedious, yeah? I mean, question after question from all these different students, offering little more than variations on the same answer. Well, here's a variation for you, a way of easing your pain. My aim today is not so much to pass European Studies as to pass the time and also to brighten your day. I'd like to try and lift you from the monotony of this repetitive process because there'll be nothing to mark here. I haven't done any work. I wanted to do Music

and RE but they wouldn't let me do that and I had to do
this instead, so as a kind of protest I used to go to the classes
without so much as a pen, let alone any books or a bag.
So now you're aware of the history, I'm going to try and
make you laugh. That's my mission here and, if I succeed,
if I can lift you from the boredom, I was wondering if, by
way of thanks, you might give me an 'A'. What do you
think? It would shock everybody, wouldn't it? It'd be really
good karma, don't you think? So that's the purpose of this
paper, just so's you know from the outset.

I remember questions along the lines of 'Who invaded what country on such and such a date and what were the immediate repercussions?' I would write something like 'Fred Flintstone invaded from Bedrock, together with Barney Rubble. He moved at night, took over the town and blew up the quarry' or some other bit of nonsense. It was all an attempt to make the examiner laugh and see if, together, we couldn't fly in the face of convention.

He gave me a 'U'. That means Ungraded – so bad it's not even worthy of a mark.

I could live with that. It was only European Studies, and if it hadn't been for Holmer Green's no Music or RE policy, I would never have taken the class anyway. The thing I'm really embarrassed about is my Drama exam.

The only coursework you had to do for Drama was keep a diary. Not very difficult. There was no structure, no right and wrong; you merely had to keep a record of what you'd done in the lessons and hand in the diary at the end of the year. But I didn't keep a diary, so I only got a 'B' when I should have walked an 'A'. Actually, it was miraculous I even got a 'B'. Mrs Roberts, my suffer-no-fools Drama teacher, told me I was a complete idiot. I must have been a constant source of frustration to her because, even though I didn't bother with the coursework, hers were the only lessons in which I paid any attention. Back in the staffroom, I'm sure she must have heard from my other teachers what a nightmare I was in their lessons, so she wasn't overcome with sympathy.

'You're an idiot, James.' I can still hear her voice and remember wilting under her gaze. 'You're so stupid. All you had to do was hand in a diary and you could have got an "A". But you just couldn't do that, could you?'

To this day I can't tell you why I didn't bother. It would be easy to say I was a maverick, that I was misunderstood or whatever, but I don't think it was that at all. I was just plain lazy.

'I know I should've handed in the coursework,' I told her, 'but I'm going to be an actor, Mrs Roberts. None of my GCSEs are going to matter.'

She looked at me long and hard. 'James,' she said, 'right now you're a big fish in the smallest pond in the world and when you get out there, you'll be a tiny fish in an enormous ocean. You're not going to know what hit you.' I remember my feeling of disappointment to this day.

When August came around and the fabled brown envelope flopped through the letterbox, I wasn't there to receive it. I was still in the Salvation Army at the time and a few of us were away at music week. I remember when the results came out, though: it was all anyone could talk about. 'Oh, I got this' or 'I got that', my friends either celebrating or commiserating with each other. But I didn't even dare to ring home. However, Dad came along to the performance at the end of the week and, with a face etched with real disappointment, asked me if I wanted to know the results. I told him that I doubted it, but he went ahead and delivered the news anyway: a B in Drama, a C in English and the rest, well, all below an E.

So that was that. It was a kind of confirmation that school was over for me. What was the point of it if it only brought disappointment or detention? But, despite his obvious frustration with me, Dad was about to prove just how much he believed in me, bad exam results or not . . .

Right, before I carry on I'm going to nip back to the hospital now to see how Mummy and the little fella are getting on. Have a cup of tea, I'll be back in a minute . . .

OK, he's doing well, but we still don't know what to call him. We're thinking Felix. I've never met a guy called Felix who hasn't been cool, so I'm liking it as a name, though Jules is worried it just sounds like cat food. It was so lovely, just now, at the hospital, holding him as he drifted in and out of sleep in my arms. It made me think of my own father, and the different times he's given me advice and really been there for us kids. I remember Dad once saying to me that 'The difference between doing something and not doing something is doing something.' He was talking to me about homework at the time, and yet I've always remembered it. I like it as a saying because it takes chance out of the equation. It says if you want to do something, if you *really* want to, and believe you can, you will.

Holding my newborn baby in my arms just now, I couldn't help but wonder what he's going to do, or who he's going to be when he's older. What will he remember as the best day of his life? I remember mine clearly, but to fully tell you about the best day of my life I kind of have to fill you in on one of the worst. Here goes:

I was walking home from school on quite a grey day, listening to Arrested Development on my Walkman, bopping like I was in some sort of music video. You know, the ones where people stride purposefully towards the camera in time to the music? That was me, all the way home. I remember the beat to 'Mr Wendal' kicking in when, out of the blue, Dad pulled up alongside me in his car and asked if I wanted a lift. Of course. I jumped straight in, but instead of talking about his day or telling him about mine, I just carried on listening to my Walkman.

We got home, and Dad said he had to tell me something. I went into the lounge where my mum was sitting on the sofa along with Andrea and Rudi. I remember asking Ange (what we call Andrea) how she got home so fast.

'Dad picked me up,' she said.

'And me,' said Rudi in her cute little voice.

At that point Dad came in and sat down next to Mum. I wish I could remember exactly what he said, or how he even began to tell us, but I can't. I can't remember anything about that moment, except one thing. Dad told us that he'd been called up to fight in the first Gulf War.

'But you're just a musician in the Air Force,' said Ange, saying exactly what we were all thinking.

'Yeah, you just play the saxophone. What are you gonna do?' said Rudi, echoing our thoughts.

Dad told us that he was going to be a stretcher-bearer and he'd be leaving in three weeks. I remember standing up off the floor (we had furniture, I just liked it on the floor) and dramatically sweeping out of the lounge and up to my room. I did this mostly for effect, but also so my mum wouldn't see me crying. The big problem with sweeping out of a room is that the moment you get out the door, you don't know where to go. I remember feeling drowned in questions to ask my dad: 'Will you have a gun? What will you eat? Where exactly is Bahrain?' But rather than go back and ask, I went to my room and got into bed. I got out pretty quick, though, 'cos to balance out the worst news we'd ever been told as a family, Mum had gone all out for tea: turkey burgers, chips and beans – I was upset, not stupid.

Three weeks came and went pretty quickly, and the day for Dad to leave arrived. I remember it so vividly. We were all in the kitchen and Dad was standing there, dressed like Action Man, with all this camouflage gear on.

We said goodbye and Dad went down the line, hugging all

of us. There were so many tears. Mum was trying her best to be strong but, the minute Ange went, Rudi went, then Mum went and that made me go. Dad stayed strong, but when he hugged Mum he was sobbing so much he held her in his chest and called the three of us over to all put our arms round each other; that cuddle felt as if it went on for ages, the whole family just clinging on to each other. I'm sure this sounds quite dramatic, but the thing about war is that it is just that. Everything feels like a huge drama. It's the unexpectedness of it. No one actually knows what they're letting themselves in for, so you end up focusing on the worst-case scenario.

Dad eventually left, and life kind of got back to normal, but to tell you the truth I was never myself during the time he was away. I couldn't cope with it. I couldn't talk to him on the phone. He'd ring every couple of days, and Ange, Rudi and Mum would chat to him, but I would just burst into tears if I heard his voice. I just couldn't adjust to where he was or what he was doing and pretend it was normal.

Some days were fine – it wouldn't feel too different to any other day, but there were times you'd really notice it. I remember being in the kitchen eating a bowl of Frosties one day, chatting to Mum, when we heard on the news that a Scud missile had been intercepted over the base where Dad was stationed in Bahrain. I just stopped eating and looked at Mum, who had gone pale. She walked over, put her arm around me and said it was good news because it hadn't hit and everyone was fine. I was down all that day; in fact, it got to a point where they were all pretty much down days in our house.

We were moving into month five when I remember coming downstairs and seeing Mum sitting on her own in the lounge. I was watching through a gap in the doorway and she was just sitting there, not crying or anything, just sitting, as if the weight of the world was on her shoulders. She looked so alone.

'You all right, Mum?' I asked.

'Yep,' she replied, and got up and left the room. She wasn't all right at all.

All a bit down this, isn't it? So I'm gonna skip forward to the good stuff, the day we were told that Dad was coming home. It was an incredible day, totally amazing. So amazing that I don't remember where I was or who told me or anything else about it. All I remember was being told he'd be home in three days. Before I knew it, we were in the car on the way to RAF Uxbridge. We got there and there were loads of other families crowding around, all waiting for the return of their loved ones.

Mum was talking to lots of other mums, and Rudi and I just sort of hung out together. Someone had tried to set up some kind of 'buffet' in the mess, but they shouldn't have bothered. There were just lots of little bowls of crisps – rubbish crisps – and two bowls of peanuts. Now that's all right, but that's not a 'buffet'. You're just getting people's hopes up for sausage rolls and picnic eggs and salady stuff when you call it a 'buffet'. Just put the crisps and peanuts out and say nothing about it; that way people thank you for it, instead of complaining about the spread.

The buffet disappointment didn't last long though, because there was suddenly a rush of activity, with everyone racing to get outside. There was loads of whooping and cheering, which was then getting drowned out by the noise of an engine and a beeping horn. I ran to the front of the crowd and could see a big blue and white coach pulling in to the car park. It drove past us a bit and I ran alongside it, looking up at the windows to see if I could find Dad. I couldn't see him anywhere and, for a brief moment, still running along, I had a pang of worry that he wasn't on the bus at all, that something had happened.

Then, just as the coach slowed to a stop, I saw him. He was right there in the window, looking straight at me. It was as if there was no one else in the world. He was smiling and looking

Me, aged three, just taking it easy on the beach.

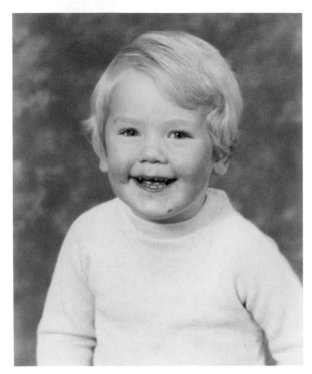

My first ever photo shoot.

On holiday at the farm.
What a dump!

Just a young guy in buckled shoes, leaning against a tree.

Inn Keeper No. 1.

Performing 'Nibble Nibble Munch Munch' at Middle School. The guy next to me was about to do a Mr. T. impression.

Aged eight, in my Salvation Army uniform.

Aged ten, Park Court Middle School,
chubby cheeks are forming.

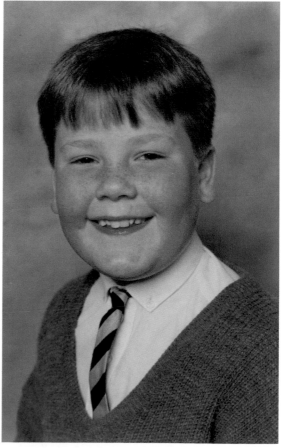

My sisters and I. Andrea (left) and Ruth (middle).

Mummy's boy.

Me, Mum, Rudi and Dad is on the right. No one has a clue who the guy on the left is. Seriously, not a clue!

Stage school agency photos. In the one on the bottom left, I had asked the barber to cut my hair like Gary Barlow's in the 'Pray' video.

tanned and, in a strange way, he didn't even look like Dad. The coach door opened achingly slowly and he was one of the first to get off.

He looked at me and said, 'Hiya, son,' and then threw his arms around me. I remember squeezing him so tight, my face pressing so hard into his shirt. He smelled like the inside of a bag that is full of your wet and musty clothes after a day on the beach. I kept holding on tight as I heard him call out to Mum and Rudi. They came over and, at first, I refused to let go. Then he picked Rudi up in his arms and held a hand out to Mum. I stepped away and Mum put her hands up to his face and just stood there, looking at him. They both smiled and almost began to laugh at the sheer joy of it all. Dad pulled Mum closer and kissed her tenderly on the forehead, and she just let out the biggest sigh of relief, as if all her worries had disappeared in that one moment. She shut her eyes and kissed him on the cheek, then Rudi leant in and gave him a kiss on the other cheek. And Dad just pulled them both closer to him, smiling all the time.

And that, right there, that moment – that was the best day of my life.

It does feel strange, looking back on that day, now that I'm a father. That the things I do and say will have a greater impact on my as-yet-unnamed son's life than I'm sure I can comprehend. I hope, like my father, that I can be a good one. I asked my dad a couple of days ago if he had always believed in me, even when things like my awful exam results happened. Whether he thought that I could do the things I'd dreamt of, the work I'm lucky enough to be doing now. Without even pausing, he said that he always had; he just hoped I would put the work in as he knew how incredibly lazy I could be. When you look at my awful GCSE results, you can't really blame him for thinking that. But, as I said previously, it was right at that moment of my exam results – when he was probably at his most frustrated and disappointed – that he was about to prove once again just how far his belief stretched.

I had already decided I wanted to go to Amersham and Wycombe College to do a B-Tech National Diploma in Performing Arts, but you had to have four GCSEs or more to get on the course. If you had fewer than that, you'd have to do a B-Tech something else for a year, a sort of access course, before going on to the National Diploma. I didn't want to waste a year, but then I didn't have the results to get me in. So I talked to Dad about it and he decided that the two of us would go and speak to the lady who looked after the admissions.

I was so nervous that I can't remember a lot of that meeting, but I do recall it not going so well from the start. At some point I started to lose it a little, and was really pleading with her to let me straight on to the B-Tech course. Dad had let me do most of the talking to begin with, but as I started to get more and more desperate, he cut in, just at the right moment, and told her that whatever my exam results seemed to suggest, I wasn't stupid; it was just that all I cared about was Drama and English. He reminded her that this was a 'Performing Arts' course and that, since the age of eleven, I'd been involved in nothing but that. He was vehement, fighting my corner, asking her what it mattered if I didn't have a C grade or above in Science or French because it wasn't relevant. And guess what? It worked. After a good old battle, she agreed to let me on the course. Dad killed it.

September came around and it felt as though a new chapter was beginning. On my first day, I got the bus to Amersham and walked up the hill to the college. It looked massive. It must've been four times the size of Holmer Green Upper, if not bigger. And the sheer number of people making their way in . . . Mrs Hatfield's comments rang in my ears. She was right: this was a much bigger pond. Four thousand people on that campus alone, and they all looked totally different to any people I'd hung out with before. For starters, everyone looked cool – lads were rolling up on skateboards, like Michael J. Fox in *Back to the Future*. I'd never been any good on a skateboard; I was always the kid lying down on it while everyone else was doing ollies and kick flips. People were smoking and wearing tour T-shirts of bands I'd never heard of. But as the day continued, my nerves started vanishing and were replaced with a massive feeling of excitement. This was all shiny and new: different people with different mind-sets from different backgrounds. I was so relieved not to be at school any more.

There were about thirty or forty kids in my class, and that first lesson we had to go round the room and say something unique about ourselves. It came to my turn and I stood up and looked around at my fellow students. 'Hi,' I said, 'my name's James and I don't care what you say, I love Take That.' I guess it broke the ice.

I met some really good friends at college. There were two guys in particular called Jack and Josh, who to this day are two of the best actors I've ever met. They came as a package, Jack and Josh, and they kind of took me under their wing. I remember one Tuesday, we had two free periods back to back, and they asked me whether I wanted to go hang out in Josh's car. 'Sure, why not?' I said, not even asking where we were going. So we went out to the car park and all bundled into Josh's beige Vauxhall Nova. I sat in the back with Jack and Josh in the front and waited for Josh to start the engine and drive to wherever it was we were going. But that never happened. Instead, Jack reached into his pockets and started pulling out various Rizla papers, half-used cigarettes and a small, clingfilm-wrapped, green wodge of something that looked like herbs, and began building what I now know is a joint. At the time I had no idea what was going on. He rolled it up and lit it, took a few deep puffs and, exhaling, said, 'Oh yeah, that's really good. Really smooth.' He then reclined his seat, closed his eyes, slid his head back and passed over the joint to Josh, who did exactly the same and then passed the joint back to me over his shoulder. I held it between my thumb and index finger and, not wanting to appear like a novice, or in any way uncool, put it in my mouth and inhaled for as long as Jack and Josh just had. Bad idea. Within seconds I was coughing and spluttering all over the place. My chest felt as if it was going to explode. Jack and Josh burst out laughing and one of them handed me a bottle of water. Once my coughing had stopped, I looked at them both in the rear-view mirror and said, 'Yeah, that's really smooth. Not harsh at all.'

They must've known it was my first time, but being decent guys, they didn't take the piss or anything; they just rolled another and for the next two hours we hotboxed in Josh's Nova, smoking joint after joint. When the time came for us to go back to lessons, Jack and Josh stepped out of the car like nothing had changed. I, on the other hand, was all over the place. I could barely feel my legs and, when I looked up, I could see two Jacks and two Joshes, which was pretty much the funniest thing I'd ever seen. I burst out laughing, then they burst out laughing, and with tears rolling down our faces, the three of us stood there in the middle of the car park and pissed ourselves (not literally) for five straight minutes. To this day I'm not sure I've ever laughed that much.

Jack went back to the car and grabbed his sunglasses. 'You'd better wear these,' he said, handing them to me. 'Your eyes are a giveaway.'

We stumbled back into class, and there I sat, right at the very back, wearing Jack's shades with the biggest grin on my face. When the teacher asked why I was wearing sunglasses, Josh jumped in quick as a flash and said, 'He's got an eye infection,' which made me crack up even more. I have no idea what the lesson was about that day. All I know is I sat at the back of that class, feeling one minute like I might die and the next like I might fly.

After class finished, I still had £1.70 in my pocket for my bus fare home, but was so all over the place that I went straight to the vending machine and spent the lot on a bag of Wheat

Crunchies, a Yorkie and a Twix. The four-mile trek home took me hours. When I got back, at 7.30 p.m., I felt so sick I went straight to bed. After that, I only joined Jack and Josh in the car on the odd occasion – and only if we didn't have a lesson straight afterwards.

I mentioned earlier that there are certain teachers who can really influence your life, for good or for bad. There was one at Amersham who was absolutely amazing: John Keats. (No, not the poet – he'd never have taught at a place like Amersham.) John had his own theatre company, which put on some really innovative productions, and his lessons had that same spark: they were like nothing I'd ever known. He had this aura about him, big-time charisma. People would be chatting away as he'd walk into a class and he'd just clap his hands and tell everyone to stand on their chairs, and – bam! – everyone would get up.

In class, we covered all aspects of performance and spent a fair amount of time on comedy. John asked us to bring in a video of our favourite bit of stand-up, so I took in Newman & Baddiel's 'History Today'. Watching everyone else's favourites showed us a broad spectrum of what made people laugh, and perhaps I absorbed more of that than I remember at the time. John asked us to follow it by bringing in five minutes of our own material. I remember some of the girls crying, completely terrified at the thought of doing it, but John was as reassuring as he was charismatic and he just told all of us we could do it. And so we did.

I loved it. To this day people still refer to me as a comedian, or ask if I'm ever going to do stand-up. My answer is always the same: anyone can be funny for ten or fifteen minutes, but that's not stand-up comedy. An hour, hour and a half – that's doing stand-up, and I'm pretty sure I don't have that skill. It takes years to get the precision needed to do it properly. I'm in awe of the people who do it: people like Seinfeld, Chris Rock or Michael McIntyre. Michael is a brilliant comedian and I talked to him the other day about possibly giving stand-up a go, obviously on a much smaller scale than he does. I'm blown away by how he can command an arena, with 16,000 people hanging on his every word. I'm not sure I have that ability, but one day I'd love to just give it a try; to do it in clubs and much smaller venues and see how it goes. That's if I can muster the courage.

John Keats didn't just talk about comedy, though. Every lesson he brought something new and even more ground-breaking to the party. For example, he took a scene from *Guys and Dolls* and made us do it as Nazis. You can only imagine how it was: Sky Masterson and Nicely-Nicely Johnson doing their scenes in stilted German accents. It was definitely different.

I loved that first term. I would look forward to the bus journey to college. I was learning so much and I was surrounded by so many talented people. Jack and Josh, for example: two brilliant, creative, original performers. I've got no clue why they aren't up there doing it now. I mean, some of the stuff I saw them do was just incredible. I suppose that was the point: everyone who was doing it really wanted to be there. I'd come from Drama classes at school where people were doing it because it was an easy GCSE, and now I was with a group of people who wanted to do nothing else. It was really magical – until John left.

Around about Easter of that first year, his theatre company just took off. We came back from the holidays and he wasn't there. It was a major blow and it wasn't the only one: Julian, another really good teacher, had gone off to study in Russia, and all of a sudden we'd gone from these dynamic young, free-thinking individuals to a guy who reminded me of Mr Hopkins. Stewart was his name and I wish I could remember his surname because as far as I was concerned, he might just be the worst teacher known to man. All we ever seemed to do was sit and read through plays, with him standing at the front giving us choice morsels like 'The first rule of theatre is you don't turn your back on the audience.'

We went from mind-blowing to mind-numbing in a

heartbeat. The new classes were painful by comparison. I remember once Julian made us do a whole lesson in the boys' toilets. The girls got all grossed out because they'd never seen how boys pee while standing at a single urinal. It was smelly, it was dirty, it *was* totally gross, but his point was that theatre is everywhere. He didn't have us in there for a laugh; he was making us aware that you don't need a stage or an interval or red velvet seats to create theatre. You can do it anywhere; you can see it anywhere. Now, with Stewart, we barely got out of our chairs.

October to Easter had been the best few months of study I'd ever experienced, so I felt doubly angry and let down when it started to go wrong. It affected me pretty badly and, to my shame, I have to admit I stopped going to college altogether.

I was living at home with Mum and Dad still, but they would be up and out to work before me. Mum was a social worker and Dad was either away working or at the Air Force base. Sometimes at college you wouldn't have to be in until ten, and being home before anyone else wasn't unusual. So when Mum and Dad left for work, I'd say goodbye, pretending to get my stuff ready, and then not bother going in. College would go on without me. I'd stay at home and just laze around the house doing absolutely nothing at all.

This went on for about three weeks before it occurred to me that I probably ought to go back in. Whatever point I was making by staying away – if that's even what I was doing – had been made, and so I knew I had to face the music. I was in the main corridor looking at the notice board for where my classes were when Stewart came up to me. He looked a little quizzical and then he asked me what I was doing there.

For a moment I just stared at him. 'What do you mean?' I said. 'I've got lessons. Your lesson actually.'

Arms folded, he shook his head. 'No you don't. You're not coming to my lesson. You can forget it.'

The corridor was busy and the way the two of us were

standing – Stewart with his arms folded across his chest, me more on the defensive – was gathering a little attention.

'What do you mean?' I asked him.

'What I said. You've not been here for three and a half weeks. No one called. Your parents didn't write in with any kind of explanation. You just haven't been here. So you're not coming back to my lesson. We're working on a show now and you're not part of it.'

He was so chillingly matter-of-fact about it that I just went cold. I stood there staring at him. Oh my God, I thought. Oh my God. What have I done?

But he wasn't finished. 'As far as I'm concerned, you're off the course. You'd better go and see the head of year. I'm sure she wants to talk to you.'

He walked off, leaving me staring at his back and wracking my brains as to what the hell I was going to do. What would I tell my dad, who'd fought for my place on the course? Or my mum, who'd always defended me when others had lost faith? I was all over the shop, so I did exactly as he told me and went straight to the head of year's office. I waited outside with my head against the wall, trying to think of something I could say that would stop her throwing me off the course altogether.

She came out to fetch me: Karen, the woman whom Dad had persuaded to let me on the course. She was cold and stern, more so even than Stewart.

'Where have you been for the last three and a half weeks?' she demanded.

I didn't know what to say. For a long moment I just looked at her. And then it came to me – I opened my mouth and out it came, one massive, horrible lie.

'I've had family problems.'

Up until this point she had been standing over me and now she sat down. 'What?' she said. 'What do you mean?'

I'd dug the hole and now I had to fill it: 'My parents are getting divorced.'

For a moment she didn't say anything, but I noticed her expression starting to soften a little and I latched on to it, pushing the lie further and further.

'It's been going on for some time now,' I said, 'arguments, fights in the house. It's been a nightmare.' I was gesturing, my eyes glassy and my voice getting smaller. 'I suppose it blew up over Easter, but it's been going on a lot longer than that. With everything that's been happening, I just couldn't concentrate on my coursework. I've been trying to take care of my sisters. I . . . I . . . I . . .' And with that I burst into tears. I've put on some good performances in my life, and that was probably one of the best; it's definitely the one of which I'm least proud.

'All right, James,' she said more gently. 'I'm sorry. I had no idea.'

'I know I should have come in,' I went on. 'Three and a half weeks is a long time. I know I should've called or written to explain or something, but—'

'It's all right,' she said, patting my hand. 'It's OK. I understand. Come with me to class and I'll explain it to Stewart.'

So we trooped down the corridor to his class and he had to listen while Karen repeated my lies. There was nothing he could do or say.

That was it. I was back. I'd survived after spouting a bunch of really unpleasant crap about my family. The whole episode nearly came back to bite me, however. About a week later a letter came through the door with the Amersham and Wycombe stamp on it. Luckily, I got to it before my parents did. It was from the head of year, saying that I was really depressed and that she hoped things could be worked out at home as I'd already missed three and a half weeks of my course. To miss any more would have serious repercussions for my future.

I burnt the letter. Obliterated all trace of it. To this day my mum and dad don't know about those missing weeks or my lie about their marriage. So here's my chance to say a massive sorry to them and to Karen and, through gritted teeth, to Stewart.

Sorry.

As it turned out, it didn't really matter. I left that summer anyway. If John and Julian had remained, then perhaps I might have stuck around – actually, there's no perhaps about it: they were two of the most radical and original teachers I've ever come across – but without them there I finished the rest of that year and then packed it in.

However, John and Julian's absence wasn't the only reason for me leaving. Something was on the horizon, something exciting. I was about to get my first big proper job – a musical in the West End.

CHAPTER 7

BEST MUSICAL ACCOMPANIMENT:
'Horny' by Mousse T.

BEST FILM TO WATCH ALONGSIDE:
Risky Business

BEST ENJOYED WITH:
oysters

Marilyn, my agent, rang and told me about an audition for a new musical that was getting a ton of early buzz – *Martin Guerre*. To save some time, let me break down the story of the play for you.

It's about this guy in sixteenth-century France who leaves home without telling his wife and kids. Everyone thinks he's dead and then out of the blue he shows up again years later with a nice big 'Hi, honey, I'm home.'

'What? Who the hell are you?' the wife asks.

'I'm Martin Guerre, of course, your husband.'

'Oh yeah, right. You don't look like him and you don't sound like him and, by the way, if you are him, where the hell have you been for the last seven years?'

'Ummm, yeah. Well, there's two ways to answer that question . . .'

You get the gist.

The story was based on real life (so Martin Guerre was actually a real guy – though the guy saying he was Martin Guerre wasn't really Martin Guerre because the real Martin Guerre turns out not to be dead and then he comes back and . . . oh, forget it) and the musical had been written by Claude-Michel Schönberg and Alain Boublil, the guys responsible for *Les Misérables* and *Miss Saigon*, two absolutely humongous hits that ran and ran and ran. Just the thought of being in a show written by those two guys blew my mind.

I'd never been so excited going for an audition. I was going for the part of one of two young boys in the chorus. I had one line – just the one: 'Roast the meats.' That was all. 'Roast the meats.' If you ever need a singing BBQ master, I'm your man.

But I wasn't singing that at the audition. For that I chose a song from the musical *Chess* called 'Anthem'. It's a standard song for West End musical auditions and I gave it all I'd got. It went well enough that the director asked me back for a dance call, along with twenty other boys of various shapes and sizes. You can imagine them wondering, can't you? Can a guy who looks like that cope with a dance routine?

Please. We all know that I'd been practising for years in the living room, studying and recreating every move Take That ever laid down; they were imprinted on my soul. So I breezed through the dancing and then later that day I got a call to tell me that I'd made it to the third stage. I was getting so close I could almost touch it. Sitting here scribbling this to you now, I can still remember that last audition as if it were yesterday.

The third call then: it was at the Criterion Theatre just off Piccadilly Circus, and I had to wait in this corridor along with a group of other actors who were there to audition for various other parts. When my turn came, I stepped onto the stage and boom, my head exploded. The size of it! It was huge, I mean colossal, monumental, enormous, really, really big. The theatre was more or less empty so there was this very noticeable echo. All I could see was this makeshift desk set up in the middle of the stalls at which Cameron Mackintosh, the biggest theatre producer in the country, was sitting. And next to him were the writers of the show, Claude-Michel Schönberg and Alain Boublil, two of the most successful musical writers in history. Then there was Declan Donnellan, the director, who ran his own theatre company called Cheek By Jowl and was – and still is – one of the best around. The choreographer, a guy called Bob Avian, was sitting next to Alain with his assistant, Craig Revel Horwood alongside him. Yup, Craig from *Strictly Come Dancing*. No pressure then.

I remember thinking that if a bomb went off at this moment, theatreland would have been in serious trouble.

So I'd made it past the first two challenges, but this, right here, was the end-of-level boss. My nerves were jangling, my palms were sweating and my legs were wobbling. I'm sure it wasn't a pretty sight. I'd prepared 'Stony Ground', a really upbeat song from a Christian musical, but the musical director had other ideas, which didn't help the nerves. He suggested I sing 'Anthem' again, as I'd done a good job on it last time around and he thought that Claude and Alain would really appreciate my vocal range. I wasn't about to argue with him, especially as he'd been nice about my performance. 'Anthem' it was.

It seemed to go down well and, when I finished, Declan came up on the stage and told me he wanted me to sing the song again, only this time belt it out as if there was an army of people in the theatre all looking to me to lead them.

'James,' he said, 'I want you to walk around this stage in a circle. I want you to imagine that this army is standing all around you. They're waiting for orders and, when you decide the time is right, I want you to send them out to war. Send them through the stalls. Send them up to the dress circle and to the upper circle. Send them out until the whole place is full of people and they're all listening to you. It's an army, James. Send them out to war!'

Right, I thought, right. OK, then. OK. I've got that, yeah – that's what you do at auditions: no matter how weird the directions seem to you, you don't question them. An army, going out to war, while I sing 'Anthem'; no worries, no problem. I can do that.

I've done a lot of auditions now and I've been asked to do some strange stuff. Auditioning for adverts is the strangest. I remember when I was about sixteen doing an advert for a Danish yoghurt company. The director – also Danish – had some interesting ideas of how to market the product. 'All right,' he said. 'Now listen to me, James, I want you to really think about this. I want you to imagine you're sitting down now, you understand. OK?'

'Yeah, sitting down. Got that, yeah.'

'OK, good. Sitting down, but not on a chair, James, not on a chair. I want you to imagine you're naked, you understand – you have no clothes on at all.'

'Naked, yeah. OK, I can do that. No clothes on. Right. No problem.'

'OK, but this is the important bit, this is where the shoot will stand or fall. I want you to imagine you're sitting on a block of ice.'

'With no clothes on?'

'That's right.'

'So it's pretty chilly then.'

'Of course. But listen, James . . .'

'Yes?'

'Here's the thing. It cannot be funny. You understand. The way you sit on the ice with no clothes. It cannot be comical, all right?' And with that, he patted me on the shoulder. I didn't get the part.

Clearly Declan had his reasons for the army, so I sang the song again, only this time I was in charge: I was in uniform, ordering an army out to war. I was Mel Gibson in *Braveheart*, Aragorn in *The Return of the King* – OK, they hadn't made that film yet but you get the picture. I went for it, singing with every bit of guts, gusto and passion I could muster. Ten days later I got the job.

Oh. My. God. *Martin Guerre*, Claude and Alain, Cameron Mackintosh – it was just the most incredible news. I'd dropped out of college and right into a West End show. And I was going to get paid.

I did get paid, £260 a week, so by the time I'd paid my agent, my rail fare and the tax and everything, I was barely breaking even. But I couldn't care less. I was so happy to be doing what I'd always dreamt of.

The first day of rehearsals came around and I was a bag of nerves. Into the toilet, out of the toilet, into the toilet again – and that was just on the train. The other young guy who'd been picked was Paul Bailey, and we hung out together quite a lot: he and I and this whole company of incredible actors, pretty much all of whom had been in other West End shows.

Ironically, we rehearsed at Sadler's Wells, in one of the rooms where I'd auditioned for *The Sound of Music* while Dad waited in the car. And now, here I was, after all those years of getting knocked back, a real-life, paid actor on the West End stage. Wow.

It's strange how things seem to come full circle. You know what I mean? I'm sure you do. The way your life seems to drift along with no set path, then something good happens to you and you can trace the line that brought you there back to a specific disappointment or rejection you suffered in the past. It's nice that things can level out that way.

My first day at work, I was so keen that I was up early, on the train early, in the loo early and, of course, I was one of the first to arrive at the theatre. I just sat in a corner as the minutes ticked by, growing more and more nervous. I had no idea what to expect. I'd signed up for a year and I just sat there thinking, Oh my God. This is it. I'm actually doing it. I thought back to that day at school when Mr Graham had told me I could forget about doing Music as a GCSE option. I thought of Mrs Roberts and her disappointment. I thought of all those times my dad had driven me up to London for auditions I never got. All I'd ever wanted was to be in a West End Show and there I was, waiting for the cast to arrive.

I want to tell you it was amazing, and that it was everything I'd hoped it would be. But if I'm honest, it wasn't. I didn't enjoy that first day at all. Usually the only useful thing about nerves is that eventually they go away, but that first day I couldn't get rid of the churning in my stomach. I was a total wreck.

At the beginning of the day, as a bit of a loosener, Declan had got everyone singing the trolley song. You know how it goes. A one, a two, a one, two, three:

> *Clang, clang, clang went the trolley.*
> *Ding, ding, ding went the bell.*
> *Zing, zing, zing went my heartstrings*
> *From the moment I saw him I fell . . .*

We had to sing it jigging around as if we were on a tram. The girls would sing a bit and then the boys would sing a bit and, when we were finished, Declan told us to take five and then talked to us in depth about a thing he called targets.

Now, this was very interesting. It reminded me of Julian and John Keats back in college. He was talking about your 'targets' as an actor. I don't mean goals or ambitions or anything like that; I mean 'targets' you're aiming for when you're acting. It's quite technical, but I'll give you a quick example: imagine you're sitting here with me now and I ask you what you had for breakfast. You'll hear the question, unconsciously glance away, with just your eyes, look back at me again and then you'll tell me. Try it with someone, see if I'm right. I bet that's how they respond. They'll listen to the question, look away and sort of visualise the answer, and then come back with it. People do it all the time. So a 'target' is something to really bring your character to life.

I know I'm going on about it and I guess you could argue I was only seventeen and this was my first proper job, but I really did feel out of my depth. From time to time, other older members of the cast would crack up at some of the stuff Declan was saying; I never seemed to get the joke. I had no idea what they were laughing about, but I laughed anyway because I thought I'd look stupid if I didn't. Looking back, I wonder if anyone knew what we were laughing about, or if everyone else's nerves were just as frayed as mine and laughing seemed the best way to hide them.

We rehearsed for three months solid. Obviously as I only had the one line ('Roast the meats') most of my time was spent hidden away at the back, watching how the actors in the bigger parts were working, but the longer rehearsals went on, the more I was getting into it. I was getting comfortable now, and with every day that slipped by the excitement around the show seemed to grow that bit more. Everyone was saying that this was going to be the biggest thing anyone had ever seen and already making comparisons with *Les Misérables* and *Miss Saigon*. It was difficult not to believe the hype when you looked at all the talent involved: we were on to another massive hit.

Before we knew it, opening night was upon us. I'd had them before with a few school plays, but nothing could prepare me for this. The buzz around the theatre was ludicrous – I thought a florist had moved in, along with a mobile champagne cellar. Backstage we were swamped with corks and bubbles and flowers of every shape, smell and colour.

It was like the school play, the bubble of attention that had created, only magnified a thousand times. I had 'Roast the meats' down to a science and I couldn't wait to get out on stage. And it wasn't just the performance we had to look forward to: there was the after-show party. Cameron Mackintosh is renowned for throwing one hell of a first-night party and, for *Martin Guerre*, he went really big. He hired Bedford Square in London – the whole place, the entire square. It was done up to look like an eighteenth-century fair. There was an old-fashioned helter-skelter, loads of marquees, goblets instead of glasses of wine and in the middle there was this massive hog roast. The attention to detail was crazy.

Mum and Dad were going to come to the party with me, which was great – I love having my family with me on really important nights. But we lived in High Wycombe, which is a good hour away, and they wouldn't want to stay at the party as long as me. That meant my ride home would be leaving before me. I had to find myself somewhere else to stay.

Becky, one of the girls in the show, told me about this great bohemian couple called Sheila and John who lived in a big old Victorian house in Shepherds Bush. As they had been in plays and shows themselves in days gone by, they liked to rent rooms to visiting actors. It was a really good deal: people in touring shows could stay with John and Sheila for about £12 a night.

Becky was sure they would rent me a room. The house was in one of the side streets and must have been very grand in its day, but by this point was a little run down – 'shabby chic', to put it nicely. Still, though, it had a great atmosphere: theatrical posters lining the walls above the staircase, loads of well-thumbed old hardbacks, the place just seemed to echo with the past.

Sheila was totally lovely and said I could have a room. I only got to the house on the afternoon of opening night, so I quickly unpacked my stuff and, as I made for the door, she asked me what time I was likely to get in.

'I'm not sure,' I said. 'About three maybe. I think the party wraps about two. Is that OK?'

'That's fine,' she said. She was a slender woman with long greying hair, who had obviously been seriously attractive in her time. 'We don't like to give keys out too readily, but whatever time you get here, don't worry, just knock on the door and somebody will come down.' She gave me a peck on the cheek.

'Have the best time, dearie, and don't worry – we're used to people coming back at all hours.'

'If you're sure,' I said.

'Of course. Go on, break a leg.'

So, the first night. How was it? Live up to expectations? Well, *yes*! It was amazing, brilliant, like nothing I'd experienced before. The place was packed and, as the curtain fell, everyone was on their feet, cheering and applauding. It was about as good a reception as you could get. And after the show finished, there was still the party to come.

Walking round to Bedford Square with Mum and Dad was such a special moment. Dad said he couldn't believe what he'd just seen and Mum grasped my hand. She had been sat next to Gloria Hunniford and because she was crying so much, Gloria had given her a tissue. The party was incredible. I'd never been to anything like it. I'd never really been much of a drinker because, growing up in the Salvation Army, you're not allowed to drink. That night, though, I went a bit overboard with the goblets: red, white, the two together, whatever I could get my hands on. I got plastered – the first time in my life I'd ever been blind drunk: mixing the grapes like that. Well, I didn't know, did I? Mum and Dad left at around 12.30 a.m. but I stayed on till the bitter end.

So there I was, staggering around at half past two in the morning. Somehow I found a cab and showed the driver the name of the road and the number of the house, which I'd had the foresight to write down on a piece of paper. Just as well as by that point I couldn't handle talking.

A little while later he dropped me off at the house. I weaved up to the front door and, at about the sixth attempt, managed to press the bell. I waited a bit, swaying like a drunk tree, but nobody came. So I rang the bell again and at last the door opened. There was Sheila in her dressing gown, hair loose to her shoulders, looking surprisingly awake.

We got inside the hallway, and even though I was totally out of it, I could tell that Sheila looked a little flushed. She was hovering at the door to the front room as if she was guarding it.

'So, how was the party?'

"Mazing. Yeah, really great. Opening night, yeah, fantastic. I think I had a little too much to drink.' I remember at that moment I hung on to the banister at the bottom of the stairs and sneezed and farted at the same time.

'That's OK. Now, do you want anything else, some water or anything?'

'No. I am ju . . . just going to bed.'

'I'll say goodnight, then.'

"K. Goodnight.'

With that, Sheila made her way down the hall and disappeared into the dining room. I kicked my shoes off and started up the stairs, but I'd forgotten the carpet was up and – 'OW!' – I trod on some little spikes poking up from the gripper rod on the edge.

'Shit, shit. Ow.' Slumping down, I felt my sock and my hand came away wet and bloody.

It was bleeding quite a lot and, even though my brain was barely functioning, I knew I ought to at least try and find a plaster. I didn't want to get blood all over their sheets, not at £12 a night. So I hobbled down the stairs and made my way along the hall to the dining room where Sheila had disappeared a few minutes earlier. The light was on and I thought she'd be reading or something.

What I didn't realise was that the wall that divided the dining room and the front room had been knocked through, so they'd become one big room, separated by an archway. And, as I stepped through the dining-room door and looked into the front room, I came face to face with Sheila's naked back.

Naked back, naked bum, naked legs, naked everything. She was sitting astride a pair of meaty-looking thighs, long grey hair flying, arms over her head, moaning in ecstasy: 'Ooh, ah, oh my God, oh my God. Go, go, go. Yessssss.'

I was literally six feet from where she was grinding up and down, her hands flailing around her, her head rocking from side to side.

I just froze.

'Ooh, ah, ooh.'

I didn't know what to do, but I knew I should get the hell out of this room. I slowly tried to make my way out of the room, but the floorboards creaked as I moved. Shit! I froze again – watching, waiting to be discovered. But Sheila just carried on.

'Ooh ooh, yes. That's it. Yes! Ooh, aah, ooh!'

I took another step: creak. Another: creak, creak.

Then, all at once, the writhing stopped. I was stood just behind the wall and for a few seconds there was silence. And then they started up again, really going for it. I couldn't move as every single floorboard surrounding me would make a noise. I didn't know what to do. Sheila was getting louder now, so I made a choice, and to this day I don't know why I thought this was the right thing to do. I sat down. There was a chair next to me, and I sat down on it. Just a few feet from Sheila and John having sex.

I tried not to move. My breathing became shorter, more panicked. What the hell was I going to do? Sheila and John were really getting into a rhythm now and worst of all Sheila was starting to talk.

'That's it. Go on! Go on! Yeeeaaahhh! Oh God, yeah!'

I was feeling less and less drunk with every second that ticked by. I decided this could go on for hours, so I had to get out of there. I peeked round the arch and all I could see was Sheila throwing her long grey hair round and round in circles. The noises were getting louder. I shuffled in my seat to try and stand without setting off the creaking floorboards, when out of nowhere a cat jumped up onto my lap! He seemed all too familiar with this routine and just curled up on my thighs and started purring away. I closed my eyes and started stroking the cat. What could I do? I just sat there with the cat on my lap while I prayed to God that they would just finish, turn the light off, leave through the other door and I could forget about the plaster and creep up to bed.

They did finish, and it was the most orgasmic climax I've ever heard. Not that I'd heard many of course. I mean, none that weren't to do with me. It was cries of ecstasy, pants of pain almost. It went on and on until with a wail of unadulterated passion, it was finally over.

Thank God. This was it: they would go up to bed now and I would remain undiscovered. But they didn't go up to bed. Instead of switching off the light and slipping away, Sheila climbed off the pair of meaty thighs, turned round and looked right at me.

I just stared at her – what else could I do when she was naked with her big grey bush all in my face? She gave a short squeal – Oooh! – tried to cover up with her dressing gown and then she started shouting, 'What the hell are you doing? Jesus Christ! How long have you been there?'

I was still transfixed by the bush. 'What?' I said, looking up.

'What the HELL do you think you're doing?!' she shouted.

'Sorry. I didn't mean to, sorry. I was . . . I cut my foot.' I was mumbling. 'On the stairs, I cut my foot. I need a . . .' I was about to say 'plaster' but before I could get the words out, John stood up from where he had been recovering his strength on the sofa.

Only it wasn't John. It was a young guy, a hunk; he looked as though he'd just walked out of a Calvin Klein underwear ad: all six-pack and biceps. Completely naked, he looked at me as he rolled a condom off his manhood. Seriously, this is how it happened. 'All right, mate,' he said, and languidly tied a knot in the condom to stop it dripping.

By now Sheila had her dressing gown fastened and went to fetch a plaster. Meanwhile, I was sitting there still stroking the cat while the ridiculously endowed Adonis casually reached for his clothes. He bent over to pick up his pants and I didn't know whether to look away or shout, 'Timber!' as it all swung about.

'Good night, was it?' he asked. 'You went to a party, right?'

Still I stroked the cat. 'Yeah, a party. Yeah, it was good.'

Sheila came back, red-faced and muttering. I sat there, as embarrassed as I'd ever been, as she fumbled through putting the plaster on my foot. The only person totally unfazed was the young dude holding the used condom.

I don't remember making it to bed. I don't remember anything but waking the following morning to a plaster on my foot and my head in a vice. I made my way downstairs to find the three of them eating breakfast in the dining room: John, Sheila and Calvin.

It all seemed very polite, so whether John was in on any of what had gone on or just didn't care, I'll never know. I didn't stick around to ask. I skipped breakfast and settled up, said my goodbyes and headed for WH Smith and the morning papers. I did look back, though, just the once, and I swear I saw that cat wink at me from where it was sitting in the front-room window.

CHAPTER 8

BEST MUSICAL ACCOMPANIMENT:
'Ziggy Stardust' by David Bowie

BEST FILM TO WATCH ALONGSIDE:
Superbad

BEST ENJOYED WITH:
a big block of Jarlsberg

In WH Smith I read the reviews of the show and they weren't very good. Actually, they were awful. After all the hype, the expectation, last night's party and everything, I was aware of a sinking feeling in the pit of my stomach. I remember calling Dad and telling him that I was mystified because the whole place had been on its feet last night. Dad's reply was as wise as ever: 'You can never tell a thing from an audience of friends and family.' He was right. Two-thirds of the theatre audience that day were probably connected to the show in some capacity. We'd been seduced by an audience who wanted us to do well. Reviews are very important, and a critic's opinion can literally make or break a show, and these were as bad as anything anyone had ever read. I knew then it was going to be a long, hard slog.

Looking back on that first foray into the West End, I made some good friends and I did enjoy it to some extent, but it was never quite what I'd hoped it would be. I suppose it taught me that – even after dreaming about it so much while growing up – I didn't actually want to be in a West End musical after all. Not just standing at the back, anyway. For so long it felt as though all I'd wanted was to appear in the West End, but the reality of doing a show eight times a week is that it can quickly become really boring.

After doing the show for a year, I learnt that loads of the actors just seemed to move from one West End chorus to the next. I didn't want to end up like that, and I knew how easy it would be to get stuck on that kind of treadmill, so I decided to talk to my agent about the possibilities of doing other things.

To get the really good jobs, whether on stage, TV or in films, I knew I needed to have a bigger profile. No one was going to take me seriously as an actor unless I put my head above the parapet. I kept my options as open as I could and, towards the end of that first year of *Martin Guerre*, Marilyn phoned about an audition for a British film called *The Church of Alan Darcy*, by two unknown writers, Shane Meadows and Paul Fraser. Shane was a young guy from the Midlands; although I wasn't too familiar with him at the time, he would go on to become one of the most exciting directors this country has ever produced.

The film was set around a failing boxing club in Nottingham, and they were casting boys mostly from that area, particularly from a place called the Carlton Theatre Workshop. Shane wanted lads who hadn't really worked that much before so he could develop what he saw as a raw kind of edge.

Bob Hoskins was playing the lead. Bob is one of the iconic British film actors of the last thirty years; the thought of appearing in a film with him was just mind-blowing. He was playing the boxing trainer who was desperately trying to set up a gym so that local lads would have somewhere to go and not end up on the streets. Shane had cast an actor called Frank Harper to play the cockney backer who helps out financially, on the proviso that his chubby son, Tonka, can train at the club. I was auditioning for the part of Tonka.

The audition was an improvisation with the casting director in London and it went really well. The tape was sent to Shane and, after watching it a few times, he liked it enough to offer me the job. I just couldn't believe it; it felt totally unreal. My second job – a film with Bob Hoskins. It was huge! However, I was still contracted to *Martin Guerre* and had to get their permission to allow me to shoot the film. After much toing and froing it all got worked out and I was allowed to do it, so I went up to Nottingham to meet everyone and rehearse.

The annoying thing was that I had to make it up and back in the same day as I had a show to do that night. We rehearsed in a cinema called the Scala, and that was where I met Shane for the first time. A young guy, twenty-four, and a skinhead, he came up to me and in his Midlands accent he just said, 'All right, mate. I'm Shane. Loved your tape by the way. Thanks so much for doing this.'

He introduced me to the other lads: Darren, Johann, Karl and Danny. For the first time I really felt like an actor. I'd been in *Martin Guerre* for months now and at no point had I ever really felt like an actor. I felt more like a warm prop, or something, whereas there was a vibe about the film that everyone could feel. Shane knew exactly what he was doing and exactly what he wanted. I don't know if I believe in genius but, having worked with him, I'd say Shane is as close as it gets. He's just got a gift. There's a purity to how he works; he thinks and talks in terms of story and character. And he's a minimalist. I mean, if Shane could tell his story in a single photograph, he'd just take that photograph.

He's an incredibly inspiring man to be around, and he made me feel welcome and at ease right from the first moment I walked into the Scala. In some respects he's a bit like me: he wasn't that interested in school; was never particularly academic. In fact, he only got into film-making because he was put on community service for stealing a breast pump from a chemist's in Nottingham. He told me he spent the community service cleaning a hall in a school somewhere and as he was working he spotted an old video camera. He asked the supervisors if he could borrow it and they told him that, if he was interested, rather than clean the hall every day, he could make a film for his community service instead. That was some kind of offer and he didn't hesitate. Over a few weeks he put together a short film where he played all the characters himself because he was too embarrassed to tell his mates what he was doing and rope them in. He would put on a wig to play one part, then switch the camera round and dress differently to play another. For one part of the film, he wanted to get a shot of himself coming out of a door onto the street, so he placed the camera on its tripod on the other side of the road and left it recording. As he opened the door, however, he spotted two lads running off up the road with it. He had to bolt after them to get it back. And, like I said, he's a big guy with no hair so, yeah, he got his camera back.

Working with Shane was a huge step forward. From the shadows of the *Martin Guerre* chorus I'd managed to end up on the set of a major British film. The problem was, I was still in *Martin Guerre*. I'd only had that one day at the Scala for rehearsal, but there was a whole movie to shoot and somehow I'd have to juggle the time. The show owed me some holiday, though, so with that, and a couple of arranged days, I could give Shane a decent-sized chunk of shooting time and the rest I would fit around the *Martin Guerre* schedule.

I'm not gonna lie to you – being in a West End show and shooting a film at the same time wasn't easy. It felt as if I was never anywhere but on stage or on the set, with barely any time for myself, but it seemed like the most natural thing in the world. In Nottingham, I'd be up at six o'clock in the morning, film all day, then I'd get on the train at half past four and be in London at six thirty that evening. Then I'd hit the stage at seven thirty, then straight afterwards, around elevenish, get another train back to Nottingham, get up the next day and do it all over again. It was tough, but I was making a film with Bob Hoskins so I wasn't going to start complaining; plus I was pocketing two pay cheques.

For the first time in my life, I had some spending money of my own.

The title of the film was changed to *Twenty Four Seven* as the producers thought it would be more commercial. Shane and Paul had written a great script, the first I'd read where the characters actually talked the way my friends and I did. They sounded normal, not fake or filmy, and there was a real heart and soul in the writing that I hadn't come across before. Every decision Shane made turned out right – especially filming it in black and white. It really pulled into focus the starkness and rawness of the town without losing any of the joy or humour in the script.

There were parts in the script where Bob Hoskins's character narrated in voiceover while a scene or montage was playing out. One paragraph in particular has always stayed with me; it's such a fantastic piece of writing. Bob says something like: 'Imagine there was a museum where a blue and green coloured football was suspended in the middle of a room, surrounded by gas so it floats. And if you look closely at the green bits, you'd see tiny people walking around, going about their day, making each other laugh and looking after each other. You could watch them, observe them: people would flock from miles around just to come and stare at these little people. Each one of them, unique and magnificent. That's what we are. That's us walking around and we can never lose sight of how amazing it is just to wake up, walk around and see things.' Those aren't the exact words, but it's close. It says so much about Shane and Paul that at such a young age they would have that kind of insight.

Bob Hoskins was the experienced old head you need to hold a film like that together, but over time he became like all the rest of us: just one of the lads. There's no better example of that than the day that Bob borrowed Ian Smith's hat.

I remember we were in the middle of filming an amazing sequence in the Lake District, which in the film is set to the Charlatans' 'North Country Boy'. Ian used to wear a woolly hat all the time; it was his trademark. You could recognise him by it. That morning he was sitting on a chair with his back to us. All us young lads were there, waiting for Shane to decide how he wanted to shoot the next scene. Justin, who played Gadget, was in one of those moods. He got up, shot me a wink, casually sauntered over to where Ian was sitting and cocked his leg over his head like a dog. Then he let rip with the loudest bomber you've ever heard, right on top of Ian's head.

For a moment nothing happened; the rest of us were wetting ourselves as Justin ambled back to his chair. Ian remained where he was, though – motionless, taking it all in. Then slowly, he turned his head round and stared down Justin, who turned white as a sheet.

It was Bob. BAFTA Award-winning, Oscar-nominated, British screen legend Bob Hoskins, sitting in a cloud of Justin's air cheese.

You could cut the atmosphere – and the air – with a knife. Justin, squirming under Bob's icy glare. And then Bob's face creased into a shallow smile; the smile got wider and wider until he started wetting himself laughing and we all just fell about.

All the time we were filming, it was like that, us lads laughing the whole time. It was just a wonderful, wonderful time and I could hardly believe it when the last day of filming came around. Looking back, I was lucky. I still had about three weeks to go in *Martin Guerre* so I never experienced that real low that can happen at the end of a shoot. I remember speaking to the other boys in the cast about how lots of them got really upset after we wrapped the film. It's understandable, really: making that kind of film is so personal and, living and working together for weeks on end, the group becomes such a tight-knit community. The film becomes your entire world and then, suddenly, it's all over. You finish filming on Saturday, have the wrap party on Saturday night, deal with the hangover on Sunday, then Monday comes around and everyone goes their separate ways. In our case the crew went off to work on other films, Shane went to the edit suite, but the cast, the group of lads who'd become such close friends, suddenly had nothing to do.

I realised then just how lucky I'd been that the producers of *Martin Guerre* had allowed me to do the two things together. But I didn't escape it entirely: the slump for me came when I finished performing in *Martin Guerre*, because I'd decided not to carry on my contract beyond that first year. Most of the cast left at the same time, and though it was sad leaving it, eight shows a week for a year had pretty much taken it out of me. It was time to stop.

When I left the show I had nothing to do. I went back to lazing around at home, playing computer games, eating Quavers and just knocking about. I would ring Marilyn and ask if there was any work around, but it seemed that there wasn't a mass of parts for someone who looked like me at the time. I did have a few auditions, but not many, and I didn't get any of them. Very quickly the money I'd earned from *Twenty Four Seven* and *Martin Guerre* was gone. I remember being £30 overdrawn and realising that this was it, the life of an actor: feast or famine. I had to find myself a normal job.

(OK, you're now going to hear the story of Ziggy, the mini-mart and the hard lads who wanted beer. This happened when I was fourteen years old, so I know it comes out of sequence in terms of the story, but stay with me, because I learn something incredibly important at the end of it. And it's also quite silly. Promise.)

The only other job I'd had was working on Saturdays at the local mini-supermarket down the road from my house. I got the job because Gemma, one of the girls I really fancied, worked on the fruit and veg stall. She had a boyfriend who was a couple of years older than me called Big Trev, who used to drive a red Ford Escort. It was just a regular Escort, but Big Trev thought he could fool everyone by stealing an XR3i badge and putting it on his car. He was a knob.

He was always parked outside the school gates waiting to pick up Gemma, the girl I thought I was going to marry. She was besotted with him and spent all her time outside of school hanging out with him. The only way I'd see her is if I went to the mini-mart and bought fruit and veg. As you can imagine, this led to some strange scenarios – Mum would often be bemused as I walked into the kitchen and handed her some broccoli and mangetout I'd bought from Gemma earlier – but I'd do anything just to talk to her. She was really funny and I used to love being around her. One day, when I was in, casually fondling a bunch of bananas, she told me that there was a Saturday job going. I knew what she was telling me – she clearly wanted me around. She wanted me where Big Trev couldn't come between us. I spoke to the manager, who said the job was mine if I wanted it. I was over the moon: not only would I now have some money coming in, I'd get to spend whole days with Gemma. She'd fall in love with me, of course, and I'd have to have a quiet word with Big Trev, but he'd understand when he saw how much in love we were.

I arrived the following Saturday at 8 a.m., ready to spend my day making double entendres about big cucumbers and avocados with Gemma, when the manager took me aside and introduced me to Ziggy. Now, Ziggy had worked at the mini-mart for as long as I could remember. He'd just always been there. So the boss turned to me and said, 'This is Chris, but call him Ziggy. He'll show you the ropes.' And he did. Except none of the ropes he was showing me seemed to be out on the shop floor near Gemma. We were stuck in the stockroom moving massive boxes of food around. It wasn't what I'd had in mind. And all Ziggy seemed to show me was how to steal things without being caught. He once bragged about how he'd stolen his family's Christmas turkey for the last three years. I asked him how one might go about stealing a fourteen-pound frozen turkey without anyone noticing, and he said, 'I just walked out of the shop and put it in Mum's car. If you're doing it wrong, do it strong.' I liked Ziggy; he was full of no-nonsense sayings like that.

One time, after we'd been working together for three or four Saturdays, we were sitting on the back wall in the storage room, eating our way through a couple of Kinder eggs and a pack of Jelly Babies that Ziggy had nicked just minutes earlier, and I asked him why people called him Ziggy when his real name was Chris. He thought for a moment, lifted his head from the Kinder-egg car he was trying to put together and said, very matter-of-factly, "Cos Ziggy plays guitar.'

'Oh,' I replied. 'I didn't know you played the guitar.'

'I don't,' he said. 'But Ziggy does.' And with that he stepped down and carried on with his day.

Working with Ziggy for a while had a bad and lasting effect on me. He'd shown me how easy it was to steal stuff from the shop, so it was only a matter of time before I started slipping the odd bag of Minstrels into my pocket. Except it didn't stop at Minstrels. If it had, I'd have been fine, but one Friday at school, I heard there was a big house party happening at Jo Toulson's house. I got on pretty well with Jo and was annoyed not to have been invited, especially as it seemed a lot of the slightly older, cooler boys were going. That afternoon in Science, a few of them were huddled around a Bunsen burner and I overheard them talking about the party, trying to work out how they were going to get alcohol. That was my way in.

'Hey guys, what you talking about?' I said, strolling over, playing it cool.

'None of your business, Corden,' said Greg Wright.

'Yeah, piss off, you fat twat,' added Alex Carver to chuckles from the rest.

'Oh, I thought you were trying to get booze,' I replied breezily. 'I can get you all the drink you want and it won't cost you a penny.'

They all turned to look at me and ushered me into the group, and I told them about my job at the mini-mart and how I could easily steal them a crate of beer. I know it seems silly that I was so keen to impress this group of unambitious, nasty berks, but I was. For some reason, my whole life I've always wanted to be around the cool guys, and it's only now, ages later, that I've realised that the cool group ultimately consists of people who are terrified of not being cool any more. I wish I'd not tried so hard so many times. It got me nowhere, and this particular jaunt was no different (as you'll find out in a bit), but I was determined to go to this party, and if all I had to do to get in was steal a crate of beer, which, as Ziggy had shown me, was easily done, then that's what I'd have to do. The prize was worth it.

I woke up that Saturday morning and was hit by the fear of what I was about to try and achieve. I hadn't thought it through: how the hell would I get a crate of beer out of the shop? How would I get it home on my bike? Alex Carver's last words as we left the school gates on Friday were ringing in my ears. 'You'd better get those beers, Corden, or you're dead.' Thanks dude.

I walked into work that day with the weight of the world on my shoulders. I kept on repeating Ziggy's mantra to myself to try and get some confidence. 'If you're doing it wrong, do it strong. If you're doing it wrong, do it strong . . .'

My first job of the day was to move five boxes of Munch Bunch yoghurts upstairs to the big fridge. I used to hate the big fridge because, every time I'd go in, one of the butchers would slam the door behind me and I'd be left in pitch-black darkness trying to find the glow-in-the-dark light switch that had ceased to glow in the dark many, many years ago. It was horrible. I'd walk into lamb's carcasses and pig's heads hanging on spikes. It was gross, like something out of a torture porn movie. One time I found Ziggy in there smoking. Honestly, smoking in amongst the raw meat. I asked what he was doing and he just said, 'It's too hot to smoke outside.'

The Munch Bunch trip went as expected. I walked into the

big fridge and – surprise, surprise – they all slammed the door behind me. I could hear them all cackling away while I fumbled around, simultaneously trying not to drop the Munch Bunch yoghurts and find the light. This wasn't helping my nerves. The day was ticking by and I'd still not got anywhere near the beers. None of my jobs was taking me near the part of the stockroom where they were kept. For some reason, all I was doing was taking endless boxes of Findus Crispy Pancakes out onto the shop floor. It got to ten to five in the afternoon and I was due to finish at half past. How was I gonna do this? I had to bite the bullet.

I marched into the stockroom and strode purposefully over ('If you're doing it wrong, do it strong . . .') to where the alcohol was kept. There were about ten crates of Carlsberg sitting there in front of me, but they were all wrapped together in cellophane. I tried to peel it away at the side of one crate, but it was tougher than I thought and I began to panic a little, worried that I wouldn't be able to get it off. I must've looked demented, trying to rip it with my bare hands. Standing on my tiptoes, I focused on the top crate instead, which should come more easily, I thought, and, eventually, I tore enough away to be able to get hold of it with my fingertips. I was tentatively inching it nearer to me when suddenly I heard, 'James? What're you doing?'

I froze. It was the boss, and there I was, on tiptoes, with both hands clutching a twenty-four-pack of Carlsberg, bang to rights. I knew that I had no other option but to confess everything, so I turned to him and opened my mouth to speak when, before I could say a word, he jumped in. '*Jarlsberg*, not Carlsberg! I told Ziggy we needed more Jarlsberg.' I looked at him blankly. 'You know, the cheese?' I couldn't believe what was happening, 'God,' he tutted. 'If you want something doing . . .' And with that he ushered me out of the stockroom and over towards the cheeses. I've always loved Jarlsberg, but never more than in that moment.

Now, in one respect, this was a miracle: I'd been caught

red-handed and totally got away with it. But, on the other hand, my problem still remained. My working day was done and I'd failed to complete my mission. I was gonna get beaten up good and proper.

I'd arranged to meet Alex, Greg and all the other boneheads on pathway 74, a secluded path through the woods between my house and Jo Toulson's. Basically, if you wanted to beat someone up, this would be the perfect place to do it. As I walked home, I couldn't think of any scenario that would prevent a beating. Except one. Our next-door neighbour Mike, who shared our driveway. He had a box of twenty-four small, stubby French beers in his garage. Now, Mike didn't like me. He thought I was trouble. I used to play football in the drive, kicking the ball against the wall to work on my touch, and using our garage as a goal. Although, as previously mentioned, I'm not very good at football, so I'd often miss our garage and hit his. One day, when I was about fourteen, he came out and threatened to smash my face in if my ball ever touched his garage again. He was a lovely man.

Often, his garage door would be left open, and a few days earlier I'd spotted the beers on the shelf right at the back. This was it – my only chance. With 'Doing it wrong, do it strong' running through my head, I walked up our shared drive, took a look back towards our house and then over at Mike's to see if anyone was looking out of the window. The coast was clear so, fast as I could, which wasn't that fast, I lifted up his garage door, ran to the back, grabbed the case of foreign beers, ran back out, closed his garage door and ran down our drive, down the road, past all of our neighbours' houses and into the woods. I've got no clue what any of my neighbours would've thought if they'd seen me, a fifteen-year-old Salvation Army boy, scampering down the street with a twenty-four-pack of beer. Once I got to pathway 74, I slowed down and checked over my shoulder to see if Mike was coming after me with an axe. No sign of him. Phew.

I hid the beers in a bush and went back home to get changed

for the big party. As I stood in the shower, it suddenly dawned on me what I'd just done. I was elated to have completed my mission, but I felt awful for even getting myself in this position. It was like that scene in *The Crying Game*, only without the . . . y'no.

I felt incredibly guilty, I really did, but I rationalised it by telling myself that I'd done what I had to do to get to the party. I gelled my hair and got dressed into my coolest clothes – a pair of cream chinos, a lemon shirt and a brown waistcoat. In my head I looked like Gary Barlow in the 'Pray' video (but I probably looked more like Ken Barlow leading the prayers at church). I got back to where I'd hidden the beers and waited for the cool guys to show. After about half an hour, I heard some footsteps coming down the path: it was Alex, his older brother Christian and Greg. As soon they saw me, sitting on the crate of beers, Alex came rushing over and started celebrating, jumping up and down. 'I told you he'd do it, didn't I?' he said to Christian. Christian was basically the reason everyone was scared of Alex. Alex was actually a bit of a weakling, but his big brother Christian was properly scary – he's since been in prison for armed robbery – so no one messed with Alex because they knew they'd be messing with Christian.

Christian took a look at the beers and started shaking his head. 'What kind of shit beers are these?' he said.

'Yeah Corden!' Greg joined in. 'I fawt you was gonna get Foster's or Kronenbourg sixteen sixty finny.'

'This is bullshit!' added Alex, who seconds earlier had been over the moon at the sight of them. I couldn't believe what I was hearing. They had no idea what I'd been through to get these.

'We can't turn up wiv these. We'll look like pikeys,' Christian said angrily.

I needed to say something fast: 'Whoa, guys, guys, guys. This is quality beer. Everyone is gonna be turning up with a four-pack of Stella or whatever. But these will stand out. They're exotic, cool. And they're stubby little bottles. No one who's anyone drinks from cans. Tramps drink from cans. I said I'd get you some beers for free and I have. I got you the most expensive beers in the shop, 'cos I thought you guys would want the best.' I was clinging on to anything to get me out of this mess.

'Are they really the most expensive?' asked Alex.

'Yeah, big time,' I replied, and suddenly they all started smiling.

'Yeah man! Wicked!' Greg said as he fist-pumped Christian.

'We got us some good shit here,' Christian agreed. What a relief. I'd passed the test. Alex picked up the beers and we all started making our way up the path and on to the party, and the girls and the—

'Umm, where you going?' Christian was looking at me in his default threatening manner.

'What?' I said, honestly confused. Now the other two stopped and turned to look at me as well.

'Where you going, *now*?' Christian growled.

I paused and thought for a second. 'I'm . . . erm . . . Well, I'm coming with you. To the party,' I said nervously. All three of them just cracked up laughing.

'Ha ha! You ain't comin' wiv us. No way!' he said through his laughter.

'But I thought . . .'

The laughter increased. 'You fawt you was coming wiv us? Ha ha! Nah, you ain't invited to this party.' Greg came over and pushed me hard in the chest and I almost fell over a tree stump. 'See ya laters, fat boy.' And with that, they walked off.

I stood on the path, on my own, more embarrassed than anything else. After everything I'd done for them, the risk I'd gone through, that's how they'd treat me? I walked home feeling a fool. Why had I gone to such lengths to try and impress people who were never, ever going to be impressed by me? It was a trait of mine that I really hated – the need to be liked by those who made it clear they had no time for me. It's gone now, thank God. Only recently, but it's gone. I've faced up to the fact that some people are going to like me and others aren't. That's all there is to it. It was the case at school and it's the same now and it will be the case throughout my whole life. In wanting to impress those guys so much, in trying so hard, all I'd done was make them think I was more of an idiot. They were never going to like me, no matter what I did or tried to do.

(Now, tell me that isn't an important lesson. See, I told you it would be worth it.)

Right, let's get back to it. I was looking for a job, wasn't I? So, after shooting a film and doing a year in the West End, I couldn't contemplate going back to work alongside Ziggy, but I did have to get a job somewhere. I went into the metropolis that is High Wycombe town centre and walked around the shops, asking to see if there were any jobs going. What came next was a succession of pointlessly filling in application forms and expecting to hear nothing. That was until I walked into Bella Pasta, where the slogan on the window read, 'The Bella Place for Bella Pasta.' Genius. They've changed their name now to Bella Italia, which I imagine means they'll have dropped the slogan. Shame really.

It was just after the lunchtime rush and I walked up to the bar and spoke to the manager, who was a really lovely woman. Our conversation went like this:

'Have you waited before?'

'I've not, no, but I'm a quick learner.'

'Do you have some black trousers, a white shirt and a black tie?'

'Erm . . . yes, I think so.'

'Well, you're in luck. I've just had two people leave – you can start tomorrow.'

So that was that; I was a waiter. Some people say it's only

when you've been a waiter that you can actually call yourself an actor. And I have to say, looking back on my month-long stint at Bella Pasta, I think I was very lucky. I really enjoyed it, it was always fun, and the people who worked there were great.

The job itself felt like the exact opposite of what I'd been doing in the West End. In *Martin Guerre* it was the same thing every night, but when you're a waiter, no two tables are ever the same. I loved the crack with the customers and I earned way more money than I ever did in *Martin Guerre*, with the tips on top of my basic pay. Whenever we had a hen night in, I'd get put on those tables and do jokes about the size of the pepper grinder and what kind of meat they wanted on the meat pizza – you know, the good stuff. I was so enthusiastic and my repertoire so varied, it almost felt like doing stand-up.

There was only one day that I really screwed up. You see, when the food was ready, the kitchen staff would put it up on the pass between the kitchen and the restaurant and if there was ever a bit of cheese or something dangling off a pizza, I'd have a little nibble, y'no, just to tidy it up. Well, this particular day, two pizzas were ready to go and the cheese was dripping off the side of one of them, so I picked it off and stuffed it in my mouth before carrying the food to the table. I went over, smiling lots and cracking gags as usual, only this time nobody was laughing. They were just staring at me instead. A little self-consciously perhaps, I put the pizzas down and then – and only then – I caught sight of my face in the mirror along the wall. There was a long string of melted cheese attached to my lower lip, with the other end still hanging on to the pizza's crust.

'Ah,' I said, lifting the pizza back off the table. 'I'll just fetch you another one of those. Won't be a minute.' Classy.

There was another reason Bella Pasta was a really happy time for me. It wasn't just because I was so fulfilled taking orders for garlic bread or the odd Fusilli Marco Polo. No, it was because it was around this time that I first fell in love.

I was under the illusion that I'd been in love before, with girls like Gemma or Claire Wyatt. But nothing prepared me for how completely bowled over I was about to be when I met Shelley. Not only was Shelley the first girl I loved, she was without question the first girl to completely love me back. She was the first girl who wasn't looking over my shoulder to see if someone better walked in, and the first girl who I could tell, when I looked into her eyes and she looked into mine, loved me like I loved her.

I met her through my friend Stuart Hay, who had been the sound mixer for both my bands, Twice Shy and Insatiable. He introduced us one day and we went for a drink after work and ended up chatting all night. Shelley was doing a degree in Film Studies and we talked for hours about our favourite films and actors. She was beautiful and funny and so bright, and I remember thinking I could talk to her every day for a year and not get bored. I was completely smitten. When the evening came to an end, she offered me a lift home in her Fiesta and, as we pulled up outside my parents' house, I thought for a moment about leaning in to kiss her. But the evening had been so perfect that I didn't want anything to ruin it. I was so used to girls just liking me as a friend, so instead I said goodnight and stepped out of the car. I took a few paces towards the front door and stopped dead: what if I never saw her again? What if this was my one chance? I couldn't let this be it. One nice evening of conversation and then a lifetime of what ifs and maybes.

I turned round, walked back to the car and tapped on Shelley's window. 'Erm . . . could I get your phone number?' I said. "Cos I'd love to see you again . . . Y'no, at some point, sometime. Anytime. Whenever. If you'd like to, y'no. Only if . . . Don't worry if you don't want to. It's cool. I mean . . . I'm not bothered, just . . . Erm. Whatever. I just think it'd be . . . nice.'

In the time I'd been babbling on, Shelley had already reached down into her bag, taken out a pen and pad, and started scribbling her phone number down. She handed it to me and I held it and looked at it for a moment, just taking it in. There it was: her phone number. Set down in ink. For me. And me alone.

I noticed in the bottom corner some small letters that said, 'P.T.O.,' with an arrow attached. I turned it over and in big letters it said, 'YOU'RE MAD, BUT I LIKE YOU.' I smiled and chuckled a little as I gazed at this amazing girl looking up at me. I didn't even think. I just leant down and kissed her. Like I'd never kissed anyone. And she, I'm pleased to add, kissed me back. It was incredible. Romantic, silly, heartfelt and sexy, all rolled into one.

It's a strange thing, kissing. We've all had good ones and bad ones. Sloppy ones and dreamy ones. I have a theory about kissing that you, like many of my friends, may think is wishy-washy and pathetic, but it's something I believe to be true. I don't think there is such a thing as a bad kisser. I don't. I just believe that there are people who shouldn't kiss each other. Because the person you've had an awful kiss with and the person I've had an awful kiss with – well, who's to say that they didn't walk away from our embrace telling their friends how rubbish at kissing *we* were? And we both know, you and I, that we are brilliant at snogging. And if, one day, those two people who didn't like kissing us should somehow end up sharing a kiss in a doorway, or on a dance floor, then there's a strong possibility that the kiss they share will be perfect. Because they were meant to kiss each other. Just like Shelley and I were.

I have to pause here for a moment because it's hard to write about Shelley. I can almost guarantee she will take no pleasure whatsoever in being written about. But I can't leave her out. I was with her too long. She was too important. We started going out when I was eighteen and we were together till *The History Boys* finished in New York when I was twenty-seven. That's a very long time, a big chunk of a young man's life: it was a serious relationship.

After that first kiss, we immediately became a couple and

were completely inseparable. Most nights I would stay at her house, which was about five minutes away from mine. Her mum and dad, Mike and Di, became like second parents to me. They were lovely and I have the fondest memories of the time I spent at their place. They came from Barry Island in South Wales and it was through them I got to know the area. If I hadn't, then things might have turned out so differently. Shelley introduced me to some of the old characters from Barry, unwittingly sowing the seed for *Gavin & Stacey* – she had a massive impact on all aspects of my life. She was my first love.

I did six months at Bella Pasta, but by then I was starting to worry a little about my career. I'd never intended to stay that long, but there was no other acting work coming in as I hadn't got any of the parts I'd been going for after *Twenty Four Seven*. That really began to bother me. I was OK for money, as I was still living with Mum and Dad, and on a personal level I was over the moon being with Shelley, but my career seemed to have come to a halt.

It was just at that point, feeling pretty low, when *Twenty Four Seven* came out to the most incredible reviews. Everyone who saw it loved the film, and Shane was hailed as the best of his generation. It was brilliant.

A year had passed since we'd wrapped the shoot; after being such a close-knit group, we'd all promised to stay in touch, like you do. It's always like that when a film is over; you really mean to keep up the friendships, but in reality that rarely happens because everyone goes off to do different projects. But here we were, a year on, all us lads having a little reunion. It was my first experience of the way that works: you shoot the film, wait what can sometimes seem like for ever, then the film comes out, and you're all brought back together to do publicity and interviews or photo shoots. If you're lucky, there might be a premiere. It's one of the things I really like about making films, that sense of continuity. Throughout the film's life, there are these constant points of excitement – getting the part, meeting the cast, shooting the film itself, seeing the finished thing and then all the reviews and press when it's released. And you get to do it – if you're very lucky – with a bunch of people you really get on with.

So, after six months being a waiter, I found myself back in Nottingham doing a photo shoot for *The Face* magazine with the other lads, who I'd not seen for a year. It was amazing: none of us had ever done a photo shoot before and there we were, this unlikely group, who were now part of this great British film success.

It was being back in the public eye that made me think about what I was going to do next. I couldn't stay at Bella Pasta for ever; I needed to get some acting work. Nathan Harmer, a friend from *Martin Guerre*, was looked after by an agent called Jacquie Drewe at London Management. She sounded like my kind of person, and he said that he'd put in a word for me. On his recommendation, Jacquie went to see the film and a few days later we met up, had a chat and got along really well. She seemed to have no hesitation in taking me on.

I was moving on but, having been looked after by Marilyn for so long, it was really traumatic to say goodbye. I'd never really left anyone before, and it was horrible having to let down a friend. Marilyn was upset, but we talked about it and I know that deep down she understood my decision. I shall always be grateful to her and to the amazing people at the Jackie Palmer Stage School. Without them, my acting career and this book might still be a far-off dream.

Not long after I signed with Jackie, she phoned me about a new comedy show called *Boyz Unlimited* that had just been commissioned by Channel 4. It sounded really exciting: it was a mockumentary about a boy band and they were looking for a guy to play a character called Gareth, who was loosely based on Gary Barlow. He was one of the main characters, the one who wrote all the songs. I nearly dropped the phone in shock. Someone had written my dream part.

I met Andy Pryor, the casting director, and he put me through a singing audition followed by an acting audition and I seemed to do well in both. We got along great and I was called back for a dance audition. It was a bit like *Martin Guerre*; with my size and everything, they made no secret of being worried whether I could pull off the routines without looking foolish.

They had brought in Paul Domain, the choreographer who at the time was creating the dance routines for all the biggest boy bands in the country. I think he was as sceptical as the rest of them, but then none of them knew that growing up I'd spent hour after hour pretending to be Gary Barlow. He started taking me through my paces, and all the moves he was showing me were ones I already knew in one form or another. I just pretended to be back in our front room with the sofas pushed up against the wall. I went for it and two weeks later I was told I'd got the job.

The show was written and produced by a great guy called Richard Osman. The script was funny and smart and I loved it; the seven weeks of filming were basically a dream come true as I spent every day either singing or dancing or acting. There were four of us in the band: Billy Worth (the cute one), Adam Sinclair (the manly one), Lee Williams (the model-looking one) and me (the fat one who writes the songs). We thought it was going to make us stars. We were in magazines and posters on the Underground; people were calling it the next big comedy of the autumn. Not for the last time in my career, I believed the hype.

It's an interesting phenomenon, hype – creating expectation, talking something up before it happens. Nothing suffers from that kind of expectation more than comedy. If something is built up to be the funniest thing since Morecombe and Wise, there's only one way it can go. That's what happened with *Boyz Unlimited*: it came out and never really caught on. Right from the start the ratings weren't good and, as the series progressed, it became obvious that it wasn't going to get recommissioned. It was a crazy time: just a couple of weeks before the show aired we'd read in the papers about a battle that was raging behind the scenes between two record companies desperate to sign us.

It's a fact of life in the entertainment business. There's no rhyme or reason as to why one thing works and another doesn't; it's always so subjective. At so many points I've felt I've been on the cusp of something, when actually it's not *something*, it's just . . . a thing. There are so many films, plays and television programmes made every year. All I wanted was to be in something that stood out and, more importantly, to stand out in it.

CHAPTER 9

BEST MUSICAL ACCOMPANIMENT:
'Get on the Road' by Tired Pony

BEST FILM TO WATCH ALONGSIDE:
Whatever Happened to Harold Smith?

BEST ENJOYED:
with a spoonful of hummus

Even though *Boyz Unlimited* didn't blow up like we hoped it would, it was another great experience – still to this day one of the best I've had – and my CV was looking more professional. I'd been in a West End musical, a really well-received film with an up-and-coming director, and now I'd played the lead in what had been pitched as a major TV comedy series.

I was still living with my mum and dad, though, and the thought of going back to somewhere like Bella Pasta didn't do anything for me. I had really believed I was on my way to superstardom and it had all ended so suddenly. Beyond the disappointment, I guess it was a little unnerving as well. It's only as you get older and wiser that you realise there is this bigger picture and each segment of life is only a part of it. For a while I was a victim of the 'Is that it?' syndrome. I'd done stage, film and TV. Had I hit the peak? Did that mean it was over?

In many ways, still being at home was a great thing because it kept me very grounded. My mum was just amazing – she always has been – and I was lucky enough to grow up in this cocoon of love and encouragement that was still there when the TV show failed to live up to expectations. It had been like that all through my childhood: my sisters and I surrounded by so much love that we felt we had total security. We went to school – we went everywhere in fact – wearing this sort of emotional parachute. I see a confidence and resilience in my sisters, Ange and Rudi, that I don't see in everyone and I'm sure it's come about because of our upbringing. How can you be afraid of failure if no one's going to tell you that you messed up?

Dad was a little different to Mum; in many ways they were the flip side of each other. I wrote a little before about how he could be a mixture of support and a sort of veiled disappointment, and I think that comes from him being so much of a realist. No matter how enthusiastic I was about a job or the potential of one, he'd always be there to add a note of caution. Dad also has a temper on him, and because I could be really irritating as a kid (you've worked this out by now, right?), I was often on the wrong end of it. I can't really blame him. I wonder what it was like for Dad, being told by endless teachers, Cub Scout leaders or members of our church congregation that I was a waster. It must've been so hard to hear. My son is just two days old and I can't imagine those things being said about him or, worse still, realising that they might be true.

He was as pragmatic about the failure of *Boyz Unlimited* as he was about everything else, though. I remember we talked a lot about hype and expectation and how damaging it could be. The real successes in British comedy are not shows that have been overly hyped – they've just sort of crept up on people. *The Office* was never hyped, *Little Britain* wasn't given a big build-up and *Gavin & Stacey* certainly wasn't in your face with billboards or adverts. That's the way it should be. Comedy is so personal, you want to find it for yourself.

With no sign of a job, I was kicking my heels again. I'd done a decent stint waiting on tables, so now I stayed at home and waited for the phone to ring. I didn't do anything much except sit around and play *Championship Manager* – which is without question the finest computer game that's ever been invented. I still play it now from time to time, though it's called *Football Manager* these days. Let me just take this moment to say thank you to everyone who ever worked on that game. You are all geniuses and I love you all – and when I wasn't at home, I'd be round at Shelley's house. I was quite enjoying the downtime actually when, out of the blue, Jacquie called me about an audition for *Hollyoaks*.

I'd better explain how the audition process actually works. Unless you're really at the top of your game, scripts don't come through specifically addressed to you. Normally, the casting director for a particular project will send agents a breakdown of the parts they're looking to fill. The agents then submit a CV and photo of the people they think could be suitable. From all those submissions, the casting director, director and producer put together a list of who they want to come in and read.

With the *Hollyoaks* audition, about thirty boys were asked to read for the part of Wayne, the janitor at the college. Wayne wasn't your typical *Hollyoaks* character. He wasn't meant to be very attractive; he smelled a bit; he was overweight. I auditioned. A week later I was filming in Liverpool.

I wasn't a fan of the show and I remember this being the first time in my career where I was doing something I didn't truly believe in. But even so, the contract was only for two months, and given it was the only thing on offer, I decided it didn't matter.

It's a soap opera, of course, and as soon as you arrive you realise why so many members of the cast stick around for so long. It's great fun, like being a student at university, only with lots of money. Everyone is young, attractive and much richer than they've ever been before. It's pretty intoxicating.

I didn't particularly enjoy the way the show worked, though, neither the atmosphere on the set nor the lack of care that went into the actual shooting of the show. It never really felt professional and, from an acting point of view, it would frustrate me. That said, I have huge respect for the actors involved and I made some really good friends there. People like James Redmond, Ben Hull and Jeremy Edwards. It was an odd experience really. I've done some interviews where I slagged the show off and I know I was quite negative. I don't mind admitting I regret them now. Looking back, I don't think it was very fair, because the show doesn't pretend to be anything other than what it is. I guess I was too young, too naive maybe to understand it. The fact is, when I did slag it off, it was at a time where I thought I could say and do what I liked, and that says more about me than it does about *Hollyoaks*, doesn't it?

There are reasons I felt negative towards the show. My character became popular quite quickly, probably because he was the only one in the show who didn't have a six-pack or chiselled jaw. It was refreshing in a way. But in one episode, my character Wayne moved in with Nick Pickard's character Tony, so the art department had to build a new set for Wayne's bedroom.

I arrived on set, ready to film about six scenes with Nick, all in the flat, when I saw something that I couldn't believe. Blu-Tacked onto the walls, in the same way you would stick up pictures of your favourite band or football player, they had placed pictures of food. Not a scene from a bohemian restaurant – actual food. Pictures of fish and chips, or a cottage pie, the odd individual sausage here and there. I was gobsmacked. What were they trying to say about the character, or, deeper still, what were they saying about anyone who was overweight? That fat people worship food in the same way that the other, 'normal', good-looking characters worship footballers or bands? I was immediately offended and I told them it was out of order. I remember looking to the crew for some support, though all I saw was a group of shifty people staring at the floor, trying not to be the person who might step out of line. I was adamant, though, and I refused to begin filming until they took the pictures down. I made a stand and to this day I believe I made the right one. I remember telling the art department guy that if he could find me one teenager in the country with pictures of food on his walls, I would go with it.

One of the producers came down to the set. He was about twenty – there were people in the cast older than him – and told me to stop causing a scene, that it was only a bit of fun, and that time-wise the crew were really up against it today and we needed to get on. I told him that the quickest way we'd shoot the scene was if they just removed the pictures and then I'd be happy and get on and do it. I didn't say another word; I just pretended to write a text on my phone. The silence went on so long that I did actually write a text to Shelley telling her I might be about to get fired.

In the end, the producer backed down and asked the art department to remove the photos. It was a strange atmosphere on set that day. I'm not sure many people ever really say things are wrong on *Hollyoaks*. Not in the cast, anyway. I felt fortunate that I'd worked professionally before and had enough experience to handle a nasty situation. What they like to do on *Hollyoaks* is cast people who haven't worked much before so that they can be moulded to their way of working. Like lab rats.

A month or so later, my contract was nearly up and I figured we'd shake hands at the end and each go our separate ways. Despite some bad moments, I genuinely had enjoyed my time in Liverpool; it's a great city and I always had fun with the cast.

I had a week to go until I was due to leave and only had three more days of actual filming on the Wednesday, Thursday and Friday. It was Tuesday night, and I was at home when Jacquie called and said that *Hollyoaks* wanted to extend my contract. I was shocked. I presumed that after the whole 'I'm not filming with food on the walls' thing, they would be happy to see the back of me. I told Jacquie that I wasn't sure I wanted to do it and she said we should wait for a bit and see what the offer was. Dad thought that was the right way to go too.

I'd never been in that position before, knowing an offer was coming and sitting around waiting for it. Previously, they'd always come out of the blue and I'd never been in any doubt as to whether I'd want to do it or not. Eventually, Jacquie called and told me she'd got them to the best money she could get. However, there was a condition: they didn't just want to offer me another couple of months; they wanted to book me for a year. The money – Jacquie paused for effect when she told me – would be £70,000.

What?! *How much?* Vividly, I remember going into the kitchen to see Mum and Dad having just got off the phone with Jacqui.

'What's happened then?' Dad asked me. 'What's the latest?'

'They've offered me a year's contract,' I told him. 'Seventy grand, Dad. Seventy thousand quid.'

He took that in his stride. 'So what do you think?'

I shrugged. 'I don't know. I'm not sure. It's such a lot of money.'

And then Dad came into his own and told me something I've never forgotten. He took a breath and said, 'Well, if you want my advice, I reckon if they've offered you seventy thousand pounds for a year, and you're not sure if you want to do it or not, I'd imagine you don't want to do it.'

'Yeah, but . . . seventy gr—' I replied before Dad interrupted me.

'You don't need it, James. You don't need that kind of money when you're nineteen and living at home. You need it when you've got a wife and a family. You're not in that position, are you? I think if you take that money and get used to all the things that come with it, then the harder it'll be to leave. So you'll stay, and stay again, and before you know it, you'll be Ken Barlow. (He actually said that, I promise you.) It's totally up to you, mate, and I'll support you in whatever you want to do, you know that. Sometimes you'll have to do things you don't wanna do for money. This isn't one of those times.'

I turned it down. I told Jacquie I didn't want to get stuck in a soap opera – though, to be honest, when I came off the phone I wasn't sure I'd made the right decision. It was true – I didn't want to get trapped on any one show, but it was very popular and it was a hell of a lot of cash. I worried about it for a week or so, and genuinely felt sad when saying goodbye to the friends I'd made there. I also felt a slight pang when the train pulled out of Liverpool Lime Street Station. A week or so went by. Just at the moment when I started to wonder if it was too late to go back, Jacquie called me with an audition for a film.

Whatever Happened to Harold Smith? was a film about a middle-aged man who starts to display psychic and telekinetic energy, causing the deaths of three pensioners when it interferes with their pacemakers. It was a comedy – you didn't guess that? – and when Jacqui told me the names of the cast, I got seriously excited: Tom Courtenay, Stephen Fry, David Thewlis, to name just a few.

Careers change direction unexpectedly. Different decisions can set you off on surprising paths. If I'd taken the *Hollyoaks* offer, that audition would never have come up. But it did and, three days later, I got the part of Walter, best mate to Harold Smith's son, Vince. If I had accepted the *Hollyoaks* offer, I'd never have been in the film and there's every chance I would still be in Liverpool now. Wayne would still be the janitor at the college and would probably have an imaginary girlfriend who looked like a Fray Bentos pie.

Harold Smith was directed by Peter Hewitt, who made *Bill & Ted's Bogus Journey*, and the thought of working with him and the cast he'd put together was totally excellent. When I first arrived at the audition, I didn't think I stood a chance. Nobody else going for the role looked even vaguely like me. My first thought was that they clearly hadn't realised I was this big from my head shot. But I really wanted to play Walter; it was such a fun part. Lulu was playing Vince's mum, and Walter and Lulu's character eventually became a couple. In all aspects, this was a dream job.

Oddly, this was one of those situations where my size really helped me out. I stood out as the only big guy up for the part. The ultra-creative Nina Gold was casting the film. Directors use people like Nina because their expertise is in knowing who is around and who is up and coming and who might be best for a certain role. With tight scheduling and budget restrictions, a director might only have one day to sit down and cast a couple of parts.

When I got the job, I remember telling Peter that I hadn't thought for a moment I'd be chosen. He admitted that he hadn't thought of Walter as a big guy either, but that the minute I'd walked in, he realised that a big lad would make the part even better. Walter was Vince's best mate and Vince was being played by Michael Legge, who had just finished three films back to back. The whole cast was full of people who were seen as the next big things. Matthew Rhys, Charlie Hunnam and Laura Fraser. All of them were in those 'one to watch' sections in magazines and newspapers. Again, just like that first day on *Martin Guerre*, I felt a little out of my depth.

The first day on any acting job is always the read-through. Everyone involved with the film sits around a table and you literally read through the script, each actor delivering their lines. I remember I was sitting opposite David Thewlis, a real hero of mine. I'm a huge fan of Mike Leigh's films – he's been a big influence ever since I saw *Life Is Sweet* – and David had played the lead in *Naked*, one of my favourites, a film about a guy on the run from Manchester in London. His performance in that film is unbelievable.

It was all a little mind-blowing. I was nineteen, I'd just turned down a year's contract with *Hollyoaks* and I was in London sitting opposite David Thewlis, who was sitting next to Stephen Fry, who was sitting next to Tom Courtenay. Crazy. I had plenty of time to just sit there and stare in awe because my character didn't appear until about fifty pages into the script.

I managed to nervously deliver my lines in the read-through without messing up too much and, afterwards, the producer invited us all to his house in Holland Park for a drinks party. That was the first I'd heard about it; no one had mentioned it before. David Thewlis asked me if I was going to go and I told him that of course I was, I wouldn't miss it, and he offered me a lift (which was a relief as I had no idea where Holland Park was). He had an old Peugeot 305 and as I sat next to him in the passenger seat, all I wanted to talk about was Mike Leigh. I imagine David had been asked the question a million times before, but I couldn't help myself. I just came right out and asked him what it was like working with him.

Mike is unique in British film-making. If you're lucky enough to be invited to work with him, your acting will be as pure as any performance you ever give. David didn't mind me asking and he told me in detail about the process: the whole thing is improvised, no script is written down and each character is developed individually with Mike. I remember sitting there thinking how amazing it would be to work with Mike, to be noticed by him. I couldn't think of anything more fulfilling or more challenging.

I remember the drinks do after the read-through for two reasons:

One, it was in the biggest house I'd ever been to – it was an amazing, luxurious townhouse, spread over countless floors.

And two, it was the first time I'd ever tasted hummus. I didn't really know what to do with it and at first I was eating it with a spoon, piling it high like it was Ready brek. After looking around at other people, I soon found out this was not a good look, and started using it as a dip instead.

Aside from the hummus embarrassment, the whole experience of making that film was great, actually. It was a brilliant bunch of people to work with and be around and the whole shoot was a really happy and satisfying experience.

CHAPTER 10

BEST MUSICAL ACCOMPANIMENT:
'Perfect 10' by the Beautiful South

BEST FILM TO WATCH ALONGSIDE:
Mona Lisa

BEST ENJOYED WITH:
canapés and sparkling wine

So, what did happen to *Harold Smith*? I'm sure you're wondering. So am I, actually. No, I'm kidding – when the film wrapped I was really hopeful it would be a success. It was quite a big British production. It wasn't a huge budget or anything, but it was big enough, and I'd almost forgotten that when the film came out there was going to be a Leicester Square premiere. It would be my first one. I remember walking down the red carpet with the TV cameras looking on and the fans screaming (none of them at me) and all the gathered press and photographers: people wanted to interview me. Me! I've got to admit that I loved all the attention.

Unfortunately, for whatever reason, the film didn't set the world on fire, which was a pretty big disappointment. It just sort of came and went, like a train arriving at the station with nobody getting on and nobody getting off. Often, that's just the way it is – most films come and go, don't find an audience, aren't through-the-roof mega-hits. It's just the occasional film that really breaks through and catches people's imagination. And who knows what that magic formula is? I find you're mostly just hoping that you've done the best job you could have and, after that, it's down to the stars aligning.

So, *Harold Smith* didn't quite hit the mark as we'd hoped, but that's not to say it was a complete disaster. There was a silver lining: because of the calibre of the cast and crew, a lot of influential people in the industry went to see the film and, soon after its release, I noticed a change in the kind of auditions I was going for.

I was auditioning a lot around this time. I remember one week when I went for six different auditions for six different films. One of them was for a film called *Dead Babies*, an adaptation of a Martin Amis novel, which an awful lot of people were saying was the hottest film in production at the time. It was going to be the new *Trainspotting*, and every young actor was dying to get a part in it. Initially, I was reading for the role of an American, but when I got there, both the director and the producer told me they didn't think I was right for it and asked me to read for another character instead.

OK, that was fine. They told me to go away for an hour, familiarise myself with the new character and come back. So I checked through the script and found the new part they wanted me to read for. Here's the description of him: 'The ugliest, vilest man you've ever seen. Less than five feet tall, his hair was falling out, he had boils on his face. A disgusting little creature.' Thanks guys. I guess I could have been offended that they took one look at me and thought I was right for the 'ugliest, vilest man' part, but it didn't cross my mind at the time. I was just concentrating on the script. I wanted to be in this film no matter what, and it didn't matter that much what part I'd be playing.

I auditioned three times for the film and I eventually got the part. The offer came through on my twenty-first birthday and I remember thinking that I was going to be in the film that everyone was calling the new *Trainspotting*, albeit playing the least attractive man in human history. Olivia Williams was already cast and she'd worked on massive Hollywood movies, and Paul Bettany was another of the leads. Paul is an incredible actor and at that moment was right on the cusp of making it huge both here and in America. I was excited about working with them both, and also with the rest of the brilliant cast that had been assembled.

But here's the thing. I've got to admit right here and now that I didn't really like the script. I didn't say anything to anyone and maybe I should have, but I never quite got it. The story was about a group of people spending a weekend in a country house, doing loads of drugs, drinking loads of booze and having lots and lots of sex. A killer is stalking the house at the same time and, one by one, the party-goers are all being killed off. The premise is great, but there was a tone to the script, a harshness, that I didn't really like. But I'd agreed to be in it, and I was still quite inexperienced at this point, so I didn't have the nerve to tell anyone what I was thinking.

We started rehearsing in a disused grammar school. My character wasn't short of scenes; he was just short. And all he wanted was to be tall. He made himself a pair of shoes with elevated heels and prayed for an *Alice in Wonderland*-style drug that would give him the extra inches. That was fine, except I'm not that short. In fact, I was taller than a couple of the actors I was sharing scenes with, so the director would get frustrated because I had to be seated all the time. It got pretty tense at times between me and Bill (the writer, director, producer and star of the film), and it all came to a bit of a head when the production team told me of their plans for the character's (or my) hair.

The designer took me to one side and told me that what they wanted to do was bleach my hair to the point where my scalp would turn red. And that, in turn, would make parts of my hair snap off so it would look as if it was falling out. Then, after that, they would shave big clumps out of my hair in various places all over my head.

Wow, I thought, that sounds a little dodgy – and painful. But it was for the film, it was in the script, so it had to be done. It only then occurred to me to think about what might happen when this film was over. I wouldn't be able to work. I would be unemployable. I mean, how many parts were there going to be for a guy with clumps of hair missing and a bleached scalp? They weren't paying me much for the film, definitely not enough to live on for the time it took for my hair to grow back.

You can see the dilemma. I spoke to Jacquie about it, told her I wasn't refusing to do it or anything, but that I was worried about what was going to happen afterwards. Jacquie had reservations as well, so she called up the producer, Richard, mentioning our concerns and suggesting we come to some sort of arrangement whereby they compensated me in some way for the hair wreckage.

It was difficult to sort out, though: the phone calls went back and forth between Jacquie and the producer, but the bottom line was they said they couldn't afford to pay me any more money. They really didn't have any more, and so suddenly we reached a bit of a stalemate. I'd never been in this situation before: the parts I'd played up until then had never called for anything quite so drastic. Ultimately, we reached a compromise where we agreed to try and achieve the same effects with prosthetics. They'd still dye and thin out my hair, but not to the point where it snapped off, and they could colour my scalp with make-up instead of bleaching it red. So, not total carnage, just a radical new look. I agreed to that happily. My make-up artist was an Australian girl who had just moved to London. I was aware that what they were planning was no easy task and so, a little nervously, I asked her what she'd been working on before she left Australia. *Home and Away*, she said happily.

Home and Away? It occurred to me, as I'm sure it does to you, that on a soap there wouldn't be that much call for crazy red scalp and fally-outy hair. I was a little worried, to say the least. I knew the budget on the film was tight, but this didn't seem the best place to scrimp on money. She did her best, though, and started by thinning my hair out to the point where you could see my scalp. I sat there watching in the mirror as she cut away, my beautiful locks floating unhappily to the floor, and when she thinned it enough, the make-up artists took over and started slapping on the red stuff. This was the part that needed to look good. Only, it didn't. It looked very not good. They kept on trying really hard to make it right, but it became pretty clear that the only way it was going to work was by going the whole hog and shaving the clumps out like they'd originally wanted.

Bill, the writer, director, co-producer and star, entered the room and stood behind me. We were looking at each other in the mirror and we both knew it didn't look right. He was looking really concerned, upset even.

'Bill,' I said, 'I don't think this is going to work.'

For a moment he didn't say anything. Then he turned on his heels as if to leave.

'Shall we just go for it?' I said quickly, not wanting to disappoint. 'Just shave and bleach it. It's OK, honestly. Shall we?'

'I tell you what,' he said on his way out, 'I think we should just hold off for a moment. Right now let's not do anything.'

A moment later one of the runners came in and told me that Richard the co-producer wanted to see me, so I left make-up and walked over to the makeshift office he was using. I went in, sat down at his desk and looked across the clutter at him.

'So, James,' he said, 'how's it going?'

'Good, I think.' I'd been smiling when I came in, happy to tell him I'd decided we should go ahead and shave my hair. But there was something about his expression that put me on edge. Coupled with the way Bill had been in make-up and the way the runner had summoned me, I knew something was up. I had the same feeling I used to get when waiting in the staff corridor at school. Pretty quickly, my smile slipped away.

Richard was looking everywhere except at me. His eyes glanced all around the room – above my head, to my left, then to my right, down to the ground; anywhere but me. Finally he sighed really heavily. 'Look, James,' he said, 'we're having problems with the way the character is going.'

'Yeah, I know. It's not really clicking yet, but we'll get there.'

'We're quite worried about it actually,' he went on, 'what with your hair, all that hassle we had with your agent.' He pursed his lips. 'You know, we're wondering whether you're completely committed to this film.'

I didn't really say anything. I was unsure as to where this was leading. I'm not committed? I thought to myself. I've just looked the director, writer, co-producer and, we must never forget, star, in the eyes and told him to go ahead and shave lumps out of my hair.

Richard was still talking. 'The thing is, I have to make up my mind whether we're going to stick with you or look for another actor, and I've got to decide that by the end of the day.'

I just sat there staring at him, completely gobsmacked. He was talking about firing me from what was rumoured to be the next big thing in British film. It had to be a joke, right? Er, no, he was deadly serious.

I didn't know what to say. I just sort of sat there, squirming. He was talking about chemistry and passion for the project and much else besides – to be honest it's a bit of a blur and I can't remember exactly what he was saying. All I remember is how he finished. 'So that's why I'm going to have to fire you, James. I'm sorry, you're off this movie.'

I felt as if I'd been punched in the stomach. I took a few moments to try and get my wits together.

'Richard,' I said, 'hang on a minute, you just told me you had until the end of the day.'

'Yeah,' he said, sitting back. 'I don't know why I said that.'

'You don't know why you said that?'

'No,' he replied, with a shrug. 'Sorry, James. I have to let you go.'

We went back and forth for what seemed like ages. It got pretty heated and, though it never broke out into a full-blown argument, it got pretty close. I was so upset. I told him I thought his decision sucked and that I'd not had any time with the director/writer/star on my own so how could anyone accuse me of not being committed. Then he brought up my height as an issue and I reminded him that I hadn't actually grown since they'd given me the job. But nothing I said was going to make any difference. No matter how hard I tried, there was nothing I could do to change his mind.

At the end of it, I left the office and went outside to the car park. I think I sort of stood there for a moment, not quite knowing what do to; then I called Shelley and just burst into tears. I bawled my eyes out. You know how it is when you can't get your breath? Well, I was exactly like that, shaking as I was talking to her.

I called Jacquie after and she told me to come straight over to the office, but that first she would speak to the producer. I stood there in the car park, my hair thinned out and tears rolling down my face, waiting for Jacquie to call back. The worst part in all of it was that right at that moment the rest of the cast were having lunch at some picnic tables across the way. It was a glorious hot August day and they were shouting and beckoning me over to them. I waved back, but I knew that if I went over to tell them what had happened, I'd find it impossible not to cry. Then Jacquie called me back and told me what I'd known all along: Richard wasn't changing his mind. It was over.

I had no choice but to head for the car they had provided to take me home. I used it to take me into London, and had it wait while I saw Jacquie. (I was getting my money's worth.) We spoke for a while and she told me I'd still get paid, which was a massive relief, and then she also told me that in all her years as an actors' agent, no client of hers had ever been fired from a film, which was a massive kick in the nuts. So I was the first, then. That was nice. What a day! As I took the car back to Shelley's, I felt beaten down; totally and utterly dejected.

At home that night my family kept trying to cheer me up, but the fact remained that I'd been fired from a film set. And not just any film set either. Remember, this was going to be the new *Trainspotting*. Ewan McGregor-style careers would be launched with this film, Hollywood would come calling, and meanwhile I'd be left in Wycombe, phoning up Bella Pasta and asking for my old job back.

I'm not exaggerating. The closest I'd come to being fired was as a teenager in the mini-mart, and I had no idea what it might mean for my career. What if this was it? What if this was the end, the last scene, the final curtain?

It really worried me because deep down I knew my attitude hadn't been right. The bottom line was, I had never liked the character and I suppose, eventually, it showed. It was scarily familiar. It reminded me of how I'd been at school: when if something didn't float my boat, I'd react flippantly; be uninterested to the point of disruption. Was that how I'd come across to the crew? Did I possess some deep-seated personality trait that was hardwired to screw me up? Would it surface to cripple me again?

I thought about that film every day for a year – the endless, painful possibilities. What if this film is the biggest British film ever? What if every member of the cast is catapulted to stardom? What if it actually is like *Trainspotting*? It was a horrible feeling that never really went away until the film was released a year or so after I'd left and made next to no impact in the cinema. I'm not gloating, truly. I just felt relieved. I hadn't missed the boat. For all its efforts, the film just sank without trace. For months I'd been preparing to be the guy who had to admit that he'd been fired from the movie that scooped all the awards and broke all box-office records.

I learnt a lot from the experience. I decided that I'd never be

The cast of *Fat Friends*, and yes, I am wearing a woman's coat.

Russell Tovey (My Russ); Sam Anderson (Zammo); Me (Levine);
Andrew Knott (Moon); Dominic Cooper (Dirtbox); Sam Barnet (Sam);
Jamie Parker (Scripps); Sacha Dhawan (Sachgelia).

The History Boys on stage at the National Theatre.

Opening night in New York, with the two men who changed our lives,
Nicholas Hytner (left) and Alan Bennett (centre).

The eight of us
on a 20ft poster
in Times Square.

And the New York
programme.
If you look closely,
I'm very subtly
giving the finger.

Mat, Joanna, Ruth and I. The first photo shoot the four of us ever did.

On set filming series one. Making script changes at the eleventh hour.

The cast and crew of *Gavin & Stacey*.
I can't name them all here, but I miss every single one of them.

Rob Brydon and I. No one makes me laugh on a set quite like him.

Ruth, Rob, Melanie Walters and I having just been on the log flume at Barry Island.

And there she is, my best friend in the whole wide world,
on a night neither of us will ever forget.

Recreating David Beckham's Armani advert for *Heat* magazine.
There are three pairs of socks in my pants.

on the outside of anything again; that if I was lucky enough to be offered a part – any part – and accept it, then I had to go for it hook, line and sinker. Good, bad or somewhere in between, I had to commit to it.

I was out of work for four months after *Dead Babies*. I'm not sure it had anything to do with being fired; it may have done, but I think it's unlikely. Most actors are out of work for long stretches and, actually, when I look back on this particular stretch, it seems like a particularly formative time for me. However down I was about being fired, I was also becoming more and more driven. Despite the disappointment, and the blow to the ego, I wanted to get back on the horse and work again.

It's hard when you're just sitting there waiting for the phone to ring for an opportunity to do things, totally at the mercy of your agent or a casting director. It's a frustrating, soul-sapping time. However, the next time the phone did ring, it was a big call. You could say it was the call I'd been longing for.

Jacquie got in touch about a prime-time series called *Fat Friends* that ITV had commissioned. It had been written by Kay Mellor, who already had *Band of Gold* under her belt, a groundbreaking piece of TV about prostitution in Yorkshire.

The series focused on the lives of a group of chubsters who attended the same slimming class in Leeds. There were six hour-long episodes, each driven by a different character. The character I was going for appeared in five of the six, and the fourth episode centred on his story. His name was Jamie; he was an overweight schoolboy with problems at home. I've never wanted a part so badly. I vividly remember reading it: lying on the floor in Shelley's parents' front room, ripping through the script, not putting it down until I'd finished the last page.

As soon as I was done with it, I rolled over on my back and stared at the ceiling for what must have been twenty minutes, and let my mind run away. This part was everything I'd waited for. There is no other way I can describe it. I mean, if you're a big guy, you're not going to be offered James Bond, are you? If it's a rom-com or a bittersweet love story, you're going to be the funny mate of the lead guy who gets the girl rather than the guy who gets the girl. I knew that when I started out. Guys like me were supporting actors, enablers – often with some of the best lines, but never with the real juice.

And yet, there I was reading this brilliant story that focused on an overweight schoolboy. His mum had been left by his dad and was depressed to the point where she was taking pills, so Jamie had basically assumed the role of a parent. He had a home life from hell, and at the same time he was being bullied at school. His story carried the whole episode – all the attention was on him. And though it might sound depressing, there was fun and laughter to go along with the tears. I'm sure you know that I'm fond of a laugh, but there's also a side of me that loves serious acting, getting into the meaty roles that really challenge you. Jamie's character had that rare mix of both.

I remember talking about it to Shelley and telling her that if I couldn't get this part, I might as well give up. It could've been written for me – I don't mean that in a big-headed way; I just really *felt* the part. Travelling up to Leeds to audition, I was totally determined to pull it off.

I thought the audition went pretty well. It was lovely meeting the production team; they made me feel very comfortable so I really launched myself into the role. But, however good you feel an audition goes, you can never be sure what the guys sitting on the other side of the desk are thinking. Each production has a different way of doing things, and this time they said they would probably call back the people they wanted for a second reading. Fair enough, I thought, now it's back home to wait and see. On the way back to the station I shared a cab with Richard Ridings, who had been reading for the part of a guy called Alan. We chatted about the day and my heart plummeted when he told me he'd been offered all six episodes, right then and there in the room.

What did that mean? Was I out already? Was that it? I didn't know what to think. They told me they were doing call-backs, but if they'd already offered a role to Richard, then maybe they were just being polite. I must have missed out. I couldn't believe it. I'd been convinced I could make that part my own. Oh well, there must've been someone out there who was better than me, that was all. What can you do but accept it and move on? It was a long, lonely journey back to London.

The next week went by slowly and, just as I'd got to the point where I'd abandoned all hope, I got a call from Jacquie. Kay had been in touch. She wanted me to meet her at the Groucho Club in Soho. I was still in with a shot.

I was really excited now: it had to be positive. I got into Soho an hour and a half before the meeting. The Groucho Club is just round the corner from the Prince Edward Theatre, where *Martin Guerre* had been on, so I knew the area quite well. During the year I'd been there I'd always enjoyed aimlessly wandering around. I love Soho. It's a fascinating place where the rich and poor rub shoulders like in no other part of London. From the exclusive members' bars hidden away behind nondescript doors to the seedy underworld of strip clubs and sex shops, it's got it all.

For some reason, on that day, I found myself wandering around the shadier part of town. There I was, minding my own business, when a voice behind me said, 'Live show? Fully nude girls?' I stopped, turned round and, through an open doorway, saw a woman sitting behind a counter with flashing lights. I'd never been down this alley before, as the walk from the Tube to the theatre didn't bring me through here. 'Only five pounds, darlin''. I checked my watch – I had an hour to kill. Maybe watching some naked women might be a nice way to pass the time.

'Come here, sweetie,' she said, beckoning me in. 'How old are you, you little cutie?'

I cleared my throat and said, 'I'm twenty-one.'

'Well, that's OK. Why don't you come in and we'll give you a nice live show.' She took my hand in hers and pulled herself slightly nearer to me.

'Would you like that? Just five pounds.' Before I could say anything, I was loosening the Velcro on my wallet and handing over a crisp fiver. She smiled at me and ushered me past the black velvet curtain and into a dimly lit corridor. 'Mind your step there, big boy,' she said as I followed her down what seemed like hundreds of steps. (There were probably only twenty.)

We walked into a small room with tables and booths set around the edges. Each table had a small lamp on it, and they were really the only source of light. I couldn't even tell you what colour the walls were, it was that dark. We walked past two angry-looking guys who were wearing brightly coloured Kappa tracksuits and then past three or four girls who were sitting in the corner in their underwear, talking and taking long drags on cigarettes. I looked around but at no point could I see a stage or any kind of strip show going on. The woman holding my hand sat me down in a sort of semi-private booth in the corner and introduced herself. 'I'm Sapphire. What's your name, darlin'?'

'I'm . . . erm . . . Mark. Yeah, Mark,' I said smoothly. We sat down and she asked me what a boy like me was doing wandering around Soho on a day like this. I didn't know what to say. I sort of stumbled and mumbled my words without much of an answer.

'Lookin' for trouble?' she said.

'Not especially,' I answered. At that moment one of the girls in her underwear came over. I felt relieved; this strip show could now start and I could get the hell out of here. So far, it hadn't lived up to the billing. I also couldn't understand why Sapphire was still sitting down next to me. I mean, who was manning the front desk?

'Hi, I'm Jade,' said the girl in her underwear, and added a 'Nice to meet you' before walking off. Then another girl came over and said her name was Bella. She leant forward and kissed me seductively on the cheek. I was about to tell her that I used to work in Bella Pasta when she just turned round and walked off too. Sapphire was still sitting next to me, not moving or saying a word. I started to feel really uncomfortable and began thinking that it might be a good idea to leave soon. I had an overwhelming sense of something not being right.

'Do you want a drink?' one of the nasty-looking blokes in the tracksuits called over.

'Erm . . . I'm OK, thanks. I'll just, erm . . . When does the show start?' I asked.

'Show starts soon,' he said, moving towards our table. 'You've got to have a drink.'

I paused and he just stared at me. 'Just a Coke then, please,' I said, in a slightly too high-pitched voice.

'How old are you?'

'He's twenty-one. I checked,' Sapphire said quickly.

'Good. Just a Coke then, is it?'

'Yes, thanks.'

As the man walked away, his shell-suit scrunching with every step, Sapphire leant in to me and whispered into my ear, 'I'm gonna go and talk to my friends. You should read the price list before I come back.'

She walked away, pulling a velvet rope across one side of the booth to the other. I looked around for a price list but couldn't see anything anywhere – no menu or drinks list on the table – until I looked at the wall in front and there, screwed in, was a framed list of drinks prices. My eyes nearly blew out of my head.

Champagne: £1,000

Beer: £500

Wine: £500

And below, right at the bottom of the list:

Soft drinks: £500

I was shocked. I mean, those were ridiculous prices, even for central London. I'd made a huge mistake. I didn't know where I was, or what was going on, but I knew I shouldn't be there. I stood up and started trying to undo the rope. It wouldn't give so I got on my knees and tried to shuffle underneath it.

'Where d'ya think you're going?' asked a broad Mancunian voice. It was the other of the two guys I'd passed near the door. I got up off the ground and said, as nicely and politely as I could, 'I think there's been a mistake. I thought this was . . . Well, anyway, I'm just gonna leave. Don't worry about the fiver.'

At that moment he grabbed my coat by the lapels and pushed me back into the corner. 'Don't worry about the fiver? Are you having a laff? You owe me five hundred quid, you cheeky bastard!'

I was shaking so much that I could barely breathe, let alone speak. He still had hold of me and, as he leant his face in to get up close and personal, I could see that he had a tattoo on his neck and his eyebrow was pierced. His breath wasn't great either.

'But . . . but I haven't had a drink,' I managed, trying to hold it together. 'I . . . I thought th-this was a strip show.'

'Leave him be, Danny,' said Sapphire, trying to help me. 'He's only young.' He put me down but only so he could push his elbow up against my chest. I didn't know what he was gonna do, but it felt as if he was shaping up to hit me. With a whimper, I closed my eyes, clenched my jaw and waited for the punch. Instead, I felt his hand rummaging around in my pocket and opened my eyes to see him pulling my wallet out of my jacket. 'So how much you got in here?' he said, pulling the Velcro open, while still pinning me to the wall.

I tried to remember. 'About twenty quid, I think.'

'Well then, my friend. We're going to have to take a little trip to the cashpoint.'

I didn't know what to do. I couldn't believe what was happening. I had a call-back for a massive TV show in forty minutes. 'I can't. I haven't got any money in the bank,' I said, clutching at straws.

'You what?' the geezer said again, applying more pressure to my chest.

'I haven't got any money . . .' I then, pretty remarkably given the circumstances, had a brainwave. Lie! 'I'm not twenty-one either. I'm only seventeen. I'm from High Wycombe. I've come to London for the day with my dad, but he's in a meeting. He's a loaded businessman. He'll give me the money and I'll bring it back.'

I was literally saying whatever entered my head. Sapphire looked at Danny. 'That's what he told me, Danny,' she said. 'His dad is loaded but he's left him to wander the streets on his own.' That was unexpected. I couldn't believe she was trying to help me.

'I promise I'll get you the money. I'll just tell him I need it for some trainers. He'll give it to me, I promise.' Danny looked at Sapphire and then carried on looking through my wallet. He pulled out my Switch card and looked at it. 'There's no money in there,' I said, panicking. 'My allowance only gets put in every month.' I truly believe that in the twenty-one years I'd been alive up until that point, this was the first time I'd used the word 'allowance.' (We got pocket money in our house, but I'd always associated an 'allowance' with something that rich kids got.)

Suddenly Danny let out a scream. 'THIS IS BULLSHIT!' He grabbed me again and slammed me back into the wall.

'DANNY, stop it!' shouted Sapphire.

I swear to God I thought I was about to cry. He emptied out my wallet and put all the cash I had, coins and everything, in his pocket. I had a picture of me and Shelley in there, which he ripped out and waved in my face. 'Is this your girlfriend? Is it? What would she say if she knew you were in here trying to pay for sex?' Eh? I didn't think I was paying for sex. In fact, that was the first time that sex had been mentioned.

'I thought it was a striptease show. That's all. I don't wanna pay for sex. Please, I just want to get out of here. I've said I'll give you the money. Please just let me go.' My bottom lip was quivering. Amazingly, he then took a Blockbuster video card out and held it up to me. I can picture it now: in big yellow letters on a blue background it read, 'Wow! What a difference,' and had 'Mr M. K. Corden' embossed underneath the slogan. (It was my dad's card but I always held on to it.) By now, he was almost spitting in my face with every word. 'I'm gonna keep this card, and if you don't come back with the money, I'm gonna find you and kill you, do you understand?' He pushed his sweaty forehead against mine and did what can only be described as a slow-motion head-butt. Y'no, a bit like footballers do when they want to look hard but just end up looking weird.

'Yeah, I understand,' I said meekly.

'Get out of here. NOW!' He let down his elbow and threw my wallet at me. I got down on my hands and knees and started scooping up the cards and receipts that had fallen on the floor, then ran out of there as fast as I could. Once I was back on the street, I ran down to Shaftesbury Avenue and for some reason nicked into the Trocadero. Inside, I walked into the first shop I could find and hid in a corner to see if anyone was following me. They weren't. The coast was clear. I breathed a massive sigh of relief, furiously started wiping the sweat from my brow with my shirtsleeve and looked at my watch – I had ten minutes before I was meeting Kay. Shit!

First things first, though. I took out my mobile and called our local Blockbuster. I pretended to be my dad on the phone. 'Oh, hello there,' I said, sounding like a character from *Dad's Army* (nothing like my dad). 'I seem to have lost my membership card. My name is Malcolm Corden . . .' I gave our address and phone number and the guy on the end of the phone said he'd send another one over. But that still didn't put me in the clear. 'Erm . . . Sorry, old chap, I'm slightly worried. What if someone were to find my card and try to get my details off your system? Could they find me? I mean, is that possible? Hey, old bean?' The old chap assured me that no one with that card could get hold of our details and that people lose cards all the time. I put the phone down and was suddenly hit with the reality of everything that had just happened. It totally frazzled me.

It remains one of the weirdest hours of my life. I shudder when I see tourists walking into those places now. For about three years after that experience, if I ever had to be in Soho, I would always be slightly on edge, worried that I might bump into Danny or Sapphire. It was, I kid you not, the most terrifying experience of my young life.

But, right then, I had bigger fish to fry. I needed to get moving, and fast. It was now only five minutes before my meeting and, if I didn't run to the Groucho Club, I was going to be late. It was just about doable. I rushed back down Shaftesbury Avenue, up Dean Street and burst in through the door. The lady on reception was – understandably – a bit taken aback by my entrance, but I told her I was here to see Kay and she let me through into the bar.

Still hopelessly out of breath, I went over to where Kay was sitting in the corner with one of the directors, called Audrey Cooke, and one of the producers. As I sat down, Kay looked at me a bit askance and said, 'What have you been up to?' If only you knew, I thought to myself. Fifteen minutes ago I was basically in a brothel that I thought was a strip joint with a bloke called Danny nicking my Blockbuster card and threatening to beat me up.

Obviously, I didn't say a word and, after I'd cooled down a little, we talked for an hour or so about the series, about Jamie's character and how they viewed him and how I viewed him, and about what I thought I could bring to the role. I suppose we reached a natural pause and they said they needed to have a chat now, just the three of them together. Fine, I said, you guys do that. I'm off to the loo.

I left them alone, and in the toilets I stood looking at myself in the mirror. What a weird day, I was thinking: one mad extreme to the other. A brothel to the Groucho Club in the space of ten minutes. This was my first time in the Groucho Club. I knew it was where famous people went – I'd seen Adam Ant standing outside it once – and so being there kind of felt important, as though I was on the right track. I was feeling pretty confident about the chat Kay and I had had too. The way the conversation had gone, I just had a feeling they were going to offer me the role.

Giving them what I hoped was a decent amount of time, I walked back to the table. My heart was fluttering a little as I sat down. For a long moment they all just looked at me and then, with a smile, the producer said they would love to offer me the role. *Yes!* There is no feeling like it – thinking you've missed out on something only to be offered it is literally the most amazing sensation. The end result is worth all the pain. I sat there tingling with excitement. I had a lead role in an hour of prime-time television to look forward to and I couldn't wait to get started.

Though I wasn't aware of it then, getting the part in *Fat Friends* would prove to be one of those pivotal moments: a real turning point in my life and the beginning of something really, really special. It was there I would find my feet as an actor and get noticed by one of my heroes. And, most importantly by far, I would meet my future best friend and, without question, the most talented person I know: Ruth Jones.

But let's not rush into all that just yet. First we had the read-through, which was back up in Leeds. As I got off the train, I spotted a woman standing in the middle of the station holding up a massive sign with the words 'Fat Friends' scrawled across it. Spotting Richard Ridings making his way over, I was keeping an eye peeled for anyone else I might recognise or who might fit the bill. There was nobody immediately obvious but, as I headed over, I found myself walking alongside a lady carrying a heavy suitcase. I asked if she needed a hand and she gratefully let me take it.

And then it hit me. Oh my God, it was Alison Steadman. Alison *Life Is Sweet, Nuts in May, Abigail's Party* Steadman. And I was carrying her case. Not only had Alison appeared in three of my favourite Mike Leigh films, she'd been married to the guy.

A sudden thought struck me. There was no way she could be in the same TV series as me, right? Could she? Nah. No way. It was just coincidence, nothing more. I was happy enough that I'd bumped into her at all and that she'd allowed me to carry her suitcase. But, as we walked together towards the lady holding the sign, Alison didn't pull away – she was matching me step for step. Still, it was only as we both climbed into the people-carrier and sat next to each other that I was prepared to believe the truth. I was going to be in a TV series with one of the all-time greats of British television.

With the show running for six hour-long episodes, there were two directors doing three each. I'd met David Wheatley at the first audition: he was directing the first three. Audrey Cooke was directing mine. I won't go into all the details of how the shoot went – it was wonderful, amazing, life-changing – apart from to say that the first time Ruth and I really got talking was after we'd finished the first read-through. Ruth, who was playing Kelly, had some big emotional scenes and had tears in her eyes as we came to the end. We had a chat about it afterwards and there was something, right then, that just seemed to click between the two of us. I'm happy to say that click has never gone away.

I couldn't wait for the series to air and, when it did, about 10 million people tuned in. I think everyone involved was pretty bowled over by the reaction. Four weeks into the series and my episode came around – my first leading role and the first time I'd held down an hour of prime-time television. I was at home in Hazlemere watching with Mum, Dad and Rudi. By the time it was over, all three of them were in tears. Almost immediately after it ended, the phone started ringing: aunts and uncles, cousins, friends from previous shows, schoolmates – it was absolutely amazing.

The show was a runaway success, which wasn't that surprising given the talent involved and all the great performances: Alison, Ruth, Richard, everyone really. By the end of the run, there were rumours flying about that the show might be up for some awards. Not for a moment did I think I'd be up for anything, so I had to be picked off the floor when Kay Mellor phoned and told me I'd been nominated in the 'Best Newcomer' category for the Royal Television Society Awards. It was a proper you've-got-to-be-kidding-me moment. I'd gone from reading the script on Shelley's floor to being nominated for an acting award. Huh?

And so it was that Shelley and I went along to our first awards ceremony. Shell looked resplendent in her evening gown, and I think I looked all right in my rented tux. The show was due to start at seven o'clock and so, being keen, Shell and I got there at 6.45 p.m. and for the next hour and three-quarters did nothing but wait for everyone else to turn up. It didn't really kick off until at least half eight, but it didn't matter – we just floated around drinking in the atmosphere (and the free drinks). This was a major TV awards do, and I still couldn't believe that I'd been nominated. Jamie Oliver, Rob Brydon and Steve Coogan were all there, people I'd admired for years, and I was there taking a seat among them.

It occurs to me now that I had no idea who I was up against until we actually sat down at the table. The other nominees turned out to be Dom Joly for *Trigger Happy TV* and Rob for *Marion and Geoff*. As soon as I saw his name on the paper, I knew Rob would win. I mean, the guy created a whole series around a guy sitting in a taxi. I certainly didn't mind losing to Rob, and I wouldn't have minded losing to Dom either. As I saw it, to be nominated along with two guys who had written and created their own shows was an achievement in itself. I was just a young actor who took the lead in one episode of a series. No contest.

Finally, the 'Best Newcomer' category came around. I remember holding Shelley's hand as our names were called and a clip from each of the shows was played to the audience. And the winner was . . . Rob Brydon, of course. The two of us spoke briefly together afterwards, and that's when I discovered that he and Ruth had gone to school together. Rob admitted he hadn't seen the show, but Ruth had told him I'd been great in it, which was very nice to hear. We got on really well – there's nothing to dislike about Rob. He's a charming, hilariously funny man.

Before he left, he made a point of telling me that I was a young guy and, though I hadn't won tonight, he was sure that my time would come. I also got to speak to Graham Norton, who hosted the awards. I'm sure he'd never remember what he said to me, but it was something I've never forgotten. He came over, introduced himself, and told me that the clip they'd showed of me crying had silenced the room and that that, in a roomful of television people, was a real achievement. I was so happy just to be talking to him, let alone receiving compliments from him. The whole night, everything about it, was so different to anything I'd experienced, and yet, at the same time, had some bizarre sense of familiarity, which must have come from me having dreamt of it for so long. Sitting in the back of a big flash car on the way home, I thought about what Rob had said, and hoped he was right; I hoped there would be many more nights like this one.

CHAPTER 11

BEST MUSICAL ACCOMPANIMENT:
'Little Bear' by Guillemots

BEST FILM TO WATCH ALONGSIDE:
any film by Mike Leigh

BEST ENJOYED WITH:
a double espresso

One statistic I remember hearing while I was growing up used to worry me quite a lot. It's this: at any one time, 80 per cent of actors are out of work. That's a scarily high number. The chances are, if ever you've been out to eat or drink in London, one of the people serving you your burger or bringing you your cappuccino will be an actor; for all you or I know, he or she might be the best actor in the world who trained at RADA and is represented by a top agent but, for whatever reason, just hasn't got the breaks. So much of acting is about luck, being in the right place at the right time and knowing the right people. And it's definitely true that the more you work, the more people you meet, and the more likely you are to get opportunities to work.

Tiger Aspect are a big production company making many varied television shows, from documentaries and comedies to dramas like *Fat Friends*. Because I'd worked with them on that show, they asked me if I'd like to audition for a new Channel 4 series called *Teachers*. It starred Andrew Lincoln of *This Life* fame and was centred around the lives of a group of young teachers in Bristol. Once again, the fact that I had experience yet still looked like I was a schoolboy played into my hands, and I was offered the part of Jeremy, the class geek. Working with Andrew was a real joy. To this day he still ranks as one of the nicest and warmest people you could ever wish to work with. So encouraging, with the perfect balance of fun and professionalism.

I made instant, lasting friendships on that job – not just with Andrew but also with the runner, a young guy called Ben Winston. There's a runner on every production and, for my money, they have the hardest job on the set. It's utterly thankless: they are the first to arrive on set and are the last to leave; they do everything, for everyone, and yet they're often treated as irrelevant. They are the worst-paid member of the film crew, but they're vitally important to the smooth running of the production and, the truth is, anyone who is anyone in film will at one point or another have been a runner. When you first start out, the best way to discover whether you're cut out for a life in TV – the shitty hours, the time away from home, the unpredictability of where your next job will be – is to become a runner. If you can hack that, then there's a good chance you'll be all right. And Ben could hack it – he could hack it ten times over. I've never known anyone light up a film set the way he did. Everyone fell in love with him – nobody more than me.

His job description involved getting tea for anyone who asked for it, bringing sandwiches, carrying messages, standing out in the rain making sure unwanted cars weren't driving through a shot . . . Any kind of crappy task you could think of on set – and there are lots of them – he performed not only with good grace, but with a laugh and a smile. To this day Ben was the best runner I've ever seen. Clearly, he was head and shoulders above everyone else.

But more about Ben later, because right now I want to tell you about a call I got that very nearly killed me stone dead. I'd just come off the set of *Teachers* when my mobile started ringing. It was Jacquie and she was phoning to tell me that she'd arranged an audition with someone I was a fan of. That got me listening.

'Who? Who is it?' I asked.

'It's Mike.'

'Mike. Who's Mike? Mike who?'

'Mike Leigh.'

I just stood there holding the phone.

'What?' I said. 'You mean actually with Mike?'

'Yeah, with Mike.'

'Mike Leigh. You're talking about *the* Mike Leigh? Basically my favourite film-maker of all time?'

'That Mike Leigh, James. Yes.'

How to explain? If you ever passed Mike in the street, you'd barely notice the little guy with dark, smiley eyes, cropped hair and a smallish, Father Christmas-style white beard. He's so un-assuming he looks like a cross between a good-natured hobbit and a monk. The reality is that Mike is probably the purest film-maker on the planet. I know that sounds a bit wanky, but it's the truth. Acting in his films is the most original, fundamental and raw experience you can have professionally. For months on end you soak yourself in the character you're about to play and get to learn them inside and out: their thoughts, their instincts, their hopes and aspirations, what they'd eat for breakfast – every-thing. You essentially become the author of a person. I'll explain that a little more later; but, right then, when I got Jacquie's call, I was still in a daze.

Jacquie told me that she'd taken a call from Nina Gold, who had cast me in *Whatever Happened to Harold Smith?* Nina was casting Mike's new film and she wanted me to come in and meet him.

Mike's office is in Soho and on the train travelling in, all I could think about was that conversation I'd had with David Thewlis back before the spoon-hummus party. I was trying to remember everything he'd told me about the way Mike works and his approach to acting and characterisation. Not a lot of it was coming back.

The usual thing you do when you're going for an audition is to read through the script and familiarise yourself with the part so you can really do it justice when the time comes. But that's not how it works with Mike. There is no script at the 'audition'; at that point I don't think Mike even knows exactly what he's looking for. It's the kind of thing that, if you over-think too much, can get very daunting; that sense of a blank page and having nothing to work from but your instincts. But if you look at it another way, it can really free you up. You're not constrained by lines that must be said in such-and-such a way or dealing with someone else's creation – the character is entirely yours. You are way more in charge.

This time, heading into London, I'd left early enough so I could navigate around the strip joints and sex shops in Soho, so as to be sure not to run into Sapphire and Danny. However, when I got to Mike's office, there was no avoiding the reality – I was right smack-dab in the middle of Soho's sex trade. The office was on the first floor of a Georgian townhouse and the bell you rang from the street had two other bells alongside it. One was for the place downstairs and the other was for the lady-of-the-night's pad on the top floor. In Soho, there are plenty of doors with the words 'Model Upstairs' printed somewhere discreetly. Here's a useful piece of tourist advice I can give to anyone visiting London: it probably isn't a model upstairs. There's someone up there; it's just very unlikely she's an actual model.

By the time I got upstairs, the nerves had overtaken me a little and I sat down in front of him, still not quite believing I was actually there, and that he was Mike Leigh.

'So,' he said in his quietly considered way, peering out from his hooded eyes, 'you were in this programme *Fat Friends*, then, with Alison?'

'Yes,' I said, 'I was.'

'Well, I don't think it was very good.' He studied me. 'What do you think?'

Mike is renowned for his no-nonsense honesty, but to be hit with that from the get-go was a little alarming. I didn't jump right in. I considered my answer for a bit and told him I could see why he might not like it, but that I was very proud of my bits.

'Really,' he said. 'I haven't seen your bits. I'll have to look them up.'

I chilled a little after that. We talked about acting and films, about my career and the kind of films I liked. I told him how important I thought films were and that I didn't have anything more valuable than my DVD collection. A lot of the films in it had been made by him, and I had to make a big effort to stop myself from telling him again and again what kind of influence he'd had on my life.

I can tell him now, though: the two greatest influences on my working life have been Mike Leigh's films and *The Royle Family* series on TV. In different ways they show you that, no matter what you might think or feel about this world, nothing is ordinary. Mike has the ability and talent to show you how people actually live, and make incredibly moving drama and comedy from it. He doesn't shy away from everyday concerns, or hardship, or even boredom; he manages to find drama and emotion in very normal places. I'm not criticising other glitzier kinds of films for their lack of realness – every movie has its place and I love my Hollywood as much as any man – but it's the genuine, challenging stuff that has always moved me the most.

It was an audition of sorts. I was with Mike for about an hour and we did a bit of background work on a character and then Nina came in. Mike told her that he thought I ought to come back again the following Thursday, when I had a day free from filming *Teachers*.

Travelling back down to Bristol, I couldn't get over the fact that I'd just spent the best part of an hour sitting and working with one of my heroes. On Nina's recommendation Mike had wanted to audition me, and now he wanted to see me again. This was the guy I'd admired all my life, the guy I'd talked about with so many other actors, the director I most wanted to work with.

When I went back to Soho again the following week, the nerves had gone. It helped that, as I walked up the stairs, I passed an Australian guy who was tucking his shirt in his trousers. 'Oh strewth, mate!' he said. 'Get yourself up there. She's a ripper!' He'd clearly had a good time.

Mike was standing in the doorway on the first floor chuckling to himself at the exchange. We sat down on the sofa in his office and he told me that he'd watched my episode of *Fat Friends* and, though he thought I was right to be proud of it, he still thought it was an awful show. I wasn't offended; in fact I appreciated his honesty.

Mike's films are entirely about the characters. Prior to their creation nothing exists at all – no story, no plot, no locations; everything takes shape as the characters develop. On that second visit he asked me to think of someone I knew who wasn't a relation and wasn't an actor either. Anyone. For whatever reason, Luke Smythson popped into my head, a guy from school who was a massive Leeds United fan. Mike told me he was going to go out of the room for a while and, in my own time, he wanted me to become Luke. He didn't tell me to do anything specifically, just to 'become'.

'All I'm going to do is step back into the room and observe,' he said, 'all right?'

'Fine. No problem.'

So for forty minutes I did absolutely nothing. I read a newspaper; I looked out of the window; I stared into space; because that's what Luke would've done. When we finished, Mike asked me to tell him about what had been going on for the last forty minutes. I amazed myself by what I started to say. I explained that I (as Luke) was reading the newspaper because a Leeds fan had just been stabbed in Turkey and the truth of it was that if I'd had more money, I'd have been there for that match, no question. He was nodding, asking a few questions, probing a little deeper, but there wasn't much more to it than that. We talked a little more and then I left. I didn't really know what to think other than that I'd really enjoyed the process. I'd had a taste of what it would be like to work with Mike and, difficult as it could be, the organic nature of the work was even more stimulating than I'd imagined.

It was just before Christmas when I got the phone call telling me Thin Man Films, who make all Mike Leigh's films, was booking me for eight months. I was absolutely ecstatic; it was a moment I will never, ever forget. I was on the set of *Teachers* and I remember telling Andrew Lincoln and him giving me the biggest hug. Ben Winston was there and he was jumping around too, celebrating with me.

It turned out that working with Mike was both brilliant and brutal. It was incredibly hard work, but also extremely rewarding. The truth is, I could write a whole book on the experience and still wouldn't be able to get across exactly what it was like. It was the most challenging, difficult, lonely, yet fulfilling work I've ever done as an actor.

You start with nothing. Absolutely nothing. Then you and Mike get together in a room and, over time, you fashion this character from birth to the age they're at in the film. It's kind of a gamble because you sign up not knowing what you're going to be doing at all, or how big your part will be. I've heard endless stories of actors signing to do a film and ending up with three lines or, worse still, being cut altogether. Fortunately, in my case that didn't happen. The film was called *All or Nothing*, and I played Rory, an overweight, angry boy who lives in a high-rise on a council estate.

If you asked me what Mike Leigh is like, I'd describe him as the nicest, warmest, funniest, most generous arsehole in the world. It's very, very hard doing his films. You never get any praise. The best you could hope for is a slight purse of the lips and maybe a quiet 'That was good acting.'

Ironically, given it was my dream job, I look back on that time with a lot of regrets. Maybe that's how it is with dream jobs, I don't know. I was so in awe of Mike that I found it hard to do my best work. When you're so desperate not to mess something up, that's all that occupies your mind, and you find yourself second-guessing your instincts and constantly questioning yourself. I find that my best work comes when I'm totally open to screwing a few things up: you accept the mistakes and learn from them. Anyway, whatever it was, I was never myself on that set. I felt out of my depth with the other actors. I didn't feel intelligent. In fact, compared to everyone else, I felt really stupid; most of the time when we'd sit round a table at lunch, they'd all be talking about things I had no clue about.

For the first time in my life, the fact that I hadn't trained professionally suddenly bothered me. Mike would tell us to warm up and send us off into a room on our own so we could get into character. I wouldn't know what to do. Once, I tried to peer under the door to watch Lesley Manville to see what she did. The really stupid thing is that, if I'd swallowed my pride and told Mike that I needed his help, he'd have given it to me. I lost something out of the experience because I was so uptight about getting it right (or at least being seen to be able to get it right). But saying that, I'm incredibly proud of the film. It's beautiful. Incredibly bleak, but very beautiful.

I remember one day – actually, 'remember' is the wrong word; it's a day that's tattooed on my mind for all eternity. It was only my second day of actual filming, and we were doing a scene between Rory and his mother, Penny, played by Lesley. Rory was an angry kid. I mean really, bitterly angry. So angry that he kicked out at every opportunity. Overweight, friendless, living on a council estate, he was a victim of his own loneliness. And the lonelier he was, the angrier he got, and vice-versa. He was big, ungainly and clumsy. Finally, in the second half of the film, he suffers a heart attack.

So, we were doing a scene in which Rory and his mum come out of a lift in the high-rise block of flats they live in. This was a real block on a disused estate. The art department managed to create the feeling that the entire block was lived in; every flat we used was fully functional so they all felt like real homes. Everything worked, from the plumbing to the lights to the cookers.

Rory and his mum had to walk along an open balcony to their front door. Rory goes to open the door, finds it locked and then just loses it. He starts banging his fist against the door, banging and banging, then yelling at his sister inside to open it. We had rehearsed this over and over again, the improvisation gradually being scaled down until we all knew exactly how the scene worked. Every gesture and every expression had been prac-tised to the point where they felt as natural as possible and had the sense of authenticity that is the hallmark of all Mike's films. Only, in my case, it wasn't quite as authentic as I thought. The line I had was simple: 'What's she doing?' The words were supposed to spill from my mouth like stones – angry, frustrated, totally raw.

Mike led us into the scene in his usual fashion, which is completely unlike any other: he'll quietly tell you to get into character and then actually give you the time to do so. Then, after that preparation time, comes the measured sound of 'Turn over the camera, cameras at speed and . . . action.' By the time you start rolling, the entire crew is absolutely focused, working as one cohesive unit.

So, I'm hammering on the door and Lesley's telling me to stop but I keep on banging, ignoring her, and then I spit out my line.

'Well,' I said, 'what she's doing?'

'Cut.' Mike stopped the cameras. And then he laid into me. Day two of filming and he's tearing this massive strip off me in front of the whole crew.

'Well!' he said. 'What's "well"? What're you saying "well" for? Where does that fit? *Well*'s not right. *Well*'s not motivated.' He shook his head and told me to 'concentrate'. Then he turned to the crew. 'Sorry, everyone, we're going to have to go again.'

The ground could've opened up and swallowed me. Please God, let me not be here suffering this bollocking from Mike Leigh of all people. I don't know if he meant to humiliate me that badly, or if he was turning my mistake into an advantage, thinking that a dressing-down would only make me – and thus Rory – angrier. Well, if that was his motivation, he was spot on. By the time we did the next take I was really angry.

You might be sitting there now with a furrowed brow wondering what the difference is between 'What's she doing?' and 'Well, what's she doing?' But in the context of the film it was massive. The word 'well' sounded as if Rory was apologising for his actions, and Rory didn't apologise for anything. By the time I'd finished working with Mike, those kind of subtleties were becoming much clearer to me. In fact, tough though it was, it was the best education as an actor that I ever had.

CHAPTER 12

BEST MUSICAL ACCOMPANIMENT:
'Club Tropicana' by Wham!

BEST FILM TO WATCH ALONGSIDE:
A Cock and Bull Story

BEST ENJOYED WITH:
baked Alaska

'd had a leading role. In a film. My name was on the posters alongside those of Timothy Spall, Lesley Manville and Alison Garland, and it all looked very promising. When they showed the film at Cannes, it received a five-minute standing ovation that sent shivers down my spine. I remember Sting coming up to me afterwards and telling me he thought my performance had been amazing. I couldn't believe it. I was so shocked I don't even think I said thank you; I just stood there open-mouthed. I remember telling myself that Sting wouldn't think I'd been rude – he was probably used to that reaction from people by now.

Critically, the film polarised opinion. There was nothing lukewarm about anyone's reaction: they either loved or hated it. But that's often how it is with Mike's films and I'd wanted to be part of it for the experience, not for where the film might take me.

He's such a phenomenal director that everyone who works with him yearns for another opportunity. There are a chosen few, I suppose, actors who get invited back: Alison Steadman, Timothy Spall, Ruth Sheen, Lesley Manville, people like that. I've got a feeling that *All or Nothing* might've been my one and only shot, though. The way my career has gone since, I'm not sure I'm what Mike's looking for.

Mike doesn't want people who pussyfoot around him and I pussyfooted around him a lot. He doesn't want people who laugh at his jokes all the time – I definitely laughed at his jokes all the time. He wants actors who challenge him and I don't know that I did that. I'm being hard on myself, maybe, but coming away from a shoot like that, you're always going to ask yourself the tough questions.

Sometimes I wonder if I might've done better if I'd gone the traditional route and spent some time at drama school. The thing about training properly is that it gives you confidence, the kind you just can't get from anywhere else. Maybe I'd become a better actor if I took a year off and went to RADA or LAMDA or somewhere, though there's always the chance I'd end up in a class full of people desperate to be in a Mike Leigh film. And that would be weird for everyone.

After the film released, nothing happened for a few weeks. I would pick up a magazine and read an article about the latest young acting sensation – the hot one to watch, you know. Generally, it would be someone I'd never heard of . . . and still haven't, come to think of it. That's the trouble with being 'hot' – what happens if you don't catch fire? So I definitely wasn't on any hot lists but, on the whole, I got good reviews for my part in *All or Nothing*.

A month or so after it came out, I went for an audition for a TV film called *Cruise of the Gods*. It was written by Tim Firth and starred Steve Coogan and Rob Brydon. Steve is one of my comedy heroes. Growing up, my mates and I would spend hours trying to out-Partridge each other, battling one another with the most obscure quotations. Instead of saying hello, we'd just say, 'AHA!' So this was a big deal for me.

The premise of the show revolved around two stars of a hit eighties TV show called *The Children of Castor*. Rob was playing the guy who'd been the lead, while Steve's character had played second fiddle. But, since the show ended, Steve's character had gone to LA and become a massive star; by contrast, Rob's had ended up working as a doorman in a hotel. He was broke, depressed and living on his own in a bedsit. Out of the blue, he's asked to be the guest of honour on a cruise in the Adriatic organised by the fan club. The part I was going for was a boy called Russell who was the fan club's chairman's assistant and, unbeknown to anyone, Rob's long-lost son.

I think maybe they had been looking for an actor who was a little better known than me, but I wanted the part so badly that I guess my enthusiasm must have shone through. Here was a chance to work with Rob and Steve and, not only that, but with David Walliams too, who was playing the chairman of the fan club. Three of the best comedy actors in Britain. Finally, they did call to say I'd got it.

I was totally over the moon. (I realise at this point I've said this a few times and it may sound as if I'm just saying it because I have to, but truly, every job I get, I still can't believe that people are prepared to pay me for something I enjoy so much. It feels as if I'm doing something illegal.)

This job, more than any other, felt like a new chapter of my career. It was the first time I'd ever had to go abroad to work. The whole shoot would take place on a cruise ship that would be sailing around the Greek Islands. I kissed Shelley goodbye and headed off to the airport. The shoot would be the longest time we'd ever spend apart since we'd been together, and I felt incredibly sad at the thought of being away for so long. This was the first time I realised that I'm someone who gets quite homesick. I love travelling, don't get me wrong, so maybe homesick isn't the right way to describe it. I get people-sick, I guess. I miss my family and my friends a lot when I'm away. (Right now, as I write this, I realise it's been six months since I've seen my mates from home – Gav, Jason and Anthony – because I've been so busy.

That's something I need to remedy. They are such great friends to me and I hope I am to them, in spite of all the craziness.)

My sadness at leaving Shelley was soon at the back of my mind, though, as I was seated next to David Walliams on the plane. Pretty much instantly, I thought he was one of the funniest people I'd ever met. Within minutes, he had me in stitches. I'd never been around such naturally funny people before and it was totally thrilling.

We got off the plane and headed to baggage reclaim. I remember, as we all stood there waiting, watching David, Steve and Rob stand around together, bouncing off one another absolutely hilariously. It was pretty obvious that they shared an easy rapport and a similar mind-set and had real respect for each other. I so wanted to be a part of that. I was standing about fifteen feet away from them, but it might as well have been fifteen miles. I had this burning desire to be included in this special band of comedy musketeers about to take to the seas.

We all collected our bags and then walked over to the coach for the three-hour trip to the port. My bag had been the last off, so I was trailing a little behind everyone else. Up ahead I could hear everyone roaring as Steve and Rob tried to outdo each other with Michael Caine impressions. Damn, I thought to myself, I don't do any impressions. I mean, the only one I could do was the same one everyone could do – the woman from Coronation Street who says, 'I don't really know.' I couldn't pull that out of the bag. Not in front of these guys. Not yet, anyway.

I was the last to board the bus and, after putting my bag in the hold, I walked up the steps and immediately felt as if I was back at school. Steve, Rob and David had taken the back seat – of course they had, they were the cool gang. But where was my place? I stood at the front and looked down the aisle. I started taking some tentative steps down the centre of the coach and then thought to myself, Screw it. Just go and sit with them. I had to let them know that I wanted to be in their gang; I couldn't wait for an invite that might never come. So I strode right up and sat down on the seats just in front of the back row, and from that moment on, and for the whole three-hour journey, all I did was laugh. I don't think I offered a single word to the conversation; I was more than happy to sit, pissing myself laughing, and be their audience. They all seemed so confident and I remember thinking that this is what it's about – creating and performing your own stuff. All three of them had created and starred in their own shows and so they weren't at the mercy of casting directors or agents if they didn't want to be. Just being around people like that made it all seem so much easier, and so much more achievable – straightforward, somehow.

We set sail on the ship and began filming the very next day. It was a great shoot. What made it so special was how confined we all were. The crew and the cast, all mixing together day and night. We filmed as we sailed, in and out of dock, down the coast and all around the islands. Whenever we had a day off I'd spend it with David or Rob, or both. Steve was only in the film sporadically so he came and went quite a lot. Russell Brand joined the cast for a while, another amazingly manic talent. I'd seen him on MTV and thought, Is this guy for real? Well, yeah, actually he was.

I'll never forget Istanbul. Not for the city so much – well, yes, actually for the city – but mostly for Russell. Istanbul is a weird place; in fact it's not like any other city I've ever been to. One minute you're in a bustling modern high street full of designer shops, and then you go round a corner and enter what looks like a war zone. One second there's all these yuppies, dripping in jewellery and leather, the next you're surrounded by ramshackle, broken-down buildings with people begging for the price of a meal. The poverty is unbelievable.

We docked for a night and stayed up drinking on the boat as we did most nights. The sense of togetherness on that shoot was fantastic. We'd work together, eat together, have a few beers together, and then, if you were Russell Brand, hit the town at three in the morning and hunt down whatever adventure you could find. That night it was around eleven when he decided he wanted to go to town. He wanted some company.

'Come on, come on,' he said. 'Gentlemen, consider. Istanbul in the dead of night. Darkened streets and dimly lit taverns where men sup and women stir.'

Russell's got a way with words, and after a few beers I wasn't going to stand in the way of Brand doing his thing.

'Yeah,' I said, 'yeah. Let's hit town and find a nightclub. Let's do it.'

A couple of hours went by and we were still on the boat, a little drunker and sleepier than we had been. But Russell wasn't finished. No bed for him (not his, anyway). I was pretty far gone by this point and the thought of leaving the boat, climbing into a taxi and heading into Istanbul wasn't doing much for me. By 1.30 a.m., Rob and David had gone to bed and Steve was about to head off. I was done too, but that didn't stop Russell trying.

'Come on, James,' Russell said, gesticulating wildly, eyes flashing, long, black hair bouncing. 'Streets black as soot, alleys lit by nothing more than the wispy flame of a gas lamp, misted windows and murky women: an adventure. Come on, come on. Come on.' Forgive me, Russell. I'm doing my best here.

I wasn't moving. Nobody was. Nobody except Russell. It was almost 2 a.m. and bed was calling us normals. But Russell Brand is just sort of, well, Russell Brand. Not normal. So out he went into the night, alone and intrepid.

He talks about that night in detail in his book, so I won't repeat what happened here. Suffice to say he showed up at breakfast having not been to sleep and looking in pretty good shape. He sat down to a coffee and began telling us, in a manner that nobody can replicate (and so, don't worry, I'm not going to try), how he'd gone looking for and found a prostitute. I remember listening to him describe the whole thing in lurid detail – how he'd gone to this squalid little room that was rented by the hour; how he and the brunette had been in the throes of lust when her mobile rang; how he'd been so furious that he'd thrown and smashed it against the wall.

As I sat there listening to him tell the story, half of me was thinking, Oh, man, this is awful, really horrible. I shouldn't be listening. I shouldn't even be in your company. But the other half of me was there, hanging on his every word, mouth open, eyes alive. 'Yeah, Russell. And then what happened? What did you do then? No. Really?'

He is, without question, the finest storyteller I have ever met. I don't know him that well, but I remember our short time on the boat fondly. He was the first person I'd ever met who was properly rock and roll. I say our short time on the boat because, well, Russell got fired. Not because of that night specifically – it was more like a football match, you know, where the ref gets irritated by a player who's constantly niggling away. It's nothing malicious – just an ankle-tap here, a shirt-hold there, a little trip now and then. On their own, they're all fine, but after a while, they build up, until the ref has had enough and breaks out the red card. In Russell's case, he was ankle-tapping too many women on the boat.

It was a shame to see him go. I kind of knew how he felt after what had happened to me on *Dead Babies*. I liked Russell. He was warm and calm yet crazy and outrageous. A great mix. No one really knew him in those days but, as we said our good-byes and watched him off the boat, none of us had any clue that in a few years' time, Russell's mayhem would make him just about the most famous person in the country.

As the shoot continued, I carried on – as I had on the coach from the airport – basically following Rob and David around. Some days I felt like a nephew they'd been told to look after. But they are both such lovely guys that they always looked after me and included me in everything. Whenever Steve came out with us, I'd retreat back into my shell slightly. As I've said, his work as Alan Partridge had meant everything to me. Like many people my age, I was totally in awe of him. I couldn't begin to understand how he'd created a character that people would talk about and love that much. So he was already instrumental in my life before I met him, and now he was about to become even more so.

One night, when we were docked in Greece, Steve suggested we head out for a lap dance after we'd finished our dinner. I'd never been to a lap-dancing club before. Unsurprisingly, the experience with Sapphire and Danny in Soho had put me off somewhat. David said he was well up for it and started making arrangements for a taxi. Rob, ever the gent, said it wasn't for him and he was gonna turn in for the night. Steve then turned to me and said, 'James? You up for it?'

I looked at him, this hero of comedy, smiling a cheeky grin from across the table, and said, 'Well, I've never been before.' On hearing that, Steve leapt up, instantly excited.

'*Never?* Well, in that case we're definitely going, and you're definitely coming.' He then shouted across the dining room to David, 'David! David!' (In my head, all I could hear him shouting was, 'DAN! DAN!' If you like *Partridge*, you'll know what I mean.) 'David, he's never been before!' David giggled a bit and, as he came over to join us, looked at me and said, 'Well, you're gonna have a good time.' And with that we were in the taxi.

I sat in the front, with Steve and David in the back, talking about mutual friends. I was so out of the loop. All I could think about was the fact that I wasn't 100 per cent sure of what I was walking into. Did I have enough money? How would we get back to the ship? What if there were no cabs? Steve and David didn't seem that bothered, so I told myself that all I had to do was stick with them and I'd get back safe.

We got to the club. It was a nondescript black door with a

white neon sign above it. I can't remember the name of it because I barely had time to look around: we were past that door in seconds. We paid the doorman and he led us down the corridor towards the club. As we got nearer I could hear the bass getting louder and louder, until suddenly we passed through some swinging doors and we were inside.

Girls in their underwear were everywhere, hanging from poles and sitting in corners chatting to guys. It was so loud I thought my ears were going to pop. I was standing in between Steve and David, who were both smiling broadly.

We saw some empty sofas and went over and sat down; within seconds we were joined by a gaggle of girls. Steve and David instantly started making them laugh. David pretended to give one of them a lap dance, which had them all cracking up and, before I knew what was happening, Steve was telling them that I'd never had a lap dance before. And that was that. Three of them jumped up and starting giving all three of us a dance. It was at that point, with three very attractive girls writhing in front of us, that Steve leant in to me and said, 'You'll never forget this.' And he's absolutely right, I haven't. Though I suspect not for the reasons that Steve was implying. I couldn't tell you what the dancer looked like, or what song was playing. No, all I can remember is thinking that I couldn't wait to tell my mates about this when I got home. And the whole thing was made ever more unforgettable because, about thirty seconds into the dance, just as the girl in front of me was lowering her ample breasts into my face, I looked over at Steve on my right and he looked back at me and shouted, 'AHA!'

I don't remember a time when I've laughed that much. In fact, the whole job was like that, just laughing all the time. Working with those guys really made me want to be part of British comedy. The way they talked about getting television shows off the ground, commissioning pilots, investing in new talent, all that had a huge and lasting impression on me.

The time I spent with David and Rob was totally invaluable, and I remember one conversation in particular that I had with Rob that stayed with me just as much as the lap dance. Part of the shoot was filming at this really tacky resort, where the only decent place to eat was a family-run taverna at the end of a dirt track. One evening Rob and I were on our way to grab some dinner there as the sun set over the sea. We were talking about our careers and what each of us was aiming to do in the future.

'I know you've done lots of different stuff already,' he said, 'but what do you really want to do? Where do you want your career to go?'

I had to think about that. Nobody had ever asked me as directly. 'I don't really know,' I said. 'I suppose comedy is something I'd like to do more of. I want to do something that people are going to remember.'

He was nodding. 'I heard Ruth wrote an episode of *Fat Friends*. Why don't you take a leaf out of her book and have a go at something yourself?'

He was totally right. Ruth was writing an episode and there was nothing, nothing at all, to stop me thinking about doing something off my own bat.

'The thing is,' Rob went on, 'you can't just sit around thinking that you want to be part of British comedy. You have to *be* part of it. Take David,' he said, pointing to Walliams, who was wandering up the track behind us. 'He's writing his own sketch show with Matt Lucas. They came up with an idea, put together a treatment and now they're making it for the BBC.'

Little Britain was about to hit our screens, the series that would catapult David and Matt into the stratosphere. Steve Coogan had created *Alan Partridge* and Rob had built his career with *Marion and Geoff*. He was right. British comedy wasn't going to come calling for me. If I wanted in, I would have to gatecrash the party.

CHAPTER 13

BEST MUSICAL ACCOMPANIMENT:
'Ready to Start' by Arcade Fire

BEST FILM TO WATCH ALONGSIDE:
The Other Guys

BEST ENJOYED WITH:
Yorkshire pudding

So with the idea of doing my own stuff firmly planted, I returned to Leeds to film the new series of *Fat Friends*. I was buzzing after those weeks on the ship. Who wouldn't be after having the chance to meet your heroes and go to a lap-dancing club with them? And after that great, inspiring chat with Rob, I was looking at the future in an ultra-positive light. I'd never felt so energised. The realisation that I didn't have to wait for parts completely changed the way I thought about work. I started actively looking for stories and dreaming up ideas for shows. No matter where I went, I would see something that intrigued me – I'd catch an interesting-looking character in a shop or waiting at a bus stop, or in a café or on the train plat-form, and start thinking about what kind of life they led, how you could make a character out of them. I tried to take in as much as I could of the world around me and then write it all down in a journal I always carried around. It's a tried-and-tested method; who was I to muck around with it?

I suppose things began to take some proper shape when Shelley invited me to a family wedding down on Barry Island. I'd never been to that area of South Wales before and I fell in love with it. We were invited to just the evening reception rather than the whole ceremony, so we spent the day walking along the beach and soaking up that special kind of atmosphere you only get from a British seaside town. You know what I mean – Skegness, Cromer, Eastbourne, all those old Victorian holiday destinations: there's something unique about them. They have a kind of era-defying Britishness that you don't find anywhere else: donkey rides, teeth-breaking rock, windbreakers all down the beach. They make me feel incredibly nostalgic for my childhood. I love those towns out of season too. They become so bleak so quickly, all shut up and empty, forgotten until the next time.

We went to the evening do as arranged, and Shelley spent some time catching up with a few friends she hadn't seen in a while. Rather than crowd her, I sat myself down at a table on my own. I wasn't fed up or bored or anything; in fact I was just the opposite. I was more than happy to sit there quietly and take it all in. Weddings are strange occasions, aren't they? I mean, the way two groups of people who don't know each are thrown together, forced to get along, and by the end of the night hopefully they're all doing the conga. That or a fight's broken out.

The party was in a hall that once upon a time had been partitioned into two rooms. The parquet dance floor and mobile disco were at one end and all the tables and chairs where we sat down to eat were at the other. The place was alive – people drinking and dancing and drinking and milling around and laughing and drinking.

Every now and then I'd pick up the odd word, or a line or two here and there, that would make me chuckle. This was a real wedding, where lots of very different people had come together (and got drunk) for a single day that would never be repeated. Sitting there, with my attention switching from one group to the next, it occurred to me that I'd never, ever seen a proper wedding on a TV show. You know, normally TV weddings are heated, theatrical affairs – say where someone busts in halfway through to stop it going ahead – and there's all this dramatic tension that doesn't exist in real life. In my experience, 99 per cent of weddings go off without a fight or a massive family fallout.

I didn't know the couple getting married; I didn't know anyone at all actually. But I did know the girl was from Barry and the guy she was marrying was from Runcorn in Cheshire, so there were two different families and two different sets of friends from two very different parts of the UK, all thrown together in this room. That kind of dynamic got me thinking and I began to wonder whether a wedding like this could be a pretty nifty setting for a comedy.

Now I really started to look around and listen in. Two middle-aged men at the next table, one from Barry, the other from Runcorn, were chatting away, a couple of pints between them. They clearly didn't know each other. I started eavesdropping and, at first, I thought they were talking about cars. You know, what they drive, what they'd like to drive, good motorway routes – it was a solid man chat. But the more I heard, I realised that they weren't talking about the cars themselves; they were using them as metaphors to describe the kind of people they were, or at least the guy from Barry was:

'The thing with me is,' he was saying in his deep Welsh accent, 'I'm a Mondeo. That's what I am. I'm not a Ferrari. I'm not a Porsche. Of course, I'd love to be an Audi, but I'm not. I'm a Mondeo and that's fine. I'm fine with that. That's who I am, see. That's who I am.'

With the kind of solemn, knowing nod you get in church, the man from Runcorn seemed to understand.

'I'm better than a Vauxhall,' Mondeo man went on, 'or a Volkswagen.'

Now Runcorn man sat forward, his eyebrows arched. 'So you

think a Mondeo is better than a Volkswagen then, do you?' he said.

'Well, yeah,' Mondeo man went on. 'It's better than a Polo, isn't it, or a Golf? A Mondeo is better than a Golf.'

Runcorn man nodded. 'Aye,' he said, 'fair enough. It's better than a Polo or a Golf maybe. But it's not better than a Passat, though, is it?'

'No,' Mondeo man admitted, 'not a Passat. I'll give you that. It's not better than a Passat. But it's better than a Golf, and a Mondeo is what I am. I'm right there in the middle, see. I'm a Mondeo man.'

I nearly broke out laughing and yet at the same time I could feel the hairs lifting on the back of my neck. This was great: this was real life in a way I understood it – a conversation about everything these two men actually were, told through Mondeos and Golfs. A wedding, I thought, a wedding. Nobody had written a wedding like this. The way the small sideline events unfold, the insignificant conversations, the nonsenses. Suddenly, I could visualise a whole set of sequences that were as crazy and hilarious as this one.

You know when you've had a good idea because it stays with you. We've all been there. You think of something, get really excited about it, then go to sleep that night and, when you wake up, you're delighted to find that the idea still feels as good as when you first thought of it. And that idea of a wedding stayed with me for ages.

Back in Leeds for the *Fat Friends* shoot, there was this one evening where Ruth Jones and I were sitting on our own at the hotel bar. There were no other cast members there, which was actually quite rare. I started telling her about Mondeo man and Runcorn man, and all the other people I'd spotted at the wedding. She got the characters immediately; they just clicked with her in the same way they'd clicked with me. Also, Ruth sort of knew them herself. I mean, she's from Cardiff and she'd known lots of Mondeo men growing up; she'd met them at countless weddings herself.

Ruth and I are really like-minded in the way we see situations and think about scenarios and character. It's hard to explain it exactly – there's no real science to it – but there are certain people you get, and who get you. I'd felt it with Ruth since we'd first met, but sitting there in the bar, that connection between us developed into something really exciting.

We started riffing, improvising, working out different characters, playing out little scenes. We got talking about two families at a fictional wedding: who they were and where they came from, who was marrying whom; who was the Mondeo and who was the Golf. Before we knew it, we came up with Barry Island and Billericay. We imagined their relatives and friends, old and young, their mannerisms, their accents, the way they spoke, the different phrases they might come out with. We decided the girl would be from Barry and the man from Billericay, and then we worked back to figure out who would be at the reception, why they'd be there, who'd arrived with whom and who was going to get off with whom. We improvised scene after scene, riffing back and forth in various characters: the drunk, the girl crying in the corner, the loudmouth and the overbearing uncle who can't tell you enough about his latest gadget.

In this case it had to be the digital camera. At the wedding on Barry Island, Shelley's uncle had sat me down and told me all about his new camera, as if he was the only man in the world to have owned one.

'See this,' he'd said, showing me the screen on the back. 'There's no film in there, no film at all. You just take a photo and if you don't like it, you delete it. See? You just delete it. No need for a film at all. The film is the camera: it's a chip, a microchip inside, and if you don't like a picture, you just delete it.'

This was 2002! I already had a digital camera. My dad had

a digital camera. Most people I knew had digital cameras. I even told Shelley's uncle that I had one, but that didn't stop him talking about it as if he'd lifted it from a NASA lab. Ruth and I named him Uncle Bryn.

The hours slipped by as we went from one scene to another, one character to the next. Later on, a bunch of office workers came into the bar for an away day or something, and we used them as substitutes for our wedding guests, picking out who was from Essex and who was from Barry Island. Then we got them involved a bit and got them laughing and joking around with us. The whole of it felt so natural and organic: pure, like the comedy I'd talked about with Rob back in Greece.

It was incredibly exciting. The original idea of the wedding had developed into something solid now, with depth and layers, and with Ruth's involvement, the scope was endless; but we both knew that a few hours of improvisation did not a TV show make – we had to write it down. Thinking back on it, that afternoon was the only time Ruth and I were ever in the bar on our own. We were in the middle of filming the series and, like I said, there would normally be other members of the cast hanging around, having a drink and a chat. But that day it was only us. Had anyone come along, the flow might have been interrupted and, who knows, maybe the whole thing would have fizzled into nothing. But for whatever reason – fate, luck, coincidence; call it what you want – nobody did come, and we both left with the same belief that we had the beginnings of something special and the promise that we wouldn't let it end there.

Timing. Most of what happens in life is timing: the fact that you leave work late and avoid a car accident, the way you bump into a particular person just when you need to, or take an important call at work when no one else is around. So much of life is about being in the right place at the right time. Had Mondeo man been down the other end of the room instead of on the table next to me, maybe none of what came after would ever have happened.

Even with all our enthusiasm, we never got round to putting anything down on paper over the remainder of the *Fat Friends* shoot. We were both very conscious of it, though, and both equally determined not to let it slide into being just another good idea that never went anywhere. On the last day of the shoot, we agreed that we'd think more about what it was we were trying to create – how it could work as a show, where the characters would go – and that we'd get together and get something down on paper.

After *Fat Friends* had finished shooting, I was out of work again and looking for my next gig. A few months before, I'd been having conversations with Jacquie about trying to get back into theatre. My only work on stage had been in the chorus of *Martin Guerre* and, though I was loving the television work and working with some real heroes of mine, I was becoming increasingly aware that my CV had a big hole in it: a proper play.

In theatreland, the difference in attitude towards doing a play and doing a musical is massive. Not everyone thinks it, but there's an old prejudice that some people still cling on to that goes like this: proper actors do plays; 'turns' do musicals. A 'turn' is a performer who sings and dances, but isn't seen as having the necessary depth to play the straighter, more challenging roles. ('Turn' comes from people calling such actors 'twirly turns'.) It's not something I agree with, not in the slightest: it's just another form of snobbery. Why should an actor who's giving a brilliant performance in a West End musical be held in any less regard than someone who's working at the RSC? These preconceptions, and that desire to pigeonhole people, exist all over the place in the arts. I've known lots of people, important people, who make the assumption that, just because someone can do one thing well, that's all they can and should do for the rest of their career. I wonder how many brilliant actors have never been able to show the world what they're truly capable of because they've been dismissed as one thing or another.

I was determined that I wasn't going to be one of those guys who did the same thing over and over, and I knew a good way of ringing the changes was to land a part in a decent play at a respected London theatre. I just had to be patient. In the meantime I still had to earn a living, so I was out auditioning a fair bit, once or twice a week for various films and tasty parts on television. In fact, I had just been offered a guest lead in a BBC drama called *Messiah*, which was really exciting. Ken Stott was in it, and he'd done a lot of work I admired – *Shallow Grave*, *Fever Pitch*, *Silent Witness* – so I was really looking forward to working with him. But, only a week or so afterwards, Jacquie phoned to say that we might have to stall on it because I had an audition coming up at the National Theatre. She was going to send the script straight over.

To my mind, the National Theatre is the greatest theatre in the world. I can't imagine there's a single actor in this country who hasn't dreamt of working there. All the greats have worked there at some point or other. What's so special and unique about the National is that it's home to three individual theatres: the Cottesloe, the Lyttelton and the Olivier. Each varies in size – the Olivier is the biggest and the Cottesloe the smallest – and each theatre houses two different productions that play in rep (which means that they alternate back and forth). With six different productions, all either rehearsing or performing at any one time, it means the whole place is constantly buzzing with an incredible creative energy. You feel it as you walk in through the foyer and you feel it even more when you go backstage.

As soon as I'd spoken to Jacquie, I started to daydream about what it would be like to work there, but I knew I had to be realistic. I'd auditioned there once before when I was about fourteen but, as you haven't come across the chapter about my big break as a child working for Trevor Nunn, you'll have worked out that I didn't get the job. As I prepared to go for another audition now, Dad made doubly sure that I kept my feet on the ground: 'James,' he said, when I told him that evening about the possible job, 'the part probably has one line said off stage and the rest of the time you'll be standing at the back wearing a mask.' Truth is, he might have been right. I couldn't get too excited before I'd read the script.

It arrived the next day and, as I opened the envelope, I needed both hands to pull out the giant stack of pages. It was the biggest script I'd ever seen: dense and heavy; literally hundreds and hundreds of pages full of dialogue. But there, on the front, were six words that any young actor (in fact, forget 'young' – just any actor) dreams of seeing: 'A new play by Alan Bennett.'

I couldn't believe it. Not just 'a play' by Alan Bennett, 'a *new* play'. There must only have been a handful of people in the world who had read it, and I was soon to be one of them. I felt lucky to be holding it; it didn't even register at that moment that I might have a shot of actually being in it. But first things first – I had to read it.

It was called *The History Boys* and was about eight young sixth-formers in the eighties being prepped and groomed to get into Oxford and Cambridge. Here's a confession: I found it really hard to understand the first time I read it through. I got totally lost: there were references to Auden, a whole scene entirely in French and lots of details about historical events that I knew very little about. More than anything else, I found it frustrating, and I got annoyed at myself for not being more intelligent, for not working harder at school. At the end of it, I put the script down, clasped my hands behind my head and let out a long sigh. Oh well, I thought to myself. That was nice. Getting to read that. Shame I don't understand a word of it.

The National was still, it seemed, a long way off. I relayed my frustration to Jacquie, but she brushed right over it and instead concentrated on which part I could play – got to love agents. But even though she was really upbeat, she was still unsure about where I might fit in. There was Dakin, the good-looking, cool kid; Posner, a young, effete Jewish boy who lusted after Dakin; Scripps, Dakin's friend and the narrator for much of the play; and Rudge, the really athletic captain of the rugby team, who wasn't the brightest. There were four other boys listed but, at that point, their parts weren't properly defined: they had character names, but many of the lines were just written as Boy 1, Boy 2, etc.

Jacquie told me not to get too downhearted and that, however I might feel about the play, I should still go and meet with Toby Whale, the casting director. If he liked what I did, then I'd most likely be called back to meet Nicholas Hytner, the director, and maybe even Alan himself.

In the days that followed I worked as hard as I could to get to grips with the scenes where lots of the boys spoke – they were brilliantly written, snappy back-and-forths between a teacher and his class of eight boys. I didn't want to count myself out of any role at that point, so I learnt as much as I possibly could of all of them. I've never worked so hard for an audition.

The week after the script came, I was in the casting rooms of the National Theatre, sitting down in front of Toby Whale. (Toby is one of the most brilliant and lovely casting directors in the country. So brilliant and lovely, in fact, that he would go on to cast a TV show you may have heard of called *Gavin & Stacey*.) The first thing he asked me was whether or not I liked the script. Like it? I said. I *loved* it; I understood every word, never got lost and absolutely knew what was happening at all times.

It's normally at this point that the casting director will suggest reading some scenes through, with him or her playing the other parts. If it's a television or film casting, they'll press record on the video camera and away you go. So I was pretty confused when Toby stood up and said, in a breezy, easy-going tone, 'OK, James. Let's go through, shall we?'

I looked up in surprise. 'Go through to where?'

Now it was Toby's turn to be confused. 'Through to meet Nick and Alan. Where else?'

It took me a couple of seconds to register the information. Toby was already heading off down the corridor, but he turned and stopped when he heard me call out, in a squeaky voice, 'Nick Hytner and Alan Bennett?' He just nodded, smiled and carried on walking.

The look on my face must've been pretty familiar to Toby by then. All day, I imagine, a stream of young actors must have been coming in thinking they were there for a general meeting with Toby before the real auditions began, and then having the rug slipped out from under them as they realised this *was* the audition and it was now or never. This was a pretty dastardly move.

But there wasn't time to debate the rights and wrongs. I was busy feeling sweatily nervous. I was hot, panicked and now, of course, wished I'd worked even harder on the script. But what could you do? I took a deep breath and stepped through the door and into the room.

I've realised in the last few years that something happens to me when I get nervous. I don't know why or how it happens, but it can either be harnessed as a force for good or it can manifest itself as pure evil. (Well, 'evil' might be pushing it, but 'not good' doesn't really work.) Basically, when I'm at my most nervous, I act my most supremely confident. When everything inside me is turning to jelly, my outer shell seems to harden and I exude this aura of confidence. Some people would say this is a good thing, and they'd be right, sometimes; but occasionally, and I hate it when this happens, believe me, those nerves turn into the kind of overconfidence that unfortunately comes across as arrogance.

Now, I don't know which level of nervousness my audition with Alan and Nick would be gauged at: confident, cocky or big-time arrogance. I don't even remember much of the meeting – I wish I could. All I know is that when Alan wrote about our meeting in his book *Untold Stories*, he said that I walked into the room and immediately took over the audition. The one thing that did stick with me was that they both laughed a lot during the read-through, which I guess couldn't have been a bad thing. But, walking away, I didn't know if I'd done enough (and I still didn't even know what part I was auditioning for); all I knew was that I'd tried my best.

I left the theatre and called Dad straight away. As he often does, he managed to sum up exactly what I was feeling. 'Well, if you've not got it, at least you've met Alan Bennett.' He was totally right; at the very worst I'd met a living legend. That was all I was thinking as I stood waiting on the platform for my train home. And then my phone started ringing in my pocket.

It was Jacquie. She sounded slightly panicked. 'Have you got on the train yet?'

'No, I'm on the platform. Why?'

'You should come into the office. You've been offered the play, but *Messiah* need an answer today, and *Fat Friends* has been recommissioned. They all clash, and we have some decisions to make.'

No way. I'd only left the audition an hour ago and I'd been offered the job already? Things like that didn't happen to me (nor has it ever happened since, incidentally).

When I got to the office, Jacquie told me that I'd been offered the part of a boy called Timms. I picked up the script and flicked through it as fast as I could. I then did it again, only this time much slower, because I was finding it hard to find any of Timms's lines. It slowly and painfully dawned on me that it had nothing to do with my page-turning pace: Timms only had four lines in the whole play, and one of them was, 'Yes, sir.' Talk about back to earth with a bump. I swore I could smell some roasting meats . . .

I didn't know what to do. I told Jacquie that it was my dream to work at the National Theatre, but to turn down two well-paid parts in successful TV dramas seemed silly for a part with four lines. But Jacquie was having none of it. She was adamant that I should do the play. She got on the phone and got busy trying to work out a way I could do all three. I sat in Jacquie's office for three hours that day, waiting for this merry-go-round of phone calls to come full circle, when, out of the blue, Alan called her office directly. He spoke to Jacquie for a few minutes before she handed the phone to me.

'Hello?' I said in a croaky, nervous-schoolboy type of voice.

'Oh, hello, James,' said Alan in his lovely northern lilt. That was basically enough for me right there. I would have dropped everything else at that point, because Alan Bennett had made the effort to call me personally. But, amazingly, he went on to say that he knew that the character of Timms wasn't written up as much as the others, but that if I were to commit to doing the play, he would write the part up and give me something I could have fun with. He ended by telling me that I would have to trust him, because he would only change it with me in mind.

Ummm . . . OK. My jaw nearly hit the floor. I couldn't believe what I was hearing, and who I was hearing it from. I looked at Jacquie and she too had the biggest smile on her face. I told Alan that I was totally overwhelmed and that I couldn't wait to be involved; then I kept saying thank you, thank you, thank you, and he told me to stop being so silly.

I put the phone down and started to smile, and didn't stop smiling for about two weeks. I felt so happy. I was going to act at the National Theatre, to work with Alan Bennett and be directed by Nicholas Hytner. This was going to be one crazy adventure.

CHAPTER 14

BEST MUSICAL ACCOMPANIMENT:
'The Boys Are Back in Town' by Thin Lizzy

BEST WATCHED WITH:
The Madness of King George

BEST ENJOYED WITH:
a ham and cheese toastie

You want real adventure? Try getting the train from Beaconsfield to London Marylebone in rush hour. It's a nightmare. Beaconsfield is basically a village made up of quite posh and wealthy people who work in London, have lived in London most of their lives, but who have chosen to move out to Buckinghamshire so they can have a big house with a nice big garden for the same price as the small but perfectly formed and well-located mews house they had just a short walk from Regent's Park.

They love it. But they also want others to love it, so they're constantly encouraging friends and colleagues to up sticks and join them out of London. They're always talking about how many en suites they have and how much better the schools are for Tilly and Oliver, or how they can be in Soho within an hour. An hour! They have achieved full-blown domestic bliss and it's the best move they ever made. All of which, I'm sure, is true.

However, on a cold February morning, when they're standing on the packed train platform waiting for the delayed 7.45 a.m. that stops at Gerrards Cross, shielding their faces from the side-ways rain that's lashing against their reddened cheeks, it couldn't look like more of a lie. Grown men and women stand shoulder to shoulder, praying that they'll be the lucky ones who get a seat, muttering under their breath that this whole move was a mistake, daydreaming of the time when they were just four Tube stops away from work, and occasionally tutting at the irritating young person standing a few feet from them who has his iPod up way too loud. And that irritating young person they're tutting at . . . well, that would be me.

(I'd like to take this opportunity to apologise to all the men and women who frequented the Chiltern Railway from Beaconsfield to London during the years 1997 to 2004 for just how loud my music was at the time. What was I thinking? It seemed the most natural thing in the world to be listening to 'Mama's Always On Stage' by Arrested Development at full volume at 8 a.m. It's only now – as a responsible father – that I can begin to see that this is the last thing you want as you try to kick-start another two-hour round trip to work in an environment that is at best uncomfortable and at worst tear-inducingly unpleasant.)

But this one morning in question, there was no overly loud music, no angry looks my way, no nothing in fact. Just nerves. I stood on the platform gripping the revised script that Alan had sent over. He'd been good to his word and Timms's part was now way more substantial, but – and you'll like this – a lot of his new lines were in French. Ahhhhh, man. Why'd it have to be French? Was this some kind of karmic retribution for all those hours I'd messed around in European Studies? Had Mr Hopkins dropped Alan a line? The only French I knew was, 'Quelle est la date de ton anniversaire?' and that wasn't even in there.

Alan seemed to have written the part as a sort of class clown. It was basically me at school: attention-seeking, boisterous, up for constant fun, but not thick or nasty in any way. I knew I could do this. Throughout the journey I flicked back and forth over my lines, hoping my northern accent was good enough and praying that I'd have the courage to just be myself when the time came and not be crippled by wanting to impress like I had when I worked with Mike.

I was so determined not to be late that I got to Waterloo Station an hour early and was the first one of the cast outside the stage door. I checked myself in on the sign-in sheet and then glanced down at the other names. Other than Frances de la Tour and Richard Griffiths, whose involvement had been announced some time before, there were no names I recognised. Richard was one of my favourite actors, who'd been Uncle Monty in one of my all-time best-loved films, *Withnail and I*, and Frances was an almost god-like figure who'd been a massive part of the success of one of the country's favourite sitcoms, *Rising Damp*. I wondered what it'd be like working with them. Generally, when you're spending time day in, day out alongside such brilliant actors, you can only ever learn from them. I hoped this would be the case with them.

But, as I said, underneath those two, there was a list of unfamiliar names; among them the seven other guys who'd be playing my classmates. The dynamic between the group of boys would be so vital to the play's success that I couldn't help but dread what the other guys would be like. Would they be a group of theatrical darlings who would look down on me for not having trained professionally? Or laugh behind my back because this was the first play I'd been in? God, this was actually *worse* than being back at school.

I sat outside the theatre, stressing over all the possible scenarios for so long that when I next looked down at my watch, it was 9.58 a.m., two minutes before I had to be inside. Shit! How had I managed to get there so early and still nearly end up late?

I rushed down the maze of corridors that run underneath the theatre until I got to Rehearsal Room Two. I stood outside for a moment, took a deep breath, closed my eyes and gave myself a pep talk: Just be yourself, James. Don't be how you were with Mike.

I opened my eyes to find a really good-looking young guy standing in front of me. 'You all right, mate?' he said in a sort of posh cockney accent.

'Yeah, I'm fine, thanks. Just a bit . . . y'no?'

He smiled, chuckled a bit, then said, 'Oh, don't be nervous. It's gonna be a laugh, this. I loved you in *All or Nothing* – it's my favourite Mike Leigh film. I grew up round where it was shot. You made me cry in that film. Amazing piece of work.'

It turned out that the young, good-looking, posh cockney was Dominic Cooper, who would go on to become my flatmate and one of my closest friends. I've told him since, of course, but I still don't think he'll ever really understand how those few words he said to me then so completely put me at my ease. My shoulders relaxed, my nerves vanished, my tummy unknotted itself and, as Dominic and I walked through the door into the vast rehearsal room, I felt calm, excited, confident and relieved, all at the same time.

The cast and stage management were standing around drinking cups of tea, being polite to each other, when Nick called everyone to sit round a long table in the middle of the room. We sat down and then, one by one, went round the table introducing ourselves and telling each other what parts we were playing. After that, we read through the entire play.

The other actors were brilliant: Stephen Campbell-Moore was already amazing as Irwin, the young supply teacher; Samuel Barnett was Posner and he read the part as if it had been written especially for him; Jamie Parker played Scripps and I remember him having the most incredible voice that made him sound as if he'd born on stage; in fact, everyone was incredible – Dominic was Dakin, Russell Tovey was Rudge, Andrew Knott played Lockwood, Samuel Anderson, who quickly got nicknamed

'Zammo', was Crowther, and the youngest of the bunch, Sacha Dhawan, played Akthar.

The read-through went really well (even the French was all right because no one, it turned out, was particularly fluent), and at the end everyone applauded; there was this wonderfully positive vibe in the room. Afterwards, the stage management crew went back to the business of building the set, which left us – the twelve cast members, Nick and Alan – all alone in this vast rehearsal room.

I reckon this is always the trickiest moment for a director. Where do you actually start? How do you begin the process of 'putting on a play'? Do you just stick the whole cast on the makeshift set and start ordering them on from stage left and stage right? Or do you insist on spending hours playing theatrical games, chucking imaginary beanbags to each other whilst pretending that the floor is on fire? Believe me, this stuff happens all the time.

But luckily not in Rehearsal Room Two when Nick is in charge. Many people regard Nick as one of, if not the best theatre director in the world. And they think this because of his amazingly varied and brilliantly received spectrum of work, from opera at Glyndebourne to Shakespeare to *Miss Saigon*, and the fact that most of his productions end each night with a standing ovation. Personally, I think Nick is the best in the world for slightly different reasons: one of the main ones being that when he was sitting round a table with a group of young, mostly inexperienced actors, some of whom had trained, some of whom had not, some of whom he knew and most of whom he didn't, he said this:

'There's a lot going on in this play and I think the best thing to do is for all of us to take a vow of stupidity. We must all agree that no one in here knows more about certain things than others. That way we can all learn together and nobody should ever have to feel stupid or be made to feel stupid about putting their hand up and saying they don't understand something. We're going to just sit here for a couple of days, and together we'll go through everything. OK?'

In that one moment he put everyone in the room on a level playing field. I know, from having spoken to the other guys, that all eight of us felt relieved that he'd said it. Feeling much more relaxed, we sat and chatted about school and poetry, but mostly we talked about history. We would pass poetry books around that were referenced in the play and each read a paragraph. There were times when some of us wouldn't completely understand certain aspects of what was written, and on those occasions we'd turn to Alan, who, in his own wonderful words, would explain it in such a way that anyone could've understood. Suddenly, dense mountains of words that had previously been closed off came alive and had meaning. We would laugh at each other's stories from school – I told some myself and, occasionally, if he liked a phrase, or found something touching or amusing, Alan would jot it down in his notebook.

There was one unforgettable afternoon when Alan read to just us eight boys, on our own in the rehearsal room, for an hour. You could've heard a pin drop. He would read different poems and then talk about why or where they were written and what he thought they meant. Hearing him read Philip Larkin's 'This Be the Verse' is something I'll never forget. If you don't know that poem, put this book down and go and look it up now. If it's not Larkin's best poem, then it must be his most repeated.

Alan has spoken many times of how rude all of us boys were. About how, even on day one of rehearsals, he overheard Dominic on the phone to a friend, talking loudly enough that Alan would hear every word: 'Oh, I'm doing a play by some bloke called Alan. Not Ayckbourn, the other one.' Alan said he found it refreshing and liked that we were making him one of the gang. And he totally was.

For all his accolades and awards, the most important thing I can say about Alan is that he still lives in the world he cares and writes about. He has seen and done it all, and yet he couldn't be more approachable and encouraging to others. There is no establishing status, no enjoyment at the fact you might feel slightly uncomfortable in his presence. He, like so many of his brilliantly written words, reaches out to you and makes you feel at home. As far as he's concerned, whether you're an actor or the security man on the stage door, you are valid and will have something to say, or something worth listening to. I asked him once why he had never accepted a knighthood or something similar, and his answer wasn't anything to do with a statement about the monarchy or a deeply held political view. He simply said that as a writer he felt he should still be a person in the world that normal people live in. Believe me, I could fill chapter after chapter of stories and conversations we had with Alan – fascinating anecdotes about Peter Cook, or the time when Morrissey called by his house. They are his stories, though, and not mine to tell here. But, I'm sure he wouldn't mind if I sneaked in just this one. (OK, bear with me on this as some of it happens a few years away from the rehearsal rooms of *The History Boys*.)

Alan had been incredibly encouraging when it came to me writing comedy. He would often tell me that I was funny and that he believed I could write. Quite near the beginning, I'd told him I was working on a script with Ruth and he would always ask about it, and we'd talk about the characters and possible scenarios. He was incredibly supportive, and said that he would always be on the end of the phone should I need any help or advice, which went way beyond the call of duty.

Fast-forward a few years to the night when episode one of *Gavin & Stacey* eventually aired on BBC3. (Don't worry, no spoilers here. You can read on.) As the end credits rolled, I was sitting there waiting for him to call. I knew he would've watched it – he'd told me he was looking forward to it – but nothing came. Maybe he'll call tomorrow, I thought to myself, or he's taped it and he'll watch it in the week. But no, episode after episode, week after week, I heard nothing from Alan. I had resigned myself to the fact that he must hate the show and would rather not call if he had nothing nice to say about it. It got me down a bit, to be honest. Alan was one of the people I really wanted to like it.

And then, as the final episode of the series finished, the phone rang.

It was Alan. 'Hello, James.' I tingled at the sound of his voice. 'I've just watched the last episode and I enjoyed it so much, I feel a little sad that it's over. You both wrote it with such love that it made me care about every single character. You should be very proud tonight.' You would not believe how happy that made me. I told Alan how relieved I was that he'd called and how I'd been worried he didn't like the show because I hadn't heard from him, and he said simply, 'Well, I wanted to watch the whole show. It's a series and I wanted to call when I'd watched it until the end.'

And that's the thing about Alan – he just makes sense. He has a way of saying things and holding himself that is so together and so precise, and yet he is completely unaware of how profound he's being. He'll be so embarrassed if he ever reads that.

(And we're back.) As we got nearer to the opening of the show, we moved out of the rehearsal room and onto the stage to begin the tech rehearsal. This is one of the most exciting times when you're putting on a play. It suddenly becomes much more real, and you start to imagine all the possible outcomes, both good and bad – the fear of everything that could go wrong, along with the excitement of everything going right. When you've been rehearsing for six weeks, you more or less lose all judgement as to whether what you're doing is any good or not: the play, your part in the play, the set, the lighting, everything. After that long, you just can't tell.

Eventually, though, all you're longing for is to get out in front of an audience. We were doing ten preview shows before press night. Nick says, to this day, that *The History Boys* had the best first preview he's ever seen. It was absolutely electric. Waves and waves of laughter in response to jokes we didn't even realise were jokes. The French scene was such a hit that Richard had to stop and wait for the laughs to die down before repeating a line that had been lost amongst the noise.

The play was a hit with the audience, no question but, as happy as we all were with how it had all gone, there was that nagging thought at the back of my mind – *Martin Guerre* had been a smash with the audience, too, and look what had happened there. Remember that saying 'Don't judge anything by an audience'? Well, it's totally true. We just had to hope the critics liked it.

Press night came. Both Alan and Nick wrote lovely cards to each and every cast member, and there were flowers and champagne and hundreds of notes from well-wishers all over the backstage area. The nerves were setting in. The funny thing is, the show was already sold out for the entire run, so I'm not entirely sure why we were all so nervous. Well, I do kind of know – the critics.

The funny thing about reviews is that they really are only one person's opinion. Of course, we take it to mean so much more than that because they're printed in national newspapers and lots of people's opinions will be determined by what the critic thinks. A couple of nights before we opened, I asked Nick what he thought the reviews might be like. Taking each one in turn, he went through the eight or nine critics who were coming and said who would like it, who would enjoy it but find negatives and who would be the one to hate it.

And, sure enough, he was absolutely right. The show opened to – by and large – the most sensational reviews you could possibly imagine. One critic described it as Alan's finest work, another picked out Richard's performance as being the best on the London stage, and one critic, the one Nick had been so sure would hate it, said it was awful and boring. I found it astounding that Nick could be so on the money with his predictions; then again, he had called it right every single step of the way.

The show was a sure-fire hit. It's so rare to be part of something that both critics and audiences enjoy in equal measure. So often it's one or the other. But here we were, twelve actors, us eight boys and the four teachers, having the time of our lives.

The only real challenge in a long run is keeping the boredom at bay. The routine can get pretty monotonous: the same words, the same action, passing people in the wings at exactly the same point, every single night. It can sometimes feel as though you're getting stuck on the treadmill – except, that is, when you're working with seven other boys who are rapidly becoming your best friends. If you happen to be doing that, well, then you embrace the boredom.

It's fair to say that for every person who enjoyed having us at the National that summer, there were two others who hated it. I can understand why – we took over the place. The canteen, the bar, but most of all the dressing rooms. The dressing rooms at the National are all in a quadrant, with the windows facing in on each other, so, at various points throughout the day, actors from different companies will be leaning out of windows talking to each other or walking around the air-conditioning units having a crafty cigarette (though never Frances de la Tour, who would literally blow smoke into the 'No Smoking' signs inside the dressing rooms).

The great thing about the whole area is it belongs to the actors and they totally make it their own. You'll see some of the strangest things you could ever see while accepting them as completely normal, like a man dressed as a First World War soldier with a gunshot wound oozing blood from his face, moaning about the fact his agent doesn't return his calls, or a dancer who's wearing a full Egyptian headpiece with tracksuit bottoms. Strange, to say the least.

I shared a room with Andy, Zammo and Sacha. Dominic was next door and Russell, Sam and Jamie were directly below us. Our room became the hub of all things *History Boys*. We would eat there together, play darts (until the dartboard was confiscated), play indoor football (until the football was confiscated), play indoor squash (you get the idea) and generally hang out.

The play was on for just over a year at the National, so we saw lots of other productions come and go over that time. For a couple of months the great Antony Sher was doing a one-man play in the Cottesloe, which had been directed by Richard Wilson of *One Foot in the Grave* fame. Our room looked directly into Mr Sher's; one night he and Richard Wilson were both in there and seemed to be very animated and passionate about something they were discussing. They were both so engrossed that they completely missed six of the eight history boys hanging out of the windows trying to listen to what they were saying. It was at this point that Andy had an idea. He bet Sacha a tenner to walk round and knock on Antony Sher's door and, when either he or Richard answered, to stare at both of them and say, as loud as he possibly could, 'I don't be*lieve* it!'

Classic. At that exact moment, this seemed like the funniest thing that anyone could do. Ever. Sacha wasn't doing it, though, and so, to make it more interesting, the money kept on going up and up. Finally it stood at £300. Three hundred pounds, for just one boy – any boy – to go, knock and say the immortal line to Richard and Sher.

I bit the bullet. 'I'm gonna do it,' I said.

The boys went hysterical. Sacha was saying that this was definitely a terrible idea, whereas Russell was egging me on, telling me that Richard Wilson loves it when people say it to him. Andy and Dominic nodded in agreement. 'If anything, it's a mark of respect,' Dom said. Like a fool, I thought this would be something fun, and might even become a nice little anecdote for my memoir.

I started to walk round the corner towards their room, the other boys giggling and scurrying around a few feet behind. 'Sshhhh,' said Jamie, who had now heard what was going on via text message and rushed up from the shower to the corridor wearing just a towel. We were close now, almost at the door, and I wanted to make sure that the money on offer was legit.

'Yeah, yeah, money's in the bank. Get on with it,' said Zammo. 'You gotta do it properly, though. A full-on Victor Meldrew.'

I looked at the door and raised my hand to knock . . . when suddenly it swung open. I stood there like a rabbit in the head-lights, completely frozen. He must've heard us talking. I hadn't even knocked.

'Yes?' said Richard Wilson, and all the boys ran off down the corridor. Jamie was the last as he was trying to pick his towel up off the floor without showing his bare arse. I took my cue.

'Look at that,' I said, pointing towards Jamie's rear end. 'I don't believe it, do you?'

Now, I think I said it casually enough that he didn't even realise. I carried on looking down the corridor as Jamie's feet slid round the corner, and then I tutted, in a 'can-you-believe-the-youth-of-today?' type of way. Richard rolled his eyes and shut the door. And I just walked away.

Needless to say, I never saw a pound of the cash. In fact, not one of the boys said they even remembered money being mentioned. Weak. The next time I saw Richard Wilson after that, he looked at me with a face that told me exactly what he was thinking: Don't, whatever you do, come and speak to me.

I couldn't believe it.

CHAPTER 15

BEST MUSICAL ACCOMPANIMENT:
'Run' by Stephen Fretwell

BEST FILM TO WATCH ALONGSIDE:
any episode of *Gavin & Stacey*

BEST ENJOYED WITH:
a refreshing, ice-cool glass of water

As the play became more and more successful, the eight history boys also became more and more in demand. Every day, Dominic was coming into work with a different film script, Sam Barnett was constantly out being wined and dined by sexy new American agents and Sacha was auditioning for epic TV dramas. Everyone, in fact, was having a good time professionally and looked as if they had a bright future after the play. Everyone, that was, except me.

I just wasn't being seen for any of the big jobs going around. I remember one day Andy, Russell and I all came into work with the same script. It was a film about two young British guys who go travelling in Thailand and end up with a girl who subsequently gets kidnapped; then they're falsely accused of her murder. It was a decent script and all three of us wanted to land one of the two lead parts. We started reading the script through together, bouncing off each other, and it was only then that we realised there weren't just the two main boys (the funny, charismatic leads in the film); there was also the 'newsagent', who had three lines on page six. I had a proper look at the note that had come with the script that told me which part I should prepare. I'm sure it's not hard to guess which one it was . . .

I tried to brush it off as being funny, but Andy and Russell must have known deep down how much it upset me. Why wasn't I being seen for the proper parts in any of these films? Why was I near the bottom of the casting ladder when I thought, after all the success the show was having, I'd be nearer the top? As I said earlier, I knew that my size would make some roles difficult to get, but it surely couldn't keep me from every decent part out there. The cast of *The History Boys* was probably the most supportive group of actors I've ever met, but at that time, and especially at that moment, I remember feeling really competitive. Not with the guys so much, more with the whole business of acting. It felt as if I was in a rut, as if someone somewhere had decided I had already reached the pinnacle of my career. Hit play, good TV drama, that's your lot: thank you and goodnight.

It seemed pretty clear what I needed to do if I was ever going to achieve anything close to the dreams I had – I was going to have to start putting the hours in and make stuff happen myself. Scripts weren't going to just land on my doorstep with wonderful parts to play. Every night, Dominic and Stephen would have their big dramatic scene near the end of Act Two and I would stand watching in the wings, wishing that it was me out there. I knew both their lines by heart. I still feel like that now, to be honest: it hasn't gone away, that desire to have a go at playing the more dramatic roles – not in Hollywood or even the West End, just . . . somewhere. I'd love someone to see that potential in me again. I'm not sure it's going to happen anytime soon, as currently I'm not sure people even think of me as an actor at all. These days, I'm a comedian (despite never having done stand-up or ever having professed to be one) or a 'tawdry celeb-rity', which was the pleasant way a journalist described me the other day. Anyway, more of that later.

So, I was on a mission and the first thing I did was call Ruth Jones to speak more about writing together and fix times when we'd both be in London. We believed in the idea we had, and the more we talked about the characters and scenarios, the more we felt we really had something.

It was around this time that I parted company with Jacquie. I think we both recognised that, although I was in this hit play, I was also in something of a rut, and that a change wouldn't be a bad thing. She was incredibly honest about the time her bigger clients were taking up and told me that she didn't want that to be a negative for me. Generously, she agreed that she'd look after me until I found someone new. We hugged and said our goodbyes and I left her office feeling a little daunted about what was going to happen next.

I met with a few different agents, and got along with them all, but then someone suggested I should meet Ruth Young at United Agents. Believe it or not, Ruth was the agent at the top of my list. She had – and still has – an incredible reputation, and the list of names the agency represented read like a who's who of British acting talent: James McAvoy, Ewan McGregor, Keira Knightley, Kate Winslet and loads more, way too many to mention here. United Agents was where I wanted to be.

I told my dad I was going in to see Ruth and he was, as ever, optimistic: 'Won't you just be at the bottom of a long list?' he said.

'I'm not sure that's how it works,' I said, hoping he was wrong.

'Well, just don't get your hopes up.'

So, bolstered by Dad's words of encouragement, I went to meet Ruth at her offices. (I'd like to take a quick time out to apologise for the ridiculous number of significant people in this book named Ruth. Sorry!) I was immediately taken by how large the agency was. Walking down the long corridors, all you can see are film posters and endless awards and, as I passed one window, I saw Kate Winslet deep in conversation with two cool guys in suits. I looked down at my scruffy jeans and trainers and thought it probably best to give her my number another time.

(I imagine if she's reading this, which I'm pretty sure she will be, given she's clearly obsessed with me, she'll be slightly disappointed that I didn't step up then. Honestly, anytime I've been in a room with her – four times in total – she's been so dumbstruck by my being there that she's not been able to utter one word to me. It's weird. It's like she can feel the chemistry but is actively making a choice to pretend I'm not there. Our eyes catch and she looks the other way. How different it all could've been.)

I got to Ruth's office and waited for her to come in. Her assistant, Heloise, asked if I'd like anything to drink and I said thanks, but I was fine, which was stupid because I was really thirsty. In fact, I was so thirsty that when I was walking from the Tube to the office, I remember thinking that I wouldn't buy a drink to quench my thirst because the chances were that I'd be offered a drink once I got there. They were a big swanky agency with loads of huge stars and they'd probably have posh juices and iced teas, or iced mochachinos. 'I really want an iced mochachino,' I distinctly remember saying to myself.

So why didn't I get a drink? I blame Winslet. Every time I've been near her this has happened. The last time I saw her at a party, she brushed past me and I spilt a vodka cranberry all over my white shirt. I was so busy looking at her, I literally missed my mouth and poured it onto my chest. She knows what she's doing; she's playing the long game with me and it's messing with my mind.

This whole being-thirsty-and-not-drinking thing was only making me more parched. I sat looking around the office. There were posters signed by James McAvoy and lots of others, advertising films I'd never heard of, with those arched gold-leaf things at the bottom that tell you they had played at film festivals and so must be good.

And then Ruth walked in. 'Hi James,' she said in her lovely

Scottish accent that immediately puts you at your ease. 'Have you been offered a drink or anything?'

'No,' I replied. What?! Why did I just say that? I'd been offered a drink and very definitely said no! Ruth looked concerned and pressed her hand down on the intercom next to her telephone. 'Heloise, can you come in here, please?'

Oh God, what had I done? This was the only agent in London I wanted to be represented by. I'd been in her office two minutes and I'd already lied to her face.

Heloise came in and handed Ruth some messages. 'Heloise,' Ruth said as she took the notes, 'why haven't you offered James a drink?' I could feel my whole face going red. *Damn you, Winslet!*

Heloise turned to look at me. 'I think I did? Didn't I?'

'No . . . no, I don't think so,' I said in a way-too-high-pitched voice. Heloise kept on looking at me, *through* me. She was on to me.

'Would you like a drink?'

I looked at Ruth. 'Are you having one?' I said, hoping Ruth would order an iced mochachino so I could just simply say, 'Make that two.'

'I've actually got a coffee here,' said Ruth, pointing at the *massive* oversized mug she was holding that I ridiculously hadn't noticed.

And then I looked back at Heloise. 'No, I'm fine, honestly. I had a drink on the way here. Thanks.' She gave me one more long, bemused look and left the room.

Luckily, the meeting only got better from there. I loved Ruth. She spoke so passionately about actors and how she represents them. We seemed to have a similar outlook on things – we both used the phrase 'in the grand scheme of things' far too much – and all in all we got on great. Just as the meeting was wrapping up, Ruth told me that she'd love to represent me, that she saw me as a good challenge and that, if I was up for it, then she was. I told her right there and then that she was the only person I wanted to represent me, and that was that – I had a new agent. We celebrated with an awkward half-handshake, half-hug that only got stranger the more it went on, and I left the room feeling as if I could walk on water – until I saw Heloise sitting outside, glaring at me. 'You sure you don't want a drink?' I shook my head, walked speedily over to the lift and got the hell out of there as quickly as I could.

So far, this whole 'taking control of my own career' thing seemed to be working out. There was still one person I had to call, though: Ruth Jones. We'd been swapping texts with little quotes and character ideas for some time, but we hadn't actually met and written anything down. I was walking back to the Tube from Ruth's office, about to press call on my phone, when it starting ringing in my hand. It was Ruth (Jones. I'm not going to apologise again).

'I was just about to call you. Literally this second!' I said, incredibly excited.

Ruth, though definitely excited, wasn't quite as moved by that as I was. There were bigger things on her mind. 'Listen, I really think we need to write this treatment. If we don't do it soon, we'll lose the momentum and it'll just disappear 'cos we'll have both moved on.'

Amazing. She was feeling exactly the same as me. That, coupled with the whole phone-ringing thing, was enough to make me go bananas. I tried to keep it together. 'But when . . .?' I said. 'When can we meet? I've got eight shows a week for the next month before we have a six-day break. I won't be able to come to Cardiff. Are you going to be in London at all?' As it turned out, Ruth's schedule was just as busy as mine, if not busier. She was filming the second series of *Nighty Night* on the south coast. We then realised we'd both agreed to do an early morning breakfast television show in ten days' time to promote the fourth series of *Fat Friends*. (We'd shot another series of *Fat Friends* shortly after *The History Boys* play opened. They worked

around the play's dates and we filmed it in Leeds. The reason I
didn't tell you any of this is because it was more of the same.
Seemed silly to keep going on about it.) So on this breakfast-TV
show, we should be done by 8.30 a.m., and we could go off
somewhere and write for a few hours, try to get as much done
as we could before Ruth had to leave London. The plan was set.

Doing breakfast television is always quite strange. It's not
what you think it's going to be. When you watch it at home with
your Coco Pops, the presenters look so relaxed and together;
their teeth are ice white and there's not a hair out of place. But
when you're on the show, you turn up at 5.45 a.m. and they're
shouting for a coffee, brushing their teeth over the sink, looking
as though they've been pulled backwards through a hedge. Once
you're on the set, what looked on TV to be a palatial lounge
filled with comfy sofas and plates of warm croissants and
Danishes actually turns out to be quite possibly the smallest
room you've ever sat in. The sofas aren't comfy, and the plate of
croissants? They're real, but have been sprayed with a disinfectant
to make them glisten under the lights. (I learnt this the hard
way, believe me.)

The show was fine. Ruth and I got wheeled on, talked about
Fat Friends, made sure we mentioned at least twice what time it
was on and then were promptly wheeled off again. Once out of
the studio, it was a short walk to the hotel where Ruth had stayed
the night before. This would be the first of many, many hotels
we would write in, but we didn't know that at the time. The
truth is, we had no idea what we were about to do. How would
this work? *Could* this work? Sitting in a hotel bar talking about
a great idea is one thing; sitting in a room and actually writing
it down is another thing altogether.

We got into the room and Ruth pulled out her laptop. Stephen
Fry once said that in all good writing partnerships, there is
someone who sits and types while the other tends to pace around,
shouting his or her thoughts aloud, occasionally looking over

the shoulder of the person who's typing. Guess which one I was? I'll give you a clue – not the typing one.

We talked about the idea we'd had back in Leeds. I think one of the biggest strengths we had in the writing process was that we never specifically talked about jokes. As both of us were actors, I think it was easier for us to focus on the characters – what they'd be wearing and how they'd speak, their backgrounds. The jokes, we thought, would arrive naturally once we'd got the personalities nailed down.

First off, we needed to think of a reason why the majority of the guests at the wedding hadn't met before. Lots of the scenes we'd worked out back in Leeds relied on people meeting each other for the first time, like Mondeo man and Mr Runcorn had back at the wedding in Barry. I told Ruth a story about my best mate, Gavin, and how he met his wife, Sara, on the phone at work. She was working in accounts and he was a buyer, or it may have been the other way round but, either way, they flirted on the phone, a lot, until one day they decided to meet. It was a complete whirlwind: they fell in love immediately. Gavin proposed soon after, and they got married straight away after that. They've now been happily married for six years and have a beautiful daughter called Ava.

Ruth agreed it could make a good back story for our characters. We knew that we weren't ever going to use it, because, at that time, we were convinced the show would only deal with the wedding day itself. It was just an exercise to help us plot out who was going to be there. At this point, Ruth was going to be the bride, and I was going to play the best man. We decided that we'd call the bride Stacey, and, in honour of my mate Gav, we'd keep the groom's name as Gavin. My cousin Lee lives in Bedford and one of his best mates was a builder called Smithy. I told Ruth about him, his mannerisms, the way he pronounced words, how he was always up for it, whatever 'it' was. We thought he'd make for the perfect best man. Then we talked about their families and friends and fleshed out the back stories so it felt as if all these characters had real lives, that they actually existed.

As we sat there, I kept thinking back to working with Mike Leigh and how it was his attention to detail that made his characters so real. It was vital to get to the point where we felt we could answer any question that the characters might throw up once we started improvising. So, we had Gavin and Stacey, we had Smithy, and now we started to sketch out the bride's best friend, who we called Vanessa. We worked everything a few more times through and began writing it properly.

It all came so quickly. As this was still just a pitch, we wanted any TV executives who were reading to get the style of the show straight away so, right at the top, we explained how we envisaged the style and pacing of the show being like *The Royle Family* meets *Marion and Geoff*. We wrote small snippets of dialogue to show the sort of tone we envisaged and, right in the centre of the page, we wrote in bold italics:

This is a wedding where nothing happens.

We were trying to get across what we believed to be the show's greatest asset – the fact that nothing obviously dramatic happened: it would simply hold a mirror up to show real people with real lives.

Before we knew it, we'd finished the treatment. It came in at about ten pages. We hoped it was good, that we'd done enough and that the TV people would understand what we were trying to do. It was in the envelope, ready to be sealed, when Ruth suggested something. Neither of us had any idea at the time what a massive impact it would have on every aspect of our lives. If we had, I think we would both have fallen over. 'Shall we put the back story in?' she said breezily. 'You know, just to give them a feel of how Gavin and Stacey met?'

I thought about it for a moment: 'Erm . . . I dunno,' I said. 'It'll make it too long, won't it? Won't it be confusing?'

'Not if we do it as two separate documents. Then if they want to read it, they can. And if they don't, they don't. I think we should, don't you?' Ruth then looked at me. I wish I could make this seem more dramatic, like one of those red-wire or blue-wire scenes in thrillers, but the truth is, it wasn't. I just sort of shrugged my shoulders and went, 'OK, yeah. Let's put it in the envelope.'

And that was that. We sent it off to ITV and waited. Ruth got on a train to the south coast to carry on filming *Nighty Night*, and I walked the few hundred yards back to the National Theatre. Nothing blew up.

I don't know why but I used to love getting to the theatre before anyone else. It probably has something to do with my constant need to feel in some way dramatic. I liked being the first in the dressing room; I liked being the one to turn on all the spotlights round the mirrors; I liked walking down to the stage and looking over the empty wings, which in a few short hours would be full of people bustling, whispering and running around; I liked walking out onto the stage, seeing the empty seats, taking in the silence. I liked all the anticipation.

That morning I followed my normal routine and ended up sitting down on the empty stage at the National. I remember thinking how much I'd enjoyed the morning with Ruth – more than I ever thought I would. Even if, as we expected, no one went for our idea, I thought that we should definitely try to do something else. However much I was enjoying the play, I knew that I was going to have to create things for myself because the good TV and film roles just weren't happening.

I sat on the edge of the stage and, as fun and positive as that morning had been, I started to feel quite down. For as long as I can remember, I've always had an inability to see the bigger picture. Rather than focusing on the good, I seek out and find the bad in me, or my career. Now, I was sitting on an empty stage in one of London's greatest theatres, having appeared on breakfast television that morning to publicise a

BAFTA-nominated drama I was starring in, and having just spent a great morning writing something new and exciting with an actress and friend I really loved and admired. And yet, all I could see was a fat boy who was never going to amount to anything. It's my worst trait, the thing I can't stand in myself – the inability to see any positives. Looking back, I can see I was the luckiest guy in the world.

Something I used to do a lot back then, and still do now from time to time, is judge my success against other people's. So, for example, just the other day someone was being incredibly kind and encouraging about my career, telling me how well they thought I was doing, and all I could think inside was, Andrew Garfield is at the Golden Globes. He's a success. If I was that good, I'd be there too. It's a ridiculous way to behave and I'm embarrassed that I'm even telling you. I wish I didn't feel like that, but I also wonder where I'd be without it. Would I have bothered to write *Gavin & Stacey*? Would I have bothered to do anything at all if I didn't feel so driven to be the biggest and best?

I'm happy to say that the jealousy and constant comparison happens less frequently these days. I hope this is because I've grown up, not because I'm more successful. The truth is, I doubt whether all the success in the world would change how I feel at certain times. It's a part of my personality that I've struggled long and hard to change. It doesn't help anyone to judge their happiness or career by looking at where others may or may not be. Dad said it best: 'All the time you're looking left and right at other people, you're neglecting what's in front of you. If you focus on looking straight ahead, you can take the odd glance at the future.' He's got a way of saying things sometimes that just puts everything into perspective.

Even with all my self-doubt, things were still going really well on *The History Boys* – so well in fact that Nick had called a meeting with the whole cast to put to bed various rumours about what was going to happen after our run at the National ended. The play had been so successful that people were already talking about transfers to the West End, nationwide tours and all sorts of other crazy things. That all sounded good to us. We loved working together so much and were having such a laugh that we were up for anything that would extend the run.

We were sitting in the theatre stalls when Nick and Alan came in. 'All right, A.B.!' came the cry from the boys. A.B. was now Alan's nickname. Yep, we gave Alan Bennett a nickname. Actually, by this point in the run, pretty much everyone in the play had a nickname: Richard Griffiths was 'Rizzo'. I came up with that one, though I'm not sure he ever really warmed to it as much as we wanted him to.

Andrew Knott ended up being known as 'Moon' and this came about organically – his first nickname was 'Anders', which then became 'Andeye', which then became 'Andeye Moon', and then simply 'Moon'. Makes sense.

Jamie Parker was known as 'Scripps', which was his character name in the play. Unoriginal, maybe, but we kept it because it just fitted him.

Sacha was 'Sachgelia'. I've no idea why.

Russell was 'Rusty', except to me. To me he was 'My Russ', and to him I became 'My Jim'. Beautiful.

Sam Barnett was, I think, 'Sam'. That's disappointing.

Sam Anderson was, and always will be, 'Zammo'.

Frances de la Tour was either 'Frankie' or 'J-Lo', on account of her occasionally wearing velour tracksuits similar to, um, J-Lo.

Clive Merrison, who played the head teacher in the play, was 'Clive-O'.

Stephen Campbell-Moore became known to all as 'Steve-Ex'.

Dominic Cooper became lovingly known as 'Dirtbox'. I wish I could tell you why, but I'm worried about how young some of you reading this may be.

And my nickname, which has stuck better than any nickname I've ever been given, was, and very much still is, 'Levine'. Or, to give it its correct parlance, 'Jimmy Levine'. I picked it up halfway through the run. Here's how it happened: I was at home one day and I called up Dominic. As he picked up the phone he simply said, 'Jimmy Levine! How's it going?' Granted, it's not the most exciting nickname-giving story. Apparently Dominic had seen some post in his house from someone by the name of 'Jimmy Levine' and then, because he's a strange and wonderful man, decided to call me that. The name stuck. Actually, it stuck so well that we have both, over time, become 'Levine'.

If my telling you about our nicknames was rather dull for you, I'm sorry. It was the simplest and most straightforward way of getting across how together we were as a company. We were strong together. There was no boy-teacher dividing line. From top to bottom, from the first show to the last, everyone was equal. It's so rare for that to happen, especially with eight young actors of similar age with similar ambitions. One older, very thespy actor in a different play at the National said we'd turned the building into something resembling a borstal. I'm not sure he meant us to take it as a compliment.

In the theatre, Nick stood up in front of us all. The first thing he did was read a lovely, handwritten note he'd been sent by Baz Luhrmann, the director of some of my favourite films: *Moulin Rouge*, *Strictly Ballroom* and, of course, that incredible adaptation of *Romeo and Juliet*. The note said how much he'd enjoyed the play and to send his congratulations to the whole cast. Of course, that was totally amazing, but I was a little worried that it might be part of a ploy to butter us up for bad news; that the rumours about the play had all been false and we'd simply be ending our run in three months' time. I so didn't want it to be over. I loved these people and I loved this play.

My worries couldn't have been more misplaced. Far from closing, Nick told us that the play was about to go on a world tour! The play would travel to the Hong Kong Arts Festival, then to New Zealand, then spend six weeks in Sydney, Australia, before embarking on a possible six-month run on Broadway in New York.

We were absolutely gobsmacked. No one knew what to say. Dominic was smiling. Sam Barnett looked at me and we both stared at each other, our eyes sparkling with excitement. Then, just as it was beginning to sink in, Alan Bennett jumped in, 'But before all that, we need to shoot the movie.'

CHAPTER 16

BEST MUSICAL ACCOMPANIMENT:
'One Day Like This' by Elbow

BEST FILM TO WATCH ALONGSIDE:
Dead Poets' Society

BEST ENJOYED WITH:
a club sandwich

What? What movie? A movie of *The History Boys*? Nahhhhh. But, as it turned out, yeahhhhh. Nick told us there had been several offers to turn the play into a film – some big, some small – and that Alan was working on the screenplay. He'd only agreed to write it on the proviso that everyone from the play would be in it. It was a very touching and very classy stance that Alan took. He'd done the same some years before with *The Madness of King George* (which Nick had also directed), saying he would only consider the proposal if the film people agreed to have Nigel Hawthorne playing the title role. It's that sort of loyalty that makes both Nick and Alan loved by everyone they work with.

It took a while for it all to sink in. So that was the next step then – a movie of the play and then a world tour with the chance of six months or more on Broadway. Exciting as that was, there were some big implications – it meant a long time away from the people we most cared about.

And specifically for me, that meant Shelley. For a while now, things had been a little hard for us. We were living together in a flat I'd bought in Beaconsfield, above a Chinese restaurant on the high street. We still loved each other lots – that was never the issue – but I'd been in the play for a year by this point, which meant I was working every evening while Shell was still working days. We were like ships in the night. We'd not been spending enough time together to make the relationship work.

The hardest thing about starting going out with someone when you're only eighteen is that you don't really know what a long-term relationship looks and feels like. You don't have a proper idea of the effort you'll have to keep putting in, or the changes you'll both go through as you grow up. And, if you're not ready to allow for those changes, then you'll be in trouble. It's not a big issue when you get together, because the intensity of your feelings for each other can pull you over any early bumps in the road. But if you don't put the effort or time in, before you know it, those bumps have become mountains and you're stuck at the bottom without the right equipment and . . . Well, you know the rest. I'll finish there before I torture this metaphor any more.

Anyway, that's me jumping ahead. The truth is, Shelley was delighted for me when I told her about the tour – she couldn't have been more excited or supportive. She told me that if I didn't go, I'd regret it for the rest of my life. So that was that. The next year or so of my life was all laid out in front of me. It seemed, right then, as if it couldn't get any sweeter – I was about to spend a year going round the world with a bunch of guys who were fast becoming my best friends . . . and then, ITV called.

As I mentioned before, Ruth and I had sent our early treatment off to ITV with an outside hope of someone there liking it. We'd sent it to Sioned William, the head of comedy at the time, because she was Welsh and we thought she'd get the dialogue and understand the characters.

We'd waited a while but heard nothing back and so we'd kind of thought they hadn't liked it. But then, out of the blue, we got a call asking us to come to Sioned's office on Gray's Inn

Road to have a chat. I remember it very clearly because the closest Ruth and I could park was outside number 3 and the office was at number 426, but that did give us time to run through what we were going to say in the meeting. And to start preparations for next year's London Marathon.

The meet with Sioned went better than we could have imagined. As soon as we sat down, she told us she loved it, that the characters were spot on and that it would be perfect as a one-off hour-long film. She went as far as asking us if we had any cast in mind, and we talked loosely about Rob Brydon and Alison Steadman. The vibe in the room was so positive that it felt as if there was a good possibility of it getting made. After that long wait for any answer at all, it was way more than we had expected.

But – and here's the kicker – nothing got green-lit in that meeting. At ITV, and it's the same with every other TV station I know of, that first meeting is only the beginning of a very long road. After the initial stages, they have what they call 'commissioning rounds', which is when a potential new show is taken to the other commissioners and controllers who decide whether it's something that they think could work.

As Sioned took it off to do the rounds, we were very hopeful. She'd been so positive about the material that we'd already been talking about potential actors, so what more was there? It was surely in the bag. Dad was, as ever, trying to make sure I didn't get carried away, and this time – annoyingly – he was right. A couple of weeks later, Sioned came back and told us they wouldn't be doing it. It was tough to hear. No matter how much you think you understand the business and all its pitfalls, when someone has been positive, it's near impossible not to get carried away. She told us that everybody appreciated there was something there, that they all really liked the characters, but the bottom line was, they didn't think it was quite right for them.

It was a setback, without a doubt, but it wasn't enough to

knock our belief in what we had. ITV hadn't gone for it, but they had said a lot of nice things about it, so we got back on the horse and sent it out again, this time to Stuart Murphy, a friend of Ruth's, who was the controller of BBC3. Stuart is an ultra-sharp, very talented guy – he'd been responsible for commissioning *Little Britain* and *Nighty Night*, as well as *The Mighty Boosh* – and was renowned for taking risks. He also has the ability sometimes to see even beyond the writers' vision – he was a godsend.

Stuart had had the treatment about a week and we'd not heard anything back when one evening I happened to bump into him in a bar. (Definitely a bump into. Honestly. I was not stalking him.) Rather sheepishly, I mentioned our treatment and, very sweetly, he told me it was on his desk and he was going to look at it the next day. I know people tell you that kind of thing all the time, but he seemed very genuine so I nipped outside and phoned Ruth.

Ruth knew Stuart better than I did, and she told me that if that's what he said, then that's what he meant. So, for the next few days we waited. We waited and we waited and we waited. I know it was only a few days – I've waited longer for a hair appointment – and I'm overdoing it, but this was big. Anyway, we waited some more and then, finally, my phone rang. It was Ruth.

'James,' she said, 'are you sitting down?'

'No.'

'Sit down.'

I sat.

'OK,' she said, 'listen to this email I just got from Stuart Murphy.' Then she began to read:

'"Dear Ruth and James, sorry about only sending this to Ruth, but I don't have James's email. I've just finished reading your treatment and I have to tell you I think it's absolutely brilliant."'

'Oh my God!'

'Wait,' Ruth said, 'there's more. "I do have some reservations, however."'

'Oh shit!'

'"The truth is,"' Ruth read on, '"we don't really have a slot for an hour-long one-off comedy like this. I also think it would be a waste of what is clearly a brilliant story with well-rounded characters and insightful dialogue. I think this could be a series. The back story you've written is as interesting as everything else. Have you thought about that? Forgive me if I'm speaking out of turn, but if you're interested in doing this as a series, I'm really keen to discuss it. Regards, Stuart."'

And then came the killer line, the line that when we were having a bad day writing would always keep us on track:

'"PS I believe this could be the best thing BBC3 ever makes."'

I don't know, maybe he puts that at the bottom of all his emails – 'PS I believe you could be the best IT person I've ever met. Now please come and sort out my printer' – but Stuart's enthusiasm and confidence were a massive help to us all throughout the writing and filming process. Right from the beginning, he saw something that nobody else did. The truth is that the treatment wasn't actually that good, but Stuart managed to see past that and grasp what *Gavin & Stacey* could become. The upshot of our meeting was that we would be commissioned to write the first episode. Boom!

Ruth really came into her own now. When there's stuff that needs doing, there is no one better than Ruth Jones to do it. When we got that email, she was shooting *Nighty Night* for Baby Cow, the same production company that had made *Cruise of the Gods*, as well as loads of other brilliant stuff. We had a chat and decided to give the treatment to Henry Normal, the head of Baby Cow. They were exactly the kind of people who would understand the show and, if a series was green-lit, we wanted them to make it.

Henry had a read of the material, got us in for a meeting and we pretty quickly sorted out all the arrangements: Ruth and I would write the scripts (with lots of helpful suggestions from Henry), Henry and the lovely Lindsay Hughes would be the executive producers and Ted Dowd, a beautiful man with a beautiful face, would physically produce it. We would all work together on crew, cast, locations, script supervision and everything else, then deliver the finished product to the BBC. It's important to remember that at this point all we really had was Stuart's enthusiasm; we were still miles away from any guarantee of a series. The BBC commissions lots and lots of scripts, with maybe two in ten actually being made. The odds were against us, but with the crack team we'd sorted, we felt we had a pretty good shot.

So Ruth and I had to write a script that would make the BBC want to commission a series. And because of all the other stuff going on – the play and Ruth's TV commitments – we only had two full days to do it: a Tuesday morning, a Thursday afternoon and all day Sunday. If we didn't get the episode written in that time, it would be six weeks until we could sit down again, and we'd lose the momentum. The heat was on.

We didn't start well. By the end of the Thursday afternoon, we'd only written seven pages. A BBC half-hour is about thirty-seven pages in length, so that meant we had to write thirty more that coming Sunday.

I got to Ruth's hotel at 9 a.m. and we both knew neither of us would be leaving until that first episode was not only finished but written to a very high, so-good-the-BBC-will-commission-it standard.

Luck was on our side. We got completely into the zone and the material started to flow, just as it had done back at the bar in Leeds. We'd already worked out the main characters: Gavin, Stacey, Smithy and Vanessa, but we now decided that Ruth would play Nessa instead of Stacey because she was a no-nonsense, straight-talking kind of woman of considerable experience.

We wanted the characters to be identifiable. They had to walk and talk the way we did, say and do stupid things, make mistakes, be like normal, regular people. We wanted the show to feel as natural as possible. For instance, if someone made a funny joke, then the people around them should laugh. Often in comedy, a character cracks a gag and you have the canned laughter, but there's no reaction from the other people on screen. In our show, the characters would laugh, and hopefully the people watching would too.

Once we'd established the ground rules, we started sketching out the families: Gavin's mum and dad should be this outgoing, flirty couple who we called Pam and Mick; Stacey had lost her father – we thought that down the line it would create a really emotional soul to the series – but she was looked after by her uncle Bryn and her mum, Gwen. Once we had all the core characters, we just started writing. Or rather, Ruth did. I paced up and down, lay on the floor, sat on the windowsill – I just couldn't stay still.

One of the first things we wrote was Smithy's introduction, when he walks in on Pam, Mick and Gavin all having dinner. Ruth suggested he should come in with a bit of a bang. I thought about it for a moment and then just opened my mouth: 'Gavlar!' I said. 'Pam-la! Mick!' I'm not sure why I said it, but Ruth liked it so we put it in the scene. It never crossed my mind that those few words might one day sort of define me. Rarely does a day go by when someone doesn't shout that line at me across the street. It's even printed on T-shirts and mugs. I have no idea what part of my brain it jumped from.

There was a lot of cool stuff going on that day at the hotel. When I arrived, I had to queue in reception to get a swipe card, and while I was standing there I noticed Guy Garvey from the band Elbow checking in ahead of me. Elbow are one of my favourite bands – they're an incredible group who make music with a heart that never fails to move me. And there he was, right there, in the lobby. It turned out he was in the room directly below the one we were writing in. We had the window open to stop it from getting too stuffy and all day we could hear the wistful sounds of an acoustic guitar, and occasionally Guy's voice, drifting up from downstairs. It was beautiful.

Two and a half years later, we were at *The South Bank Show Awards*, picking up the award for 'Best Comedy', on the same night that Elbow won for their album *The Seldom Seen Kid*. I spoke to Guy and told him that I'd seen him in reception on the day that we wrote the first episode. Guy told me that he'd been writing some songs for the album at the time and that he remembered writing some of them in that very hotel. Imagine that, *The Seldom Seen Kid* and *Gavin & Stacey* both being written in the same place on the very same day. Cool.

I didn't leave Ruth's room until nearly midnight. We spent all day riffing in character, improvising, getting the dialogue first, then working out the mechanics of the scene after. Once we had all that, we'd finally write it down. It's the only way we can do it. We have to be physically together and bouncing off each other in order to get the level of spontaneity.

By the time we finally finished that day, we were totally exhausted, but we were pretty sure that we'd written a good episode. We sent out the two copies to Henry and Stuart, necked a couple of club sandwiches and went our separate ways – I went off to *The History Boys* shoot and Ruth went back to the *Little Britain* set. We'd done all we could – we were back to waiting.

The History Boys shoot was filmed over the summer at some grammar schools in Watford, as well as on location in Harrogate. Escaping from the confines of the National Theatre seemed to reinvigorate us all. There was a football pitch at one of the schools and whenever we weren't filming we would be out there kicking a ball around. All the old jokes and nicknames were still there – 'Dirtbox' was still 'Dirtbox' (and I still can't tell you why) – only now we had more room to spread our wings and our friendships became even deeper.

The laughs we had on set were perfect for taking my mind off the *Gavin & Stacey* script. Over the summer we didn't hear anything back but, right at the end of the shoot, when I'd almost given up again, Ruth, Henry and I all got called into the BBC to have a chat about the first episode. It was the first time I'd been to Television Centre. Since then I've been loads of times, but nothing changes – I still get that tingle of excitement walking through the doors. I even got it the day Smithy pulled up outside in the Volvo with George Michael in the passenger seat. (Well, probably more so then, 'cos I was sitting next to George Michael.) It's the history of the place, all the incredible shows that have been made there, like *Blackadder*, *Porridge*, *The Two Ronnies*. I always love going there.

Ruth and I were both quite nervous going into that meeting – it felt like the culmination of a lot of work and thought, and neither of us wanted it to end here. But, as it turned out, we had no reason to worry. Cheryl Taylor and Lucy Lumsden, the two comedy commissioners we met with, told us from the very start how much they loved the material and that they were really keen for us to write more. Initially, they asked us just to do another couple of episodes, but Henry managed to persuade them to commit to us writing a full series. Six episodes. That meant a lot of work. Then, for the first time, they mentioned shooting it, which made it much more real. We were no longer just talking about words on a page: this was gonna be a TV show – *our* TV show. But with that came the problem: they wanted us to think about filming it in April or May of the following year.

'Ah,' I said, 'in January I'm going away for an eight-month tour with *The History Boys*.'

Silence.

'It might not be eight months,' I added quickly. 'I mean, the show could flop and I'll be back much sooner.' I thought about that for a moment and knew I had to be honest. 'On the other hand, it's done really well so far and if that's the case in New York, I won't be back until the end of September.' I waited for their answer, biting my lip. Surely my schedule wasn't going to screw us now.

'Well,' said Lucy, 'let's just see how it goes. Go ahead and write the series and we'll take it from there.'

Phew.

We left that meeting totally elated, and with a whole lot of work to do. This was the end of October and in roughly four months' time I'd be on my way to Hong Kong. We had to get this baby written, and fast. We quickly got a routine together. Ruth would come up to mine in Beaconsfield for two and a half days, she'd sleep on our sofa bed and we'd write in the kitchen. Then she'd go home, we'd give it a day and then I'd drive down to Cardiff and we'd do another couple of days at her house.

So that's how the first series of *Gavin & Stacey* was written, back and forth along the M4 between Beaconsfield and Cardiff. It worked. We would spend entire days just laughing together. There were the big landmark moments, like when we decided that Stacey had been engaged five times already before Gavin popped the question, or when we first thought up the fishing-trip subplot. Those days were some of the best. As time went on, we built up such a deep affection for the characters that we more or less fell in love with them. And Ruth and I kind of did the same. (Whoa, not like that.) The more time we spent together, the more we became part of each other's lives. It's inevitable really, when you work that closely with somebody. There was an openness and honesty to our relationship that was absolutely vital to making the show as good as it could be. If you think something doesn't work, especially in comedy, you have to be allowed to say so, and Ruth and I never felt as if there were any no-go areas with each other.

We worked solidly for those two months but, by the turn of the year, and with me off on tour in a couple of months, we hadn't quite finished episode six. We had the first five in the bag, but we'd just run out of time with the last. And that was the one we'd been working towards – that the whole series had been working towards – the wedding. Christmas came and went and when we spoke to Henry about the last episode, he said not to worry too much about it. He thought that what we were delivering would be enough for the BBC to make the call on whether they wanted to shoot it or not. So we sent everything in and, before I knew it, it was time to go on tour.

Looking back, the build-up to leaving was a very emotional time. I was going away for eight months – maybe more – and I had no idea what that would do to Shelley and me. That was the big downside of the tour: it meant having to leave behind the girl I'd fallen in love with. By this point, Shelley and I had been together for almost eight years. We'd never been apart from each other for that long before; we'd had this agreement that the longest we'd ever spend without each other was a month, never any more.

To say goodbye, we had a meal together at the little pull-out table in our kitchen, the table where I'd been writing *Gavin & Stacey*. It was so romantic, but heartbreaking at the same time. Shelley was absolutely wonderful. She'd put together a playlist of songs that meant so much to both of us and created a photo album with pictures of us together, along with pictures of my family, my sisters and my nephew. She fell asleep before me, so I slipped quietly out of bed and wrote hundreds and hundreds of little 'I love you' Post-it notes and hid them all over the flat, in every nook and cranny. I hoped that as the months rolled by, she'd still be finding them and be reminded of how I felt.

CHAPTER 17

BEST MUSICAL ACCOMPANIMENT:
'New York' by Stephen Fretwell

BEST FILM TO WATCH ALONGSIDE:
When Harry Met Sally

BEST ENJOYED WITH:
pastrami on rye

The car came to pick me up the next day; after wrestling my enormous suitcase into the boot, I turned to say goodbye to Shelley. We held on to each other for as long as we could, tears rolling down our faces, both of us shaking like leaves. I finally got in the car and waved sadly to her as we pulled away. I cried all the way to Heathrow. I cried because I knew how much I'd miss her but also because, deep down, there was a part of me that knew things would never be the same again.

I remember sending a text to Russell Rook, a really close friend who works for the Salvation Army. I told him I was leaving to go on this great adventure and yet there I was in the taxi unable to stop crying. I asked him what on earth I could do. Russell tried to call, but when my phone rang, I just couldn't answer. I knew if I did I would burst into even more tears and never be able to get a word out that was even vaguely intelligible. I sent him another text explaining that I couldn't speak; I was too upset. Bless him, he sent one straight back. 'Just let the tears flow,' he told me. 'Don't try to stop them because in a few weeks' time it's important you remember why you were crying. It's important you remember who and what you're missing.'

He was absolutely right. I knew I was crying because I'd miss Shelley, but more than that, I really didn't know if we could get through this. I remember thinking that New Zealand, where we were going after Hong Kong, was as far away as it was possible to be.

When I got to the airport, I found that I wasn't the only one struggling to hold it together. All the other guys were just as upset as I was. We saw each other in a completely different light that day; usually, when we were together, we were the most confident, happy, piss-taking group of boys you could imagine. On that afternoon, however, as we were all standing around glumly waiting to check in, it seemed as if we'd lost a layer or two of skin.

Things calmed down as we boarded the night flight to Hong Kong. I was in a row of three together with Dominic and Stephen Campbell-Moore in economy. (This was a play, not a Hollywood movie.) We decided that the best way to deal with our emotions and the long flight ahead of us was to get totally hammered and film ourselves doing it. Why not? What else were we gonna do? Cry for the next thirteen hours?

Dom and I borrowed a camera from Andrew McDonald, one of the producers of the film, who'd lent it to us to film the tour for extras on the film DVD. We have hundreds of tapes and Dom and I have promised ourselves that one of these days we'll sit down together and edit all that footage. We filmed ourselves getting drunk. When we touched down in Hong Kong, we were all wearing high-altitude hangovers.

We were only in Hong Kong for a couple of weeks and, to be honest, I didn't have the greatest time, but that's probably because I hardly saw any of it. Let's put it like this. If you need any good tips on where to go drinking at three in the morning in Hong Kong, I'm your man. It didn't help that we were booked into the YMCA in Wan Chai, which is about as 'real' as Hong Kong gets, so going to bed was never the safe option. On our first night there, Zammo found a pile of human hair crumpled among his sheets, and the morning after, when Jamie Parker turned the shower on in the bathroom, the water was the colour and consistency of chocolate Angel Delight.

But if it was good enough for Richard Griffiths, it was good enough for us lot. Sometimes, other people's bed hair and skiddy-brown water are the realities of working in a touring theatre company, and the best thing to do is suck it up and just get on with it. Anyway, it was such a laugh being together again that our one-star accommodation wasn't going to spoil it.

It had been a few months since we'd finished filming the movie and since then we'd all been doing different things. Dominic had been offered film after film after film, Sam Anderson had been in a show called *Trapped*, I'd been writing with Ruth and (oh, I forgot to mention this) I'd also had a small part in a film called *Starter for Ten*, which Tom Hanks had produced. Dominic had been in that too, only his part was much bigger than mine. He'd played James McAvoy's best mate and I'd played a long-haired rocker mate of Dom's. Thinking about it, that film had a seriously talented young cast. I mean, James McAvoy has become a proper, bona fide movie star, Alice Eve and Rebecca Hall have done fantastically well and Benedict Cumberbatch is being talked about as the best actor of his generation. And then there's Dirtbox, but more on him later.

Hong Kong was a difficult place to kick off the tour. In a way, we weren't properly prepared for it. We were so used to the massive success back home, all the awards and the great press, and the roars of laughter rolling back from the audience every night at the National. The problem in Hong Kong was that the play was subtitled into both Mandarin and Cantonese, and so, as a consequence, it lost some of its spontaneity. There were two giant screens on either side of the stage translating all our lines as we spoke them. We'd say our words and, instead of that instant feedback of a big laugh, there would be this stony silence. Then, moments later, when the translation came through, the audience would get the joke and start cracking up, but by that point we were on to the next line. It was no one's fault, but it ended up feeling stilted. We had to adjust our performance to pick up the extra beat, which meant it didn't flow as it normally would have done.

But, as I said before, Hong Kong was more about what happened after the show than what happened during it. Most nights – OK, every night – after the show was over, four of us would pile into Jo-Bananas, the nearest bar, and get the party started. There was Zammo, Dominic and Andy, three good-looking guys, along with a chunky lad from Beaconsfield. Before we'd even ordered a drink we were surrounded by the most beautiful girls we'd ever seen. I just gawped at them, naively thinking that they must have an incredible infatuation for English guys, and for about twenty seconds, I knew what it felt like to be James Bond. Slowly, it dawned on me that it wasn't just the English guys; every westerner in the place was sitting with two or more scantily clad girls around them.

It was the same every night. It didn't matter what street or bar or restaurant; we were swamped by prostitutes looking for business. In the end I developed a fool-proof way of keeping them at bay: as soon as one approached me I explained that like them, I was working, that like them I sold my body for sex and whenever they saw me out at night they should know that I was working. If they wanted any action, they would have to pay me $1,000. No discounts. Pretty quickly word got around about this slightly mad English boy and they left me well alone.

I don't recall seeing Hong Kong at all in the daylight. We'd do the play, be out all night, then crawl back into bed at nine the next morning. Then do it all over again the next day. The whole place just passed me by. It was kind of a relief to get out of there to be honest.

After all that debauchery, New Zealand had real appeal – for starters, it just seemed much healthier. This was the place out of *The Lord of the Rings* with the amazing waterfalls and mountains – wide open, beautiful countryside compared to the densely packed high-rises of Hong Kong.

Landing in Wellington, I made my way to baggage reclaim and switched on my phone and immediately a text from Ruth popped up. I hadn't heard from her for a while, so this must be something big.

'Oi, Smithy,' it said. 'We've got a green light, a'righ'.' Written as Nessa – nice touch.

Not even thinking of the time difference, I phoned her right away. It was late morning in Wellington and almost midnight in the UK and Ruth was just about to go to bed when she picked up.

'What's this?' I asked her excitedly. 'I just landed in New Zealand and I got your text. What green light?'

'We've got the green light, James,' she told me. 'The BBC are going for it. They want the whole lot. The whole six episodes. They want us to start shooting as soon as you get home.'

I love you, New Zealand! If you ever want to remember a place fondly, I'd recommend getting some amazing news the first moment you touch down there.

Ruth and I shouted at each other for a bit down the phone, then I let her get off to bed. I hung up and stood fixed on the spot by the baggage carousel, my mouth hanging wide open. Jamie Parker was standing next to me, looking a little concerned.

'Levine,' he said, 'you all right? What's up?'

I stared at him for a while before answering. 'The show's been picked up,' I mumbled. 'Our show. *Gavin & Stacey*. The BBC's picked it up.'

'You're joking,' he said, beginning to smile. 'You're kidding me.'

'No.' I shook my head. 'That was Ruth on the phone. They've given us the green light.'

Telling Jamie made it real and – boom! – like that, suddenly it hit me. I was gonna make my own TV show! Jamie grabbed me, hugged me, slapped me and kissed me and then the two of us started jumping up and down and round and round with the whole baggage reclaim area looking on. It was a beautiful moment.

Hearing that fantastic news really chilled me out – in fact, everyone was more relaxed once we got to New Zealand. We had three days to ourselves before the play opened, and we decided to hire a camper van to check out some of the countryside. If you've seen *The Lord of the Rings* movies, then you'll know what it's like, so I won't bore you with all the details. All right . . . quickly, though. It is really, really beautiful. There, said it.

In Wellington we were back in front of an English-speaking audience, which made our performances all the better. We were performing at the St James Theatre, a proper old vaudevillian design that hadn't been touched for nearly a hundred years. It had a very intimate stage, creaky wooden floors with old-fashioned bench seats and was a really romantic place to perform. At the end of each night, the audience would stamp their feet on the wooden boards, which sounded like an onrushing wave of water. It was a lovely noise.

From New Zealand we moved on to Sydney for a six-week run, which meant renting apartments. I shared with Dom and we really lucked out. Our place was massive: twin balconies overlooking the city centre, and only a few minutes down to the waterfront. There wasn't a lot not to like about our time there: the theatre was great, the show got a fantastic reception, and on our days off we'd hire a catamaran and sail under the Harbour Bridge or just lie out on the beach and listen to Arctic Monkeys' *Whatever People Say I Am, That's What I'm Not*, which kind of became the soundtrack to the whole tour. The only problem I can remember was the poster. Before we got to Australia, every promotional poster of the show had had a picture of us boys as the central image. But in Sydney – and you've got to wonder whether there wasn't a sneaky call made – it only had Richard Griffiths on it. Rizzo absolutely loved it, thought it right and proper given his age, ability and standing, and, of course, was always lording it over us lot every time we went out. You've gotta love that man.

The night before we were due to leave for New York, Dom and I went out for an all-nighter, which made the flight very rough. We had a two-hour stopover in LA but, before that, there was a painful fourteen hours of being squeezed in with no legroom. Happily, on the connecting flight to New York, I managed to wangle three seats to myself and, within seconds of taking off, I was out for the count. I've been lucky enough to have been on some pretty expensive flights since, but I promise you, nothing has ever compared to the relief of stretching out over that row of seats and passing out.

So, New York. Broadway . . . it was totally awesome. It's New York. When we landed, Richard Griffiths told us that we had no idea how brilliant this was going to be, and he couldn't have been more right. We were staying in some serviced apartments in Midtown to begin with as we had no idea how long we'd be staying there. We were booked in for six months, but that was only if we made it past the critics. I mentioned earlier that in London, theatre critics really can make or break a show. Well, in New York, they can murder it. In the week we got there, David Schwimmer had just opened a play; a week later, after some pretty nasty reviews, the play had already shut. New York is the most demanding city in the world and the theatre's no different.

We were playing at the Broadhurst Theatre on Forty-Fourth Street between Eighth and Broadway, directly across the road from a restaurant called Angus McIndoe's. That first day is one I will never forget. We'd been in this play for twelve months in London, shot a movie of it and taken it to Hong Kong, New Zealand and Australia, but that first morning we went down to the theatre in New York will always be one of the highlights for me. We all came out of the subway at Times Square and there, right in front of us, was a *History Boys* poster the size of a London bus – it was of all eight of us and I get a tingle down my spine just thinking about it.

It didn't take very long to fall in love with the city – New York is New York, after all – and the vibe was great from the start, with the week of previews going really well and the New York producers proving they were at the top of their game. They had fought really hard to get us out there and I can't thank them enough for what they did. They made sure the production was as good as it could be and they backed Nick's directorial decisions to the hilt.

We had a couple of early nights where the critics came in, but all the reviews were embargoed, as they always are, until after opening night. That's one of the strange things about theatre in New York compared to London: everyone knows what kind of reviews you're going to get long before anything is published, and long before you do. You find out which way it's going to go at your opening-night party – if no one turns up, then the news isn't good. New York is brutal: succeed and the city's there at your feet; fail and you'll overhear them in the restaurants marvelling that you've dared to show your face.

We all brought our families over for opening night, which was wonderful. Mum and Dad came out together with my sisters and my nephew; having not seen them for so long, it was lovely to be together again and catch up. We'd had a few nerves in

Sydney but, compared to New York, that was a breeze. It felt more like it had when we opened in London, only much, much worse. We were desperate for this to work, but we were more than aware of the pressure. If the critics didn't like it, we'd be on our way home.

As it turned out, we weren't gonna get kicked out anytime soon. The play was a hit – I mean, a *major* hit. It went down as well in New York as it had in London, maybe even better. The reviews were great and a couple of days later we were told that we'd definitely be on for the full six months. Amazing! You can imagine how it was. You're in your mid-twenties; you're in a hit play on Broadway; you're living and working with your best mates in one of the greatest cities in the world. If that isn't living the dream, I don't know what is.

We were told that one of the really cool things about being in a hot play on Broadway is that lots of famous people come and see it and they'll often pop backstage to say hello. And the thing is, you know when a famous person is in because the front-of-house team tell you about it. So, we'd get told that Philip Seymour Hoffman or Jennifer Aniston or Bill Murray were in and after the show we'd all anxiously wait for them to show up at the stage door. But none of them ever came. It seemed as if every night there'd be someone in the audience we wanted to meet, but for whatever reason they never turned up backstage. Well, there was one occasion, but it didn't quite pan out as we'd imagined . . .

It was a midweek show and we were told that Harrison Ford and Calista Flockhart were in the audience. If you're a child of the eighties like me, then Harrison Ford means something: *Indiana Jones, Star Wars, Blade Runner*. He *was* the eighties. I remember even being nervous that I was going to perform in front of him. You can always spot the famous people because they're generally near the front of the stalls and they always sit on the aisle, for the quick getaway. That night, just before the show started, I peeked out of the wings and caught a glimpse of Harrison and Calista. There he was, Indiana Jones, about to watch me do my thing on stage. Cool. Very cool.

After the show, Russell and I were coming down the stairs backstage, desperately hoping they'd be the first to come back. We both let out simultaneous gasps when we saw them waiting just inside the stage door. This was my one and only chance. I walked up to Harrison and grabbed his hand and started shaking it like a loon. 'May I just say,' I began, 'that we've had a lot of extraordinary people come to see the play and we were always told they'd come back to say hello. But you guys are the first to actually do that. Thank you so much. The boys will be so excited to meet you.'

So far Harrison hadn't said anything. He'd just sort of awkwardly looked at me with a nervous smile while Calista hovered around behind him. I was waiting for him to say something – anything – when a security guy stuck his head round the stage door. 'Your car's here, Mr Ford,' he said.

'Thank you,' Harrison muttered, and without a word to me, he and Calista left.

Now that was embarrassing. To gush that much and be met with nothing. Oh well, at least they came to see the show. And they weren't the only ones: one Sunday matinee we had David Bowie, James Taylor, Steven Spielberg and Steve Martin all in the same audience. It was really humbling to have so many incredible people come and watch the play. Steven Spielberg is in my opinion the greatest film-maker of all time and David Bowie and James Taylor are some of music's biggest names too, but for me, Steve Martin being in the audience was absolutely huge. *Planes, Trains & Automobiles* and *Dirty Rotten Scoundrels* are up there among my favourite films and I couldn't let him come and go without somehow marking the occasion.

Lily.
The love affair
that never was.

And Mat.
The love affair that
very much was.

Wii scream This child's reaction to his Christmas present is a hit on the internet telegraph.co.uk/tv

Worth his weight in gold to the BBC

PROFILE Told by Alan Bennett that he had a gift for making others laugh and should start writing, James Corden could be the star of 2009

AT HIS 30th birthday party earlier this year, James Corden was given a copy of an old school report. "If he just gave the same level of commitment to work as to trying to make others laugh he'd be a grade-A student," wrote one exasperated teacher.

Belatedly, it seems Corden took those words to heart. If 2008 was the year his career took off, 2009 should see it go stratospheric. BBC bosses have singled him out for major stardom. The third series of his Bafta-laden sitcom, *Gavin and Stacey*, is heading for a prime-time slot on BBC One after the Christmas Eve special pulled in an impressive seven million viewers.

He has also produced a sketch show with his comedy partner, Mathew Horne, which executives are mentioning in the same breath as Morecambe and Wise. His forthcoming feature film, a comic horror about lesbian vampires, already has the makings of a cult classic. He has been offered a job co-hosting this year's Brit Awards, and will also be an executive producer on a US version of *Gavin and Stacey* after NBC snapped up the rights.

All this while juggling dates with a string of famous beauties, from singer Lily Allen to *X Factor* winner Alexandra Burke. Not bad going for a former Salvation Army kid who cheerfully admits to having been overweight for as long as he can remember. "I wasn't picked on at school because of my weight and that's probably because I was the first to make a joke about it. I realised that if you're funny, even the bullies will want to hang out with you," he has said.

"But my size was never an issue for me because my parents' attitude was: 'You are who you are and you have the capacity to be brilliant.'"

Most of his acting roles have played upon his size, including his television breakthrough as a bullied schoolboy who joins a slimming club in the ITV1 series *Fat Friends*. There, he met Ruth Jones, a fellow cast member, and they hatched the idea for *Gavin and Stacey*.

The show started life on the digital channel BBC Three and became a word-of-mouth hit, spawning catchphrases ("What's occurring?") and internet fansites galore. By series two, ratings had quadrupled to two million.

Realising it had a hit, the BBC repeated the show on BBC One. At last year's Baftas it beat *Cranford*, *The Apprentice* and *Strictly Come Dancing* to win Programme of the Year, while Corden was named Best Comedy Performer. The finishing touches are being put to a deal for series three, which will make Corden a rich man.

For the uninitiated, Gavin is a boy from Billericay in Essex and Stacey a girl from Barry Island in south Wales who fall in love over the phone and marry after a whirlwind courtship. The leads are played by Mathew Horne and Joanna Page, but the real stars – and the ones with the funniest lines – are their respective best friends, Smithy (Corden) and Nessa (Jones). The supporting cast includes Alison Steadman, Julia Davis and Rob Brydon.

Nothing much happens in *Gavin and Stacey* and that's the point. "It's all about finding the extraordinary in the ordinary," Corden has said.

On the surface, the plots are so conventional that they bring to mind *Terry and June* or *The Good Life*. But the delight is in the detail: in what other show could the two perfectly harmless families be named the Shipmans and the Wests?

In a year that proved a tipping point for crude comedy – think Jonathan Ross, Russell Brand and the vulgarity of *Little Britain USA*, which appalled even the most hardened critics – the BBC found that what viewers really wanted was something more gentle and warm-hearted about old-fashioned values such as love, family and friendship.

> *It feels as though people are asking me why I think I'm attractive. No one asks Brad Pitt that*

After throwing money at big-name stars only to see them sully the BBC's reputation, there is no small irony in this low-budget and most understated of shows (it is filmed in a real terraced house on a Barry Island backstreet) becoming the success story of the year.

Perhaps the only person not taken aback by the popularity of the programme is Corden himself. By his own account, he was "the cockiest child" in class and that self-assurance has carried through to adulthood.

Raised in Hazlemere, near High Wycombe, Bucks, Corden is the son of a social worker mother and a musician father who was a stretcher-bearer in the first Gulf War and now has a second career as a Christian bookseller. A born performer, Corden sang at family get-togethers, played the cornet in the Salvation Army band and eagerly signed up with a local drama school.

His career as a child actor was a failure, but he was undeterred. "I never worked at all, I don't know why. I think it was the best thing that could have happened to me because it taught me about rejection from a really early age."

He eventually landed a role, aged 17, in a West End production of *Martin Guerre*, but found it boring and walked out. "You've got to have a ridiculous ego to be 17, on your first job, thinking, 'What's this – why am I just stood at the back?'" he admits.

At 19, he made his film debut in the Shane Meadows film *Twenty Four Seven*, followed by television appearances in *Teachers*, *Dalziel and Pascoe* and an ill-fated stint in teen soap *Hollyoaks* ("I'd actually rather die than go back ... all these people walking around with this chicken-in-a-basket fame, talking about going to LA").

He proved his serious acting chops in Mike Leigh's *All Or Nothing* before coming to national prominence in Alan Bennett's *The History Boys*, first on stage and then in the 2006 film version. Bennett told Corden he had a talent for making people laugh, and should try his hand at writing.

With the popularity of *Gavin and Stacey* comes a celebrity lifestyle and Corden is regularly pictured out on the tiles with a succession of pretty girls on his arm. He admits that stardom went to his head for a time, prompting his co-star Brydon to give him a pep talk on the perils of believing his own hype.

"I think I started to believe I was a bit more of a dude than I really was," he says now. Those who know him well say there is an element of bravado to his persona but that he is a kind, thoughtful type. Family remains the most important thing in his life. Despite having the money to afford a luxury London pad, he still lives near his parents in High Wycombe.

That self-confidence never wavers though. The one thing that angers him is the suggestion that he is an "unlikely" sex symbol. In every interview, he is asked what makes him so irresistible to women. He is genuinely affronted: "It's odd because it feels like people are asking me why I think I'm attractive. No-one is asking Brad Pitt that question."

CV

Name: James Corden

Born: Aug 18, 1978

Education: Holmer Green Senior School and Jackie Palmer Stage School, High Wycombe, Bucks

Television career: *Fat Friends*, *Hollyoaks*, *Teachers*, *Gavin and Stacey*

Most famous creation: Smithy in *Gavin and Stacey*

Famous fans: Noel Gallagher, Rio Ferdinand, Jackie Collins

Forthcoming projects: *Gavin and Stacey* series three, BBC sketch show, film about lesbian vampires living in Wales

Romantic history: Previous relationship with actress Sheridan Smith. Regularly spotted in the company of beautiful women, including Lily Allen, Alexandra Burke, Leona Lewis, Alesha Dixon and Agyness Deyn.

January 2009.
Build 'em up.

Catch a falling star

How can Mathew Horne and James Corden recover their nosediving careers? **Mark Lawson** has some suggestions

From toast-of-the-town to toast ... Mathew Horne and James Corden on stage at the Royal Albert Hall last weekend

PHOTOGRAPH JO HALE/GETTY IMAGES

There is a convention in showbusiness journalism that says acts who are performing for charity are treated more kindly than if they were performing for profit: even Jonathan Ross's most severe critics were relatively generous about his recent fronting of Comic Relief. But this rule seems to have been suspended for James Corden and Mathew Horne, who have received a string of stinkers (including a one-star review in yesterday's Guardian) for the sketches they performed at the Royal Albert Hall in aid of the Teenage Cancer Trust.

This week's reviews are the latest instalment in one of the steepest and quickest falls from grace in showbiz history. Until a few months ago, the biggest problems the 30-year-old friends had was finding a shelf big enough to hold the awards for their sitcom, Gavin & Stacey. Since then, they have followed a universally slated movie, Lesbian Vampire Killers, with a generally hated TV sketch show, flopped as presenters at the Brits in February, and now can't even get a laugh for sick children.

The causes of this fall are the most familiar snakes on the ladder: overexposure and overconfidence. Performers, knowing that careers can be brief, seize work when it's there, but Corden and Horne have made the mistake of moving too far from the circumstances of their breakthrough work. In Gavin & Stacey they performed words written by Corden with Ruth Jones; for their BBC3 sketches, Jones was replaced by Horne, while their film was scripted by two inexperienced writers, Paul Hupfield and Stewart Williams. The moral seems to be that they need Jones.

Another factor in the backlash is clearly a perception that Corden, in particular, has not taken well to sudden celebrity. Accepting the second of two Baftas for Gavin & Stacey on the same night last year, he seemed to express resentment at not also having been considered in a third category. The actor has since tried to explain that he was wryly commenting on the illogicality of prize ceremonies; nonetheless he created an impression of arrogance, for which some of his bad press is a punishment.

At least the pair have the comfort of knowing that other comedians have gone from toast-of-the-town to toast and recovered. Ricky Gervais was written off by many critics after a bad Live Earth charity gig, but went on to make a hit movie, Ghost Town.

So how might Horne and Corden recover? The first strategy a Max Clifford might suggest - doing something for charity, possibly involving kids with cancer - has already failed. Another tactic often recommended to public figures in trouble, a spell of quiet isolation, is risky for showbiz casualties: absence from the headlines is a mark of disaster.

The best approach for them is the mantra often quoted by businesses: maximise your assets. In their case, this would mean concentrating on Gavin & Stacey: creating another series and a couple of specials so impeccable that these recent blips will be bracketed by new awards. Of course, this creates its own problems by inviting critics to conclude that the project that made them famous is the only thing they can do well (see the eagerness of Sacha Baron Cohen and Steve Coogan to escape from Ali G and Alan Partridge). Also, the revisionism the duo has suffered has been so severe that the reviews for series three of Gavin & Stacey wouldn't fail to point out that this hit had been overvalued.

What would a spin doctor advise? That they should seek their salvation through theatre. Although many of Corden's fans think his career began in TV, he had achieved substantial theatrical success, in particular in Alan Bennett's The History Boys. Horne has also recently pleased large audiences (and some reviewers) in a London revival of Joe Orton's Entertaining Mr Sloane. The smart move might be pairing them under a strong director with a script of proven quality. When I interviewed them recently, they expressed an interest in Tom Stoppard's Rosencrantz and Guildenstern Are Dead, which would suit a physically and vocally contrasting double act.

As it happens, that play contains a scene in which an actor outlines his company's recent projects. "Is that what people want?" he is asked. "It's what we do," he replies. For Corden and Horne, that answer may no longer be an option. They badly need to start doing something that people like

April 2009.
And knock 'em down!

Smithy and the England team.

David and I. Putting towels on our heads was his idea.

Sport Relief 2010
Smithy giving his speech.

Jenson and I didn't actually know we were being photographed at this moment.

Me with Andy Murray and the great Ben Winston.

On the high board with Tom Daley. Tom's the one on the left.

(*Facing page*) 2010 was a busy year to say the least.

Fulfilling my childhood dream of actually being Gary Barlow!

Smithy with George Michael and Sir Paul. Two of my heroes and I'm hugging them both a bit too tight.

Jules tucking into the best steak she's ever had on the first of many nights in.

Me and Jules in the Maldives, jumping into the rest of our lives!

My loving sisters, and my best friends. I'd have been lost without them.
Me and my Bubba. She is the best person I've ever met.

There was a scene in French where I pretended to be a prostitute and I had a line that always got a really big laugh. I'd say the line, look at Dominic and then look away; it was the way I looked away that got the laugh. So, on this particular Sunday afternoon, I could see Steve Martin watching from an aisle seat close to the stage. I gave the line, looked at Dominic and then looked away. The laugh came as it always did – it was a big one that day – and, very deliberately, and totally unprofessionally, I looked straight to where Steve Martin was laughing his socks off and gave him the biggest grin. I mean, come on, I just made Steve Martin laugh and he'd been doing that to me all my life.

The play went on to win six Tony Awards in the United States, more than any play had ever won until then. That whole time in New York was magical; I just loved being there. Six incredible months living in an uptown apartment with Russell next door and Central Park just over the road. My apartment was on West Seventy-Fifth and Central Park West, number 7½, on the third floor. It wasn't particularly big or nicely kitted out or anything, but it just felt like a real Manhattan apartment: from the tiling in the bathroom to the sort of half-bath and the a/c unit fixed in the window. Being neighbours, Russell and I became very close. On matinee days, we'd walk the thirty-odd blocks to the theatre and afterwards the eight of us boys would go for a drink somewhere. We'd sit down and, before we could order, the waiter would bring a tray of drinks that somebody had already bought for us. It was nuts. A fan site started up on the internet and every time we'd finish a show, there would be more and more people crowding around the stage door. It was my first real taste of fame, and being someone who likes a spot of attention (check out the title), I revelled in it. It wasn't just the attention though. Living for six months in a city like New York, away from my family and friends back home, gave me a sense of freedom and possibility that I'd never really had before.

As the months rolled by, I found myself thinking more and more about that last episode of *Gavin & Stacey*. Ruth and I still hadn't finished it, and we didn't want to keep the BBC waiting any longer than they had to. We were always chatting on the phone, discussing it with each other, but we both knew we needed to be in the same room together to get it done. Ruth had some time in between TV stuff, so I suggested she come out and stay with me to finish it off, which she did.

We had five days to complete that last episode and, just as we had done back home, we'd sit in my apartment and start riffing, improvising and getting into character. We'd write all day, then I'd go and do the show; when I got back, we'd plough on into the night. It was hard, energy-sapping work and I was nowhere near getting enough sleep. To compensate I started taking a sneaky little nap at work.

There was around a thirty-minute gap between the last scene of Act One and the second scene of Act Two, where I wasn't on stage at all, and I used it to catch up on all the sleep I was missing out on. Normally, I'd have been watching that final scene of Act One from the wings because it was my favourite of the whole play. It's a really poignant moment where 'Drummer Hodge', a poem by Thomas Hardy, is being discussed by Richard Griffiths's Hector and Sam Barnett's Posner. Hector is talking about writing; how there are times when you think you might be the only person ever to have experienced a particular kind of emotion, only to discover it had been written down, word for word, by someone long ago. Someone you don't know, even long dead, had experienced every single feeling you were going through and, in writing it down, had reached out across time to clasp your hand in theirs.

It's one of the play's most moving moments but, when Ruth was in town, I was so tired that I'd roll up my blazer to use as a pillow, lie down, close my eyes and nap right through it. Act Two started with this loud burst of music so I wasn't afraid of not waking up, and there'd be enough time before I was on stage to get my head back in the game.

But this one Thursday matinee it didn't quite pan out as I'd hoped. I was so far gone that I slept right through the music. I woke up to hear someone else speaking my lines. I'd missed my cue. Worse than that, I'd missed the entire scene. What a dick! I felt horrible, like I'd let everyone down. There was nothing I could do but wait in the wings until I could apologise to Richard. Earlier I told you he'd played Uncle Monty in *Withnail and I*, one of my favourite films. I'd never stop asking him questions about it: what it was like filming it, who he'd based his character on – anything you can think of. When I went up to him at the end of the scene, full of apologies, he just put his hands on my shoulders and studied me for a long moment. Then, in his best Uncle Monty, he said, 'I'm preparing myself to forgive you, boy. I'm preparing myself to forgive you.' After that, I kept the sleeping to my bed.

Ruth and I were halfway through the week and making great progress with that final episode, but it was hot in New York that summer, so we ended up writing a fair bit over the road in Central Park. Together we would sit on a bench with Ruth's laptop, do some people-watching and get the last bit down. That's where we wrote the wedding scene in which Uncle Bryn gives Stacey a letter her dad had written just days before he died. It's one of the scenes I'm most proud of.

At the end of that writing week, Ruth flew back to the UK, but we stayed in constant touch. We'd call each other or text back and forth, but either way, because there was still so much we needed to be on top of, we'd always get back to each other right away. One day, however, I got one of Ruth's texts as I was carrying my shopping up the stairs, so I couldn't reply. By the time I'd got inside and packed it away, I'd forgotten all about the message. It was the first time I hadn't replied immediately, which obviously spooked Ruth, so when I woke the next morning there was another text asking me if I was all right. I smelt an opportunity.

I texted back, 'Actually, Ruth, I'm not.'

'Why? What's up?' was her reply.

'There's no easy way for me to tell you this and I can't believe I'm writing it, but two days ago I was involved in an accident at work. I've lost my hand.'

I even went to the effort of using my left hand to write the text. It's all about authenticity. I know, I know. It was mean and silly and poor Ruth must have been going totally mad with worry. She was. Another text popped up on my phone: 'Please, James, tell me you're joking.'

I wrote back, 'I'll call you in five minutes.'

Five minutes ticked by, six, seven maybe. Then I called her. She answered before the phone had rung twice.

'James . . .' she said, her voice hollow, frightened.

'Hi.' My own voice was so solemn it was all but cracking.

'Oh my God,' she said, and at that moment I knew she really believed me. 'James, what on earth happened?'

I couldn't string this out any longer, it would just be too mean, so I burst out laughing instead. Ruth got the joke – only just – and told me that when she'd read the text, she'd run upstairs to her husband, David, and they'd both started praying, which made me feel like a right spanner. She was imagining herself having arguments with the BBC about the show: 'Well, why can't Smithy just have one hand? So he's disabled, so what? What do you mean? *No.* That's just discrimination.'

Ruth says that I have a childlike streak in my personality that means that I'm in constant need of entertainment. And so, if nothing fun is happening, then I'll make something happen myself. I'm not exactly sure why, and I hope I've calmed down a bit now.

After six months in New York, and a one-month extension

to the run, the play was finally coming to a close. What we hadn't realised was that *The History Boys* film was coming out on the day we got back to London. There was going to be a royal premiere and we were flying out literally after the curtain came down on our last show. It was an incredible way to end the run on Broadway. The rush was perfect too. If we'd had time to sit there thinking about it and discussing it, we'd probably never have left the theatre. We'd been together off and on for so long it was agonising to think it was almost over.

Our bags were packed, we'd checked out of the apartments, and our dressing rooms had been cleared of all the bits and pieces we'd acquired over the last months: the good-luck cards, the photos, all the other mementoes. Walking in there for the last time, it felt completely alien, as if we'd never even been there in the first place.

We were determined to make that last show the best we'd ever done. And it was a very special night. We were sure that most of the audience had seen the play at least once before, but just wanted to be there for the very last performance. Their energy and laughter and sheer positivity were totally infectious and pushed our performances up one more notch.

The last scene, after Hector is killed, the boys all sit at the front of the stage and sing 'Bye, Bye, Blackbird' and if you've seen the play or watched the film, you'll know that Frances de la Tour's character explains what happens to the boys after going to university. One of us is a journalist; another is a property developer; my character owns a chain of dry cleaners and takes drugs on the weekend. Finally, as she gets to Posner, Richard's character appears at the back of the stage. 'Pass it on, boys,' he says, 'pass it on.'

That Sunday, that last ever performance, the last time he spoke those words, Richard's voice cracked. This was an actor who had been on stages all around the world, yet he was so moved his voice just started to go. *Pass it on, boys.* That line, and specifically that moment, just seemed to capture the spirit of the whole production, and an incredibly special time in our lives. This wonderful, momentous, brilliant play, which had taken us all on such a journey, was finally coming to a close.

When the lights came up, Russell was the first to go. He started crying and then we all started crying. We did the curtain calls, three or four of them, but the audience just refused to leave. The house lights came up and they were still out there, screaming for more. The stage manager told us that we couldn't leave them like that and had to go out again, so we sort of ambled back on stage. We didn't bow, we just stood there taking it all in. Everyone was on their feet. Most of us were in bits; I know I was a total mess.

Then Richard, ever the professional, stepped forward, put his hand up and eventually the audience quietened down. 'Thank you,' he said. 'Thank you so much for having us in your incredible city. We've been blessed to be part of this play, and to do it in your city has been amazing. Thank you for taking us to your hearts. We have to go and get a plane now. We have to be back in London for the premiere of our film. Thank you, New York. Thank you.'

Zammo did a back flip. I ripped off my tie and, like a pop star, jumped down into the aisle, where I gave it to a girl who must've come to see us at least fifty times. Sacha was running up and down like a crazy person high-fiving everyone, and by the time we finally pulled ourselves away, we were all so overcome with emotion, we could barely see straight. I'm never going to forget that night; thinking about it still gives me goose pimples.

It was time to go home, so we grabbed our bags and bundled into cabs to JFK. We'd flown in from Sydney in economy, but we were flying out first class, courtesy of the film's distributor, 20th Century Fox.

I was sitting next to Sam, sipping on a tasty rum cocktail. 'Sam,' I said, 'I've got a question for you. I wanted to know, what do you think the difference is between film and theatre then?'

'I don't know,' he said. 'I have no idea at all.' And with that he pressed a button and disappeared from view as his seat turned into a bed.

CHAPTER 18

BEST MUSICAL ACCOMPANIMENT:
'When You Wasn't Famous' by the Streets

BEST FILM TO WATCH ALONGSIDE:
Notting Hill

BEST ENJOYED WITH:
cocktails

We touched down in London and were driven straight to the Dorchester Hotel, where we caught up on a little sleep for an hour or two. Then we slipped into the Giorgio Armani suits that had been made specially and out to where a pair of limos were waiting to take us off to Leicester Square. Less than twenty-four hours previously we'd performed for the last time on Broadway, and now we were on our way to meet Prince Charles. This was totally ridiculous.

As the *Gavin & Stacey* scripts had developed, I'd asked a few of the boys to play various parts in the show. At the premiere we did that thing where you line up and Prince Charles walks along, being introduced one by one, shaking hands and asking questions. He asked Zammo what he was up to next, and Zammo told him that he was going to be in my TV show. So, when the prince got to me, he said he'd heard I was making a programme set in Wales.

'That's right, sir,' I said. 'We've not cast all the parts yet so there's a part for you if you want it. We'd love you to join us if you're available.'

'Really?' he said. 'Well, if this job ever goes wrong, it's good to know there's something to fall back on.' I liked him, and Camilla. I told her that the dress she was wearing was a triumph and she seemed to like that.

We watched the film and then headed off to the after-show party, which turned into this wonderful reunion with all our families and friends. Most of us hadn't seen our families since opening night in New York, so this was our first opportunity to properly catch up. It felt so good to be home. We felt like heroes. Looking back now, I realise that that night was the last time we were all together in the same room. There've been various points where all but one or two of us have been together, but since that night, it's never been all eight of us. *The History Boys* was such an unforgettable, magnificent and life-changing journey that we all now have a romantic attachment to the National Theatre, and to each other. There's an unspoken understanding between us that I hope will never leave.

With the film now out, work-wise I was concentrating all my energies on *Gavin & Stacey*. While I'd been in New York, Ruth and Henry had been sending over casting tapes of various people to start filling the roles. As soon as I saw their tapes, I knew that Mat Horne and Joanna Page would be perfect as Gavin and Stacey. Ruth had phoned to tell me about Christine Gernon, who she thought would be good as our potential director; the two of them had worked together before and Henry was also keen, but they both wanted me to meet her before we firmed it all up. So while I was in New York, I'd caught a night flight one Sunday that got me to London on Monday morning to grab an hour or two with Christine. She was great, really enthusiastic and full of ideas about how she saw the show and how she'd like to shoot it, all of which I agreed with. We offered her the job there and then, and then I went straight to the airport and back to New York. I didn't even have time to go home. With Christine on board, she and Ruth continued to send over DVDs of people they liked, and that's basically how we cast the show.

We cast Larry Lamb as Gavin's dad. Alison Steadman had agreed to play Pam, Gavin's mum, which we were over the moon about. Alison playing that part was all we'd ever wanted. We'd already worked out that Ruth was Nessa, I was Smithy, and we got Rob Brydon to complete the set as Stacey's Uncle Bryn.

A couple of weeks after the premiere, we organised a read-through of series one with all the cast. It's still one of the best I've ever been to. I am, of course, incredibly biased, but it was a magical day, particularly for Ruth and me. To hear those words we'd so lovingly laboured over for so long being read aloud was a big moment for the two of us. People at the BBC told us afterwards that they were taken aback by the laughter in the room, that the way all the personalities had just clicked was incredible – and pretty unusual. Ruth and I kept glancing at each other, mouths open, neither of us quite believing that it was actually going so well. There were all kinds of indicators and little moments to let us know we were on the right path, jokes that we'd thought might be a touch subtle, but which worked in the room. For example, someone asked Smithy, who's in his mid-twenties at this point, where his girlfriend was. 'Doing her Duke of Edinburgh,' is his reply. As the series plays out we find out Lucy is young, we just never know quite how young, but the joke got the laugh and on it went from there.

The read-through honestly couldn't have gone any better; more or less as soon as it was over, we all went off to Cardiff to begin shooting. So I'd barely been back a couple of weeks – one of them spent travelling all over the country promoting *The History Boys* film – and I was already leaving again to go off working. Eventually, it took its toll on my and Shelley's relationship.

To this day that break-up with Shelley makes me feel so sad. Since I'd got home it had become clear that the relationship had nowhere else to go. There's no question it was absolutely the right thing to do, but that didn't change how difficult or painful it was. We'd been together since we were eighteen. I was twenty-seven now and the emptiness I felt after she was gone was just awful. Break-ups are never good, no matter how amicable they're supposed to be, and ours dragged on a little, which it shouldn't have done. To be honest, I was so busy that it wasn't for quite some time afterwards that I actually grieved for what had happened to us. I threw myself into work and it became my entire focus. All I can say is, Shelley, if you're reading this, I'd like to take this moment to say thank you. Thank you for being the first person I ever loved and the first person to love me. You are one of the best people I've ever known. Your love, support, friendship and care have in no small way shaped the man I am today. I'm sorry if it ever felt like I didn't miss you. I did, though it hit me later. I'm sorry if there were times I wasn't a good enough boyfriend, if I put work before you. I have so many fond memories of our time together. You will always have a special place in my heart.

It was such a strange time, with so much going on, and I used all those other distractions to take my mind off what was happening with me and Shelley. And one of those distractions was a new love – come on! I'm not that callous. No, the new object of my affection was a certain man by the name of Mat Horne. Our man-love became so intense so quickly that – I'm not gonna lie to you – it turned into my next big affair. I'd seen him on tape back in New York and then we'd met for the first time at the read-through; after that we had our first phone call, which lasted for an hour. It was a beautiful thing.

Mat and I got each other immediately and, as we got deeper into filming the first series, we became absolutely inseparable. It was ridiculous. I think the entire time we were shooting we were never more than three yards from each other, and by about week four we'd got so close that we were finishing each other's sentences. Prior to *Gavin & Stacey*, Mat had been part of a double act called Mat and MacKinnon, so he was a natural when it came to riffing ideas and scenarios, and as the shoot went on we started doing these little improvised sketches together in our downtime. On more than one occasion, people commented on the chemistry between us, which got us thinking about working together on another project after *Gavin & Stacey*, maybe some kind of sketch show. There were a few out there at the time, plenty of competition, but we both liked the idea. In the meantime, though, filming was going well and we were getting some really good stuff in the can. Within a couple of months the shoot wrapped, we began the edit and, before we knew it, the first show was ready to air.

Our show, the one we'd dreamt up in a hotel bar in Leeds, was about to be broadcast. *Gavin & Stacey* by James Corden and Ruth Jones. There it was, on a black card, with Stephen Fretwell's piano chords playing underneath. I couldn't help but think back to the days and nights I'd sat with Ruth writing the show. The way we'd laugh and get excited at the thought of people maybe seeing something we'd written. I remembered back to that day at the airport in Wellington when Ruth sent me the text, and also how she'd come out to New York and we'd written some of our very best stuff on a bench in Central Park.

It was such a proud moment – probably the proudest I've ever had – sitting with Mum and Dad on Sunday night at our family home in Hazlemere. It felt like my very own opening night. The next day, I got down to the newsagent's first thing to read the reviews: I remember the *Guardian* and the *Daily Telegraph* specifically, but it seemed as if everyone was talking about the show with such affection, and that never really disappeared. In fact, from the moment the first show aired in May 2007, the show just took on a life of its own; the ratings started at 500,000 viewers, and by the time the last episode of the last series went out on New Year's Day 2010, the figures were over 12.5 million. It still takes my breath away that so many people took the show to their hearts.

The people at the BBC were so excited about the show that, before the first episode had gone out, they'd commissioned a second series. I was staggered that they could have that kind of faith, but they did, and so, weirdly, Ruth and I ended up writing the second series while the first one was still being shown on TV. In some ways, that was actually quite difficult. It's very hard to emulate success, especially when that success is happening at the same time as you're trying to emulate it. It wasn't a position either of us had been in before. When we'd written the first series, there had been no comparisons and nobody was telling us how good we were. This time round, the pressure was really on.

We were determined to get the second series right. We wanted to use all the positivity the first series was enjoying to help us write the best second series we could. So, every Tuesday we'd nip down to the shops, buy a copy of the *Radio Times* and read the review about the previous week's show. Jack Searle, the reviewer, was a big fan, and each week he'd tell his readers to make sure they caught it. The plan kind of backfired. As lovely as it was to read all the nice things Jack wrote, it made the prospect of writing the second series doubly scary: not only did we have to repeat what we'd done, we wanted to do better.

Gavin & Stacey seemed to be growing into something special; the characters had struck a real chord with lots of people, so Ruth and I didn't want to disappoint anyone who'd taken the show to their heart. With all those thoughts whirling around my head, all that pressure Ruth and I were putting on ourselves and each other, writing that second series was bloody difficult. I'd drive down to Cardiff and we'd sit for five or six hours at a time, trying things out but often coming up empty. Writer's block: up until that point I hadn't believed it really existed, but I became pretty familiar with it during that time.

On the other hand, everything else seemed to be going along well. My love affair with Mat was in full swing and rarely a day would pass when we didn't speak or text each other. And, alongside the man-love, I was about to fall for a new girl I'd met while filming *Fat Friends* a few years back, an actress called Sheridan Smith. She had been in *The Royle Family* and *Two Pints of Lager and a Packet of Crisps* as well as loads of other things. She is an incredible actress. Unbelievably talented. Funny, and absolutely intoxicating to be around. It would be wrong and distasteful to go into detail about our relationship – some things have to remain private. All I can tell you is I loved her more than I ever knew was possible. I was head over heels in love with her and, for the next two years, on and off, off and on, we were together.

With the first series doing well, more auditions started rolling in and Mat and I both found ourselves up for a British film called *Lesbian Vampire Killers* (of which more later). I don't think either of us could believe that we were being considered for the two leads in a film. I thought back to how I'd felt when Andy, Russell and I had all been given scripts for that Thai kidnap movie and I'd been asked to audition for the newsagent. Suddenly, from being the guy to ring up twenty Bensons and a scratchy, I was being considered for leads in films.

It was such a strange time for me. Professionally, it couldn't have been better and yet personally, I was starting to feel quite lost. My relationship with Sheridan was either up or down – true love or the deepest heartbreak – and so I lost that stability that I'd known for most of my life. Everything that I knew, everything that was familiar, seemed as if it was drifting away. I know, I know, you're going to tell me you hear this kind of thing from people in books all the time, but it's the truth when I tell you that the next couple of years all went by in a bit of a blur. So many things changed so quickly. I was up. I was down. I was up again. *Gavin & Stacey* was swiftly becoming the kind of success Ruth and I could only have dreamt of, but the reality is, I don't remember a lot about it. It sounds crazy, but sitting here now,

I find it hard to remember exactly what happened, when and where.

By the time Ruth and I were writing the second series, in the summer of 2007, Shelley had long since moved out of the flat in Beaconsfield. Since the day she left, the place had a lingering air of emptiness: the shelves were half-empty, the drawers half-full; the home that we'd worked so hard to create together had lost its heart. For some time, I'd been on and off and on again with Sheridan. When we were on, we spent a lot of time together in London, and when we were off, I had no desire to be on my own in Beaconsfield, so I'd crash wherever I could.

Dominic Cooper had recently broken up with his girlfriend, and so we spent a lot of time together. I don't think Dom felt as lost as I did, but he was still going through a little heartache and we clung to each other like a couple of lost boys. He had moved out of his girlfriend's place and was living in a self-contained studio at the top of Nick Hytner's house. As for me, my car boot was always full of clothes because I never knew where I was going to end up. I'd either stay with Dom or I'd wind up in beds I'd never slept in before, with girls I'd never met before. I was single at the time, so I wasn't doing anything outrageous, but I'd never been a womaniser, and the longer it went on, the emptier my soul felt.

I remember one morning specifically. I'd done a shoot for *Heat* magazine wearing only my underpants. It was a laugh, a mock-up of the famous Armani David Beckham photo shoot. Well, that night I went to a party thrown by Tom Vaughan, who had directed *Starter for Ten*. He had a new film opening and he'd invited Dom and me along to watch the premiere and, of course, we were well up for it. The great thing about my relationship with Dom is that at various times in our lives, we've known exactly what each other have been going through and been able to lean on each other for support. That night was about us forgetting all the crap and going out for a big night. I remember getting steadily pissed during the premiere itself as Dom and I sat there putting away a bottle of wine. Afterwards we went to the party and drank plenty more and when that wrapped up, we headed for Soho and the Groucho Club.

By now, the Groucho had become pretty familiar to me. From meeting Kay Mellor there to talk about *Fat Friends* a few years back, it had become one of the places where I spent a fair number of nights out. That night (as with a few nights like it), I don't remember what happened after I got there. I don't remember getting there, drinking there or parting company with Dom, but I definitely do remember waking up the next morning completely naked, in a strange flat, without a clue as to the name of the girl I was lying beside, or where the hell I was. What I did know, however, was that I had a day of radio interviews lined up with Mat Horne and I was already an hour late.

The girl lying in bed next to me was still fast asleep, so I crept out of the room and got dressed in the hallway. I walked down the stairs and standing right there in front of me in the kitchen were two girls holding the *Heat* magazine centrefold. I had no idea what their names were either. (I didn't even remember getting back to this flat, so names were unlikely.) They asked me if I was OK and I said I was fine, but that I had to leave as I was already late for something. As I was walking out, one of the girls pointed to the magazine picture and commented on the size of the bulge in my pants. 'It's mostly all balls,' I said as I left and went downstairs.

Outside, I looked around a bit but realised I had no idea where I was, so I went back to the flat and knocked on the door (which hurt a lot because that had been a great line to leave on). One of the girls opened up. 'You're back,' she said. 'Are you all right?'

'Yeah, I'm fine,' I said. 'I just wanted to ask you where I am.'

She looked at me as if I'd grown another head. 'You're in London.'

'Yeah, I know that, but what part of London?'

'Oh,' she said. 'Chelsea.'

Chelsea, right. I'd never been to Chelsea before. Here I was, walking down the King's Road in last night's clothes, searching for a cash machine so that I could get a cab to where these interviews were taking place. I was an hour late and I stank of booze. Scrubbing up good.

I guess it would have been all right if it was just a one-off, but it wasn't; this was happening a lot. Most nights I'd be out on the town somewhere, getting drunk, hanging out with different people who seemed to like me. And I still didn't really have anywhere to stay. The last train to Beaconsfield was at midnight or it was £80 in a cab so, instead of trying to get home, I started staying at the Soho Hotel. I would literally check out every day and tell myself I would go home that night, but then inevitably I'd be back there checking in at 4 a.m., needing to sleep before another day's work and another day's hangover. I'd buy clean pants and socks every day. That was how things were for a time.

Success can be giddying, if you know what I mean. I was a young guy, in the public eye for the first time, and I no longer had the stability of a settled home life as back-up. And in terms of the show, the good news just kept on coming. It had been nominated for seven different British comedy awards, which was not only a record, it also added more media interest about the people in it. In the end we won three of the seven: Best New Comedy for the show, and both Ruth and I won Best Newcomer. We were named the Writers' Guild of Great Britain's Comedy Writers of the Year. The Critics' Choice, *The South Bank Show* Award for Comedy. The plaudits and praise just kept rolling in. Ruth took it all in her stride. She enjoyed it and found the fun in it. I, too, relished it. But the difference was, I started to believe the hype.

I began this book by telling you that my family is due home in a couple of days, and I guess it's from that perspective that

I'm looking back on the guy I was then. I'm a dad now, with all the responsibilities that suggests. I'm in the relationship I always dreamt I would be in. I'm calm and comfortable and very, very happy. Back then, though, I was anything but. I was floundering. I'm not saying I regret all the experiences I had because I don't. I definitely regret certain things I said and did, but it was a wild time – and there was nothing more wild (or totally confusing) than the couple of months I spent sort of hanging out with Lily Allen.

I first met Lily at the premiere of *The History Boys* film back in 2006 and immediately thought she was great. She's confident, funny and fiercely intelligent. We got talking at the party after the film and she asked me for my phone number. On one hand, this was very cool, but on the other, just a little embarrassing, as I was standing next to Shelley at the time. Anyway, we hadn't really seen each other since that evening, and then I got a call asking if I'd go on her chat show.

The second series of *Gavin & Stacey* was out and they asked me if I wanted to go on and promote it. Did I? Of course I did but, more than that, I wanted to see Lily. The attention and awards and everything else that was going on in my head had convinced me that I could pretty much have any woman I wanted. I know. I can't even believe I'm typing that myself. It's so ridiculous for any man to think that, let alone me.

A couple of days before the interview I did a pre-chat on the phone with a researcher and told him about the time I'd first met Lily and that she'd asked for my phone number. He told me that Lily had told him that too. ERM, WHAT? Lily was walking around the office telling everyone that she'd wanted my number? I was amazed she even remembered. I immediately started to build this whole thing up in my head, even more so when the researcher told me that one of the ideas they'd had for my appearance was a game where they tried to find out how compatible Lily and I would be.

'Compatible? As in a relationship?' I asked the researcher.

'Yeah!' he replied excitedly.

Well, given where I was at the time, with my ego starting to spiral out of control, a broken heart trying to nurse itself with empty one-night stands and a complete lack of understanding of my position in the world, this was right up my street. I made it my aim to make Lily mine.

It was a BBC3 show and a pretty crazy affair all round, with a young studio audience and a seventies retro circular bed with cushions, rather than the normal chat show couch. Lily and I were up there together, nestling into the cushions, chatting for a bit about how we'd met at *The History Boys* premiere when she'd been absolutely off her tits. Then she showed a clip of the first series of *Gavin & Stacey*, where Nessa slaps Smithy on the bum, and after that there was another clip showing me snog the face off Daniel Radcliffe at an awards do. Lily commented on how sweetly I kissed Daniel, and that, right there, is when I went for it. Resting on one elbow in the cushions, I looked into her eyes and said, 'That's just what happens when you kiss me.' She giggled. 'Are you all right?' I added softly as she fell about. 'Difficult to hold it together, isn't it?' Lily was laughing and I got the impression that she was flirting back, but I wasn't finished yet. 'Your dress is a triumph,' I told her, my gaze fixed on hers now. 'D'you want to know the truth?' I said. 'I don't think you know how lovely you are.'

That last line drew a massive 'Aaahhh' from the audience. They seemed to be getting into this as much as I was. 'Let me tell you this,' I said, 'and you can cut it out of the show if you want, but on my life, truly, without irony or agenda' – yeah, right – 'I don't think you know how lovely you are.' Lily was doe-eyed at this point. 'You know,' I told her, 'you could do with someone to tell you how lovely you are every day.' She kept staring into my eyes as I drowned in the applause. 'Ignore all those people,' I told her. 'I mean, I don't know you, but—'

'Oh, just fuck me,' she cut in.

OK!

I'd never flirted with anyone quite so blatantly and definitely never so publicly. It was electric, it was brilliant and it was all on TV. I would never dream of doing it now, but back then, in the state of mind I was in, it seemed the most natural thing in the world. When the show was over, I asked Lily if she wanted to go for a drink. She said she'd love to but she had somewhere else she had to be. So I left on my own, still buzzing, and instead of heading out to some club or bar like I normally would, I finally went back to Beaconsfield. I felt at that moment that I wanted to be at home. As it turned out, on my way back I got a text from Lily thanking me for coming on the show and saying that she'd love to see me soon. Wow. I thought about her all the way home, and when I woke up the next day she was the first thing in my head. Was what happened real? Could it ever be real, or was it just some TV show? I thought, whatever that had been, the best way to make it real would be to impress her. I couldn't just leave this up to fate. I had to act now.

In her dressing room before the show we'd chatted about life and the jobs we used to do and Lily had told me she'd done some work experience once where basically her only task had been to laminate stuff; she'd loved it. She said that now she was doing other stuff, she missed the laminating; she'd found it therapeutic. (If you have never laminated anything, I would wholeheartedly recommend it.) The laminating was my 'in'. I rang up a mutual friend, who gave me the address of Lily's mum's house, which was where she was staying at the time. I had an idea of how I was going to surprise her – it involved buying her a laminator. And I mean the greatest laminator money could buy, all the equipment and some laminating sheets and every-thing else. I wrote a note and I dropped it round to the house.

Later that day I got a text from Lily telling me that she loved it and it was so cool of me to have thought of it. I was beside myself. I knew she'd just come out of a really serious relationship and I'd been hurting like you wouldn't believe over Sheridan, but none of that mattered then. I was like a lovesick teenager. Looking back, I reckon we were both just having a good time, enjoying the fact that we could flirt with each other and not worry about the consequences. But I wasn't thinking that clearly then. Not even close. I'd already convinced myself that we were meant to be together.

I really wanted to date her, of course I did. Who in my position would not want to date Lily Allen? Phase 1 of my plan had been to deliver the laminator. Phase 1 was complete. Phase 2 was waiting for Lily to phone and ask me out. Phase 2 was not complete. I remember walking around with my tummy in knots, checking my phone every other minute for a missed call or another text, until, a few days later, Phase 2 finally kicked into gear. Lily phoned and asked what I was doing the following night.

'Er, not much actually,' I said about as nonchalantly as I could while trying to figure out how I could cancel the thing I'd arranged to do.

'Listen,' she said, 'I'm going to the Teenage Cancer Trust comedy gig at the Albert Hall and I was wondering if you fancied coming with me.'

'Yeah, cool. Why not? That would be great,' I said breezily, trying to sound like I was down with the kids.

'OK then, let's meet in the Groucho Club and we'll take my car.'

I rang Mat Horne; I rang Dominic; I rang just about everyone I could think of to tell them I had a date with Lily Allen. I've never been known for my subtlety.

So the next night there I was sitting in the Groucho Club, waiting for Lily Allen to show up to our date. Finally she walked in, sporting a new blonde hairstyle that really suited her. I stood up and was about to greet her with a hug when I noticed someone quite familiar over her shoulder. It was her assistant. That's a bit weird, I thought to myself, bringing your assistant on a date. But then again, maybe she was just dropping Lily off, or meeting friends of her own here and was gonna say a quick hello and then go her own way, so that the date could begin.

'Would you like a drink, James?' Lily's assistant asked me.

'Erm, no, I'm good, thanks,' I said, and then turned to speak to Lily. 'So, is it just the three of us, then?'

'No, actually,' she said. 'We have to pick up my friend Miquita on the way.'

So four, then, not three at all. Ah. How could I have got that so wrong? This wasn't really what I had in mind. I mean, I've got a lot of love to give, but I'm only one man and three women . . . Let's not go there. Lily, if you are reading this – that was not what I had in mind at all. I'd actually been thinking you and me, you know, quietly together, yeah? No, let's not go there either. Moving on . . .

We left the Groucho Club and drove across town in Lily's convertible, picking up Miquita on the way. We went to a gig but only stayed until the interval; then Lily asked me if I wanted to make a move. Right, so this was the part of the date where it would just be the two of us. I tried to play it really casually. 'Whatever you want.' Now, maybe that was my mistake right there. And that wasn't the only one. The whole time I was hanging out with Lily, that's how I'd be. I was so desperately trying to look cool that I'd go where she wanted to go, I'd do what she wanted to do, I'd drink what she wanted to drink – anything to please. I'd gone from being this assertive, cocky flirt from the studio couch to what was basically this obedient puppy. She'd ask me a question and I'd always answer with something along the lines of 'Yeah, Lily, sure. Whatever you want.' Not cool. Very not cool.

Anyway, we left the gig and I was still hopeful because it

was just the two of us. I was getting all ready to spend some quality time alone when suddenly, as we were walking back to her car, about twenty paparazzi ran up to us and started taking our pictures. I'd had a bit of experience of this sort of thing, but nothing like this; there were all these guys calling our names, asking us to hold up, snapping away like you see on the telly. Only this was me, and this type of thing didn't normally happen. In the car I told Lily it felt pretty weird, but she just shrugged it off. 'James, it happens all the time,' she said. 'Don't worry, you get used to it.'

Used to it? Did she say I'd get used to it? What did that mean . . . ?

We went to a casino where Lily played roulette while I just watched. After that, we headed back to the after-show party at the gig. The photographers had all followed us to the casino; when we came out, they followed us back to the gig. And I don't mean on foot. As soon as we were in the car, this whole fleet of scooters assembled and started tailing us across London. I have to admit to quite enjoying it at first, though it soon got a little tedious. It's so intoxicating to feel as if you're at the centre of something, that what you do on a night out is suddenly worthy of being news. Basically, there's a lot of attention coming your way – I think we've already established that this is something I've been known to revel in. In just one night, we became one of those 'are they or aren't they?' couples you read about in magazines.

The truth is, I probably went out with Lily four or five times in total, and not once was it actually a proper date. I guess we were friends – like she's friends with lots of guys – although for my part I definitely wanted more than that. I had been so heartbroken that the idea of going out with someone like Lily only made me fancy her more. However, it's for that reason, among others, that I'm sure Lily didn't really have much interest in me. I was nothing like I'd been on the TV show. That was a totally different guy. On the odd occasion when I actually thought there was a possibility of something happening between us, I just turned to jelly.

I remember one night we went to a party and, from there, on to the Groucho. We were sitting having a drink when out of nowhere, she suddenly said, 'Do you want to come back to my house?'

I was so stunned I just stared at her. 'Back to your house, sure, yeah, why not? Whatever you want.'

I nipped to the toilets to try and calm myself down. Here's what was going through my head right then: Well, she has been giving me really flirty eyes and now she's finally asked me back to hers. OK. This is good. I guess ever since we met each other at *The History Boys* thing we've been building to this. Thank God she finally asked me back. I was never gonna ask her back. All right, be cool, be cool. How am I gonna play it when we get back . . .? Oh, man. This is good.

What I didn't know was that while I was thinking about what it might be like when we got back to hers, Lily was inviting about forty other people from the club back to her house for an impromptu party. I didn't even share a cab back with her. No, in my cab was me, Noel Fielding, the legend that is Louis Weymouth and Robbie, the lead singer of a band called the Big Pink. I sat, slightly dejected, as Louis tried to cheer me up with his hilarious stories. When it came to the crunch, there was no relationship. There was no Lily and James. It was all in my head. It didn't matter if the national newspapers were talking about us, the truth is that we never even shared a kiss. I don't think there was ever a time when it was just the two of us alone anywhere, except perhaps the odd moment driving, but that doesn't count.

The last time I went round to her place was when the reality finally dawned on me. That night, it was Lily and me and a couple of her friends and we were sitting around chatting and drinking until, eventually, Lily let out this massive yawn, looked at me and said, 'I think I'm going to go to bed now. What about you?'

My heart stopped. This was it. After all this time, all the false dawns, this was the moment.

So she walked up the stairs with me padding behind, my mouth dry, my stomach churning, my hands sweating: I was all kinds of sexy. Play it cool, I told myself, you can do this. She is just a girl, just a girl. It was all going through my head now: Jesus, did I smell OK? How was my breath? What underpants was I wearing? Were they clean?

Finally, after what seemed an eternity of staircase, we got to the landing. There was a bedroom on our right and Lily pushed open the door. My heart was pounding: it was so loud I could hear nothing else. Slowly, languidly, she turned to me and looked deep into my eyes.

'You can sleep in there,' she said, pointing to the room opposite, and then pecked me on the cheek. 'Night, night.'

And that was it. Off she went into her room. I went into mine and closed the door. Never have I felt like such a douche bag. Who was I trying to kid?

I remember it as if it were yesterday: lying in that strange bed in Lily's house, staring up at the ceiling and realising how badly I'd misread the signs. This was never going to happen. This had been a bit of fun on the TV and that was all. There was no me and Lily – it was all in my mind. I suppose I felt more foolish than gutted. Looking back now, though, I can actually say I'm glad that's all it was. I like Lily very much, she's a friend, and I know that if push came to shove that night, I'd have been awful in bed. I would've been so nervous that nothing – and I do mean nothing – would've happened, so I want to take this moment to say thank you to Lily, for sparing a lovesick fool that kind of embarrassment.

CHAPTER 19

BEST MUSICAL ACCOMPANIMENT:
'Lose Yourself' by Eminem

BEST FILM TO WATCH ALONGSIDE:
8 Mile

BEST ENJOYED WITH:
humble pie

Despite the lack of any real sexual chemistry between Lily and me, all of the newspaper interest had meant that my profile had gone up considerably. I was on the cover of *Esquire* magazine and various newspapers were describing me as the hottest property in television. It was so strange, yet very exciting . . . I'm finding all this stuff hard to write if I'm honest. It was only a few years ago and yet it seems so far away. I can remember the moments from school that I've already written about much more easily than I can recollect this period. I was in a haze, I guess, a whirlwind where everything rushed by me so fast.

Every article that was written seemed to push me further and further away from the person I had always felt I was. I remember Ruth Jones calling me one day and asking if I'd seen that morning's *Daily Mirror*. I hadn't. She suggested I might want to but also warned me to sit down when I did. She was right: it did come as quite a shock to be staring at a double-page spread announcing me as a 'babe magnet'. There was a series of photographs of me with various different women, only one of which I'd had any sort of thing with, but it was making me out to be some kind of love god. It felt as if both tabloid and broadsheet were proclaiming me as a 'hot' thing – in different ways and in different contexts, but 'hot' either way. I have to be honest and say that I found it all. I'd been waiting for so long to be *the* guy, *the* thing, and suddenly it felt as though that was happening.

I was on and off with Sheridan again throughout this time, most of 2008. Each time we got back together the love would be more intense, and then, of course, the break-up would be all the more heartbreaking. When I was single, I would go out all the time. And I mean, all the time. I couldn't really see the point of staying in.

The night that *Gavin & Stacey* won *The South Bank Show* Award for Comedy sticks out in particular. I loved *The South Bank Show*. Every Sunday night, growing up, I would watch it with my family, really enjoying how openly people would talk about the love they had for what they did. I must have watched the episode in which Damon Albarn from Blur goes and looks around his childhood school about twenty times. For whatever reason, it struck a real chord with me.

The ceremony took place on a late January afternoon at the Dorchester Hotel. The awards were, and still very much are, a wonderful thing to attend. It's an amazing buzz to be in a room with a whole mix of people from Tracey Emin to Ken Loach. Art and artists everywhere. Year after year I'd watched the ceremony on TV and seen the likes of *The Office, The Royle Family*, Steve Coogan and *Little Britain* all win the award for comedy. So for us to win and follow in the footsteps of that lot was mind-blowing for me. I celebrated by having a glass of champagne on my own. And when I say a glass, I mean a bottle. And when I say on my own, I mean On My Own. I'd lost Ruth, who I think had gone to the bar with Alison Steadman, and I couldn't get hold of anyone I knew, so I just sort of wandered around the room drinking. I got to speak to Vic Reeves, which was fantastic, and I met Alex Turner from Arctic Monkeys, who was incredibly nice and humble, but sooner or later the realisation hit me that I didn't know any of the people in the room – or any of the people I was climbing into a taxi with later. (I didn't know where we were going either.)

This was not a one-off; it was happening almost every night: parties after parties after after-parties. House parties of people I didn't know; back rooms of pubs and other crappy dives. I wish I could remember more about it so I could better understand why I was behaving like that. Every single one of my dreams was coming true and yet I couldn't have been more miserable. I think most of all I felt lonely, which is why I wanted to surround myself with people, even if I didn't know them at all. In one sense, I must have appeared supremely confident, walking around with my silly swagger and seemingly being in demand, but I was crumbling inside. The woman I thought I loved was with someone else at this point and it was killing me. Everything I did – all the showing off, all the partying and drinking – was just compensation.

They say you should never believe your own publicity, and they, whoever they are, are absolutely right. But the truth is it's really, really hard not to absorb some of it, at least when your picture is being plastered across the covers of major magazines and when everyone and their uncle is lining up to tell you how great you are. I'm sure that if I'd been more grounded and surrounded myself with the people who really cared about me, I might have behaved differently. I'd gone from talking to my dad almost every day to not speaking to him for weeks. I was ignoring the people who had known me growing up, who had been such a huge part of my life before all the fame stuff. I don't know why; I wish I did. It's something that will always confuse me. Why didn't I just stop and look around at what I had and see how lucky I was?

This was the spring of 2008. I was coming up to thirty and

my career was all going as well as I could have hoped. The second series of *Gavin & Stacey* was running and the viewing figures were way better than the first series and steadily growing. I said earlier that a few people had made comments about how well Mat and I bounced off each other on set. Well, after the success of the second series, we began talking with the BBC about the possibility of doing a sketch show. Mat and I were really up for the idea, but on the condition that we'd make a sketch show that our parents wouldn't want to watch. It had to be something for us.

Originally, I thought we should try and make a pilot. We'd not made one for *Gavin & Stacey*, but then Ruth and I had lived with the characters for so long, and we were working with such experienced actors, that it didn't feel as if we needed one. This was different, though: this wasn't a sitcom with a developing story; this was a series of sketches. Time was a big factor, though. Mat and I had both just been offered the leads in *Lesbian Vampire Killers* (which, remember, we'd auditioned for after series one happened) and so we, the BBC and the producers decided to push on without a pilot. So, we had to write and shoot the sketch show, shoot the movie, and Ruth and I had a BBC1 Christmas special of *Gavin & Stacey* to write. The rest of 2008 was shaping up to be plenty busy.

But the cherry on top of the cake was about to arrive. I awoke one morning in March to a few voicemails and text messages, all saying congratulations. I didn't know what they were for until I scrolled further down to find one from our producer, Lindsay Hughes, which said, 'Well done. You've been nominated for a BAFTA!' I honestly nearly fell out of bed. The first thing I did was call Ruth Jones. I couldn't wait to share the excitement of it all with her (and I also just wanted to check that this wasn't a massive wind-up). Some people had predicted we might get nominated after doing well at other awards dos, but I never thought it would actually happen. I found it hard to believe that our show had been nominated for 'Best Comedy' at the BAFTAs. Except, well, it wasn't. Ruth told me that *we* hadn't been nominated as a comedy, no. The show was up for the Audience Award for Television Programme of the Year, and *I* had been nominated for Comedy Performance. It never even crossed my mind that I might have received a nomination for my performance. I always felt that if anyone from our show was going to be nominated, it would be Ruth. Her performance as Nessa is, in my opinion, astounding. So understated and yet rich to its very core. It couldn't be further away from who she is as a person and, when I catch moments of the show now, I am still in awe of what she did with that character. It felt strange to have been nominated when she wasn't. I guess the only slight disappointment was that we hadn't been nominated in the 'Best Comedy' category. It seemed strange to be nominated for a massive award like the Audience Award, alongside shows like *Britain's Got Talent*, *The Apprentice* and *Strictly Come Dancing*, and not to have been recognised as a comedy. But, with all the other good news, it wasn't something I was going to dwell on.

When the night came around, it was tremendously exciting. I was flying. It started off with Ruth and me walking down the red carpet and all the fans screaming our names, which was a very weird experience. Then, when we got inside, I was sitting behind Piers Morgan, who I didn't know at the time but who I'd always liked – his books are great – and I kept leaning forward, tapping him on the shoulder and saying, 'This is huge, Piers. This is bigger than all of us. Tonight. Tonight is huge.' Piers and his lovely partner (now wife), Celia, kept looking round. I'm sure they were both thinking, Who the hell is this guy?

The ceremony started and quickly came to the award for Comedy Performance. I was up against three incredible actors in Peter Capaldi, David Mitchell and Stephen Merchant, so I never, even for a second, contemplated winning. Simon Pegg was giving out the award. (Simon's one of my heroes. Everything he's done, the choices he's made and the paths he's taken. He's someone I really look up to.) He read out the nominees and then they played the clips. (Mine finished with a shot of my bare bum, which made Piers turn round to me and say, 'Now that's huge!') As Simon said the words 'And the BAFTA goes to . . .' I was getting ready to clap the winner up onto the stage. And then . . . I heard my name. Simon had just said my name! I sat there in such a state of shock.

I was sitting next to Rob Brydon, who had his hand on my arm, and I vaguely remember him telling me that I'd done it. Suddenly, I was on my feet and hugging Ruth, and then I was making my way up to the stage to collect the award. I was trying to keep my nerve. I was about to receive a BAFTA! Even now I can't quite get my head around the fact that it actually happened.

I think my speech was good. It went exactly how I hoped an acceptance speech might go, when I was dreaming of giving speeches back when I was a kid. I thanked my mum and dad, I thanked my sisters, and then I thanked Ruth, for not only being a brilliant actress and writer, but also being the best friend I could wish for. I said that I was sharing the award with her, and I meant every single word. There'd be nothing without Ruth, and I really do think of that award as half hers and half mine.

It was everything I'd wanted to say. Normally, when you win, you go out the side of the stage and they take you round to the press room where you do a short interview and they take a few pictures. But when I came off, they ushered me straight back to my seat. That got me suspicious. Why were they rushing me back? Unless, unless . . . No, it couldn't be, could it? It wasn't possible. The competition was too strong, surely. Wasn't it?

Sitting down, I remember my palms were tingling. I waited nervously until it came to the Audience Award. I can still hear them announcing it. 'The Audience Award for Television

Programme of the Year goes to –' and I'm thinking, *Britain's Got Talent* or *Strictly* or *The Apprentice* or any other show that isn't – '*Gavin & Stacey*.'

I clean jumped out of my seat. I hugged Ruth and Rob and Joanna. None of us could believe it. We'd won. We'd won a second BAFTA.

What happened next . . . No, I'll rephrase that: what *I did next* I will regret as long as I live. We walked up to collect the award and, as we got on stage, I opened my gob. Instead of being gracious, or delighting in the fact that we'd won a second BAFTA, I asked a question. Remember when I said that I wasn't going to dwell over the fact we hadn't been nominated in the 'Comedy' category? Well . . . here's how my question went: 'How can what is apparently the best comedy performance and the television programme of the year not even be nominated as a comedy?'

Instead of applause or nods of agreement, I was met with silence, shock and disbelief. Now, of course, I can see why and how it must have looked – ungracious, ungrateful and brattish. Rather than using my speech to thank everyone who'd helped on the show, I'd ruined the moment and belittled myself in the process. I was so full of myself, so much in the bubble of my own importance, that I thought I could stand up there and ask why our show hadn't been nominated for Best Comedy. The two awards had given me this huge sense of entitlement and I'd acted like a fool. But more than that, I'd taken the gun that a lot of people already had pointed at me and loaded it. Who on earth did I think I was? Two amazing prizes, and yet there I was, apparently demanding another one.

I regret it – I will always regret it – but it just summed up where my head had been for months. I'd lost all sense of the grounded person I thought I was. It's only now, a couple of years down the line, that I can look back and see what a prat I was. Back then I honestly couldn't see the problem everyone had with me asking the question. I wish I could tell you that this was a wake-up call for me, that I immediately saw what a fool I had become and set about righting my wrongs. I truly wish I could say that – I would've been so much happier had this been the case – but unfortunately I can't.

The truth is, my behaviour probably got worse. As 2008 wore on, it got so bad I was being rude to my agent, and I even started being rude to Ruth. If I was in company and the conversation wasn't revolving around me, I would just switch off. I was the youngest person on the *Guardian*'s Media Power List, I had a new sketch show lined up, I had the lead in an upcoming film and, on top of that, I'd been asked to host the Brits with Mat and Kylie Minogue. I had everything I'd ever dreamt of and yet I was behaving like an oaf. Deep down, I was the unhappiest I think I've ever been.

What happens to the dream part of a dream when it becomes a reality? What happens to the bit of you that had the capacity to dream the dream in the first place? Did all that hope, desire and ambition just sort of vanish? Did my ability to dream again vanish with it? I had no idea, but for me the dream had been exciting, tense, beguiling even and yet the reality just felt incredibly hollow. It seemed to me that all my life I'd been looking at these goalposts; they'd dominated the horizon for so long that I hadn't been able to see beyond them. My dreams had come true. I'd kicked that goal, but when I ventured beyond the posts to retrieve the ball, not only could I not find it, it was foggy out there and I sort of lost my way.

I was in a very bad place indeed. I had an entire sketch show to write but instead of knuckling down and really focusing on it, I put in probably a third as much work, effort and time as I should've done. I didn't understand that with such incredible success under my belt already, the expectation would be so much greater and actually I needed all the help I could get. Once you've had success, you have to go to ground, dig really deep – deeper than you ever did before – because that's the only chance you'll have of beating or even emulating what you achieved the last time. I just assumed we could put a show together without too much thought and we'd be the toast of the town all over again.

I truly believed in what Mat and I were trying to do. I do still believe that we could've been, or maybe one day still could be, a good double act. We certainly had the makings of one. But to form a double act, to stand up there with the greats, the thing you need most is time. Lots and lots of time. You need to find out what it is that makes you tick, what is unique about you as a duo, a twosome. If I could have my time again, then I would've liked Mat and I to try and find who we were together. Most great double acts have been together for years, experiencing triumph and disaster together, working comedy clubs night after night. Ours was a friendship where there were definitely sparks showing we could have the kind of chemistry to make something great together.

Instead of testing the material unannounced at comedy clubs like we should've done, we took the show to a handful of student unions where our audiences were really only people who wanted to see a couple of blokes from off the telly. They loved it. We went down a storm, but it was no yardstick. I was complacent. I can't speak for Mat, I only know how I was, and I was far more interested in how many girls I could get back to my hotel room than I was in making sure we had a show we could be proud of. Now, the thing is, obviously I'm writing all of this after the event, in hindsight. I'm trying my best to remember what it was like at the time and mostly I remember it feeling incredibly exciting.

Lesbian Vampire Killers was directed by an incredibly bright and talented man called Phil Claydon, and he'd been trying to make it for so long. He was so passionate about the project that you couldn't help but fall in love with him. The film had a budget of about £2 million so everyone felt fairly confident that it was going to do good business. Mat and I were now doing almost all of our work together for the next year or so. Not that either of us minded. I loved working with Mat. We were so incredibly close. We'd finish each other's sentences and know exactly what the other was thinking almost all of the time. We had a confidence when we were together and a closeness that, looking back at now, may well have from time to time been seen as arrogance.

So we shot the film, the sketch show and the Christmas special and all the time, both together and apart, our profiles kept raising. The success of *Gavin & Stacey* had grown to such a point that the show had 7 million viewers on Christmas Eve. I had secured an American agent and just been offered my first part in a Hollywood film with Jack Black, so professionally things couldn't have been better. In many respects, however, it felt so hollow. The better things got at work, the worse they became personally. I had once again been on and off in my relationship. I felt further and further away from my friends and family, and was still continuing to go out like my life depended on it. Christmas came and went and in January, Mat and I had a meeting where we were told that the Brit Awards, the sketch show and the film were all going to come out within the same month. We looked at each other, both of us thinking the same thing. I was the one to say it out loud. 'God, we're gonna be everywhere.'

'I know,' said one the sketch show or film promoters, 'it'll be great. There's going to be a bus campaign for the sketch show and posters all over bus stops for the film. You're not gonna be able to miss it.' At that moment Mat and I weren't feeling quite as excited; don't get me wrong, we weren't unexcited, but there was also trepidation on our part. All of them coming at once. It was all going to be a bit in your face. There was nothing we could do about it, though. We didn't have the sort of power to be able to change it. We had no choice but to go with it.

The Brit Awards came first. I've always loved the Brit Awards.

Being such a fan of pop music, it was a must watch for me when I was at school, so to be asked to host it alongside Mat and Kylie Minogue was a dream come true. The best thing about hosting the Brits is that on the day of the awards there is a dress rehearsal in the afternoon where basically the whole of Earls Court is empty and these huge acts – U2, the Pet Shop Boys, Lady Gaga, Take That and plenty more – all come out and basically perform for the host, and the host alone. All day it felt like such a privilege. We did the show and thought it went well. People were coming up to us afterwards and saying it was great. Helen Terry, who had produced the awards for the past twenty years, pulled Mat and me aside and said that we shouldn't be surprised if in the next day's papers we were being called the greatest presenters ever. We went off and danced and drank well into the night. Mum and Dad came to the show and were crying throughout – it had been a momentous night.

And then the next day arrived. No one could have predicted what the press response would be. The reviews were awful. We were called the worst hosts of all time. Mat and me – not Kylie, she didn't really get mentioned, which was probably fair as she hadn't written the script. No, it was Mat and me and this was strike number one. It was the first time I'd ever been on the end of criticism like that and it was strange. 'Bring back Sam Fox and Mick Fleetwood' was a popular remark. It didn't bode well for the next two weeks, when the sketch show and film would both be coming out.

A few months ago, I watched the Brits 2009 back again and I have to say that all of the criticism was absolutely right. Harsh in tone at times, but of course I'm going to think that. The truth is, I was bad, really bad. I've no idea what we were thinking. Some of the choices we made were disastrous. We were under the illusion that people cared that we were hosting the Brits, when the truth is the host should be almost invisible, just ushering the show from one performance to the next. You don't need to be funny, it's a music show. It's the worst room you could ever play and the best thing to do is ignore the people who are there and play it all for the cameras. I was lucky enough to be asked back in 2011 and thankfully, I got good reviews second time around.

The sketch show aired on Tuesday nights on BBC3 and had the most phenomenal ratings. It is still, as I write this, the highest debut comedy in the history of that channel. In fact more people watched the first series of *Horne & Corden* than ever watched series one of *Gavin & Stacey*. But none of that mattered, because when it came to reviews, we had the worst. Worse than I've ever read before. From broadsheet to tabloid it was open season. It was awful. 'The worst show that's ever been made,' said one. 'Puerile and disgusting,' said another. It was endless. We were called homophobic and talentless, and from there, it just kept getting worse.

The film then came out a week or so after and brought with it another round of awful coverage. The most embarrassing film since whatever the last awful film was seemed to be the gist of most of the write-ups. In three weeks, we'd seemingly gone from heroes to zeroes. It hurt. It really did. It was a huge wake-up call. The hardest part was that because the three things had come so quickly after each other, it led to profile pieces being written about us. Day after day, another thing would be written. I remember going to meet Mat one day and he was sat reading a piece in the *Telegraph* that said, 'The backlash begins for the cocky princes of comedy.' It went on to say that we were basically awful, our careers were finished, that I was arrogant and mentioned my BAFTA speech. Mark Lawson, a broadcaster and journalist whom I really respect, wrote a piece in the *Guardian* entitled 'Catch a Falling Star. How can Mathew Horne and James Corden rescue their nosediving careers?' He wrote about our overexposure and overconfidence and how we had had the worst reviews anyone had ever seen. This was probably the fifth or sixth of these articles that had been written in the few weeks since the film was released.

The truth is – and it's taken a while for me to realise this – that the reviewers and other journalists writing these things were right. Unkind at points? Sure. Enjoying our fall from grace a little too much? Absolutely. But most of all, they were right. The Brits, the sketch show and the film. Not one of those things was good enough. There were moments in the sketch show I'm proud of, and the character of Xander I still like very much. The British Olympic team sketches are good as well, but that's not enough. The show lacked vision; it lacked heart and soul. Mostly, though, it wasn't funny enough.

It's difficult writing this. I could go the other way and defend the show, talk about the great ratings, and how when I meet the people who were the target audience for the show, they all tell me they enjoyed it. And I'm pleased they did. Truly. But ultimately, deep down, I know that all of those reviews were right, and worse than that, I know that I was to blame. The person I had become wasn't the person I had wanted to be. I had drifted so far from my close friends and family that I didn't really know how to pick up the phone and talk to them any more. I was lost and I needed to find myself again.

I thought it would blow over quicker than it did, but it seemed to go on and on. The easiest thing to do in these circumstances is not to read any of the papers, but there was so much being written, so consistently, that if I tried to ignore them, it wouldn't be long before someone would come to me and say, 'That piece in the such-and-such newspaper is horrible. Just ignore it. Tomorrow's fish and chip paper.' All I'd want to do is say, 'I'm trying to ignore it. I didn't even know it existed, but now I do. Thank you.'

It was a testing time, to put it mildly. I was now back in my on-and-off relationship with Sheridan and was only staying at the flat in Beaconsfield very occasionally. It was as if walking back in through the front door of that flat reminded me of a time when I was a different person, someone I'd drifted from somehow. I would go back every now and then to sort out my post or wash some clothes. One day, when I was sitting in the kitchen going through a mound of bills and bank statements, I found a postcard with a beautiful picture of an old seat on the front. On the back was written, 'I'm sorry to read that you've been going through a tough time. I've no advice other than to say, "Screw 'em." It's always stood me in good stead. All my love, Alan Bennett.' I sat staring at it and was so touched that he'd bothered to do such a thing. And over the next couple of weeks he wasn't the only one. Lots of people called and sent messages telling me to keep some perspective on this. Piers Morgan, despite what he'd have you believe, is an incredibly nice guy. He sent me texts with wonderful nuggets of wisdom from his days on Fleet Street. He told me I was due a kicking, that this was how the press roundabout worked. He called me a few days later to talk the whole thing over. He is just generally a great bloke.

So I became totally focused on the third series of *Gavin & Stacey*. Ruth and I had to make the best series we ever had. The show had become bigger than we'd ever dreamt possible and the reviews for the sketch show had told us that the knives would be out again if series three wasn't up to scratch. My agent and I agreed that I shouldn't be on television for a while, so we said no to any offers that were coming in. However, there was one TV appearance I just couldn't say no to and that I was very passionate about: Comic Relief.

For as long as I can remember, I've loved Comic Relief. I'd been involved in some small way ever since I was a kid. Red Nose days were always a laugh at school – you'd be allowed to wear your home clothes and there was inevitably some kind of mad fundraising event that involved getting wet or really messy. There was one time when my band Twice Shy charged a pound a head for a lunchtime concert, with all the money going to

Comic Relief (that was the most we ever made from a gig, and we didn't even get to keep it), and I vividly remember sitting with my mum and being incredibly moved by watching a Billy Connolly appeal film back when I was around ten. It had always been something I'd hoped to be a part of one day.

Richard Curtis had been in touch about doing something, and Ruth and I were thinking of doing a *Gavin & Stacey* special. We had this idea where all of the characters were heading to BBC TV Centre in White City to watch Bryn hand over a cheque for £45 that he'd raised from doing a sponsored swim. All the characters would be there, but in one way or another they would all get lost whilst walking around TV Centre. This is easily done, I might add. I've been lost in there for hours before. The idea was that Bryn would end up on the set of *Strictly Come Dancing*, Gwen would show Jamie Oliver how to cook the perfect omelette, Gavin and Stacey would try and have a quickie in the Blue Peter garden, Nessa would keep bumping into famous old flames and Smithy would walk onto the *Match of the Day* set, meet the England team and give them a team talk.

Richard loved the idea and we tried to put the wheels in motion, but it soon became clear that logistics would make it too difficult. Getting everyone together in the same place at the same time would be impossible. I was still really passionate about trying to do something for Comic Relief, though, so I suggested we concentrate on Smithy and the England team – make it bigger, do it with the whole squad. Smithy could say to the England team what every fan would dream of saying if they were face to face.

I remember Richard shaking his head. 'James,' he said, 'I've got to tell you there's no chance of getting anywhere near the England team. We've tried to do stuff with the FA before and got absolutely nowhere. It's a no-go. It's a bit like trying to do something with the Royal Family – it just never happens.' But I was insistent, and Richard came around to the idea that asking

again wouldn't do any harm. He also asked if I had any prefer-
ence about who should direct it. I knew instantly. Remember
the runner from *Teachers*, Ben Winston? Well, we had stayed
friends and he'd since gone on to become one of the most
exciting directors/producers you could wish to meet. I told him
about the idea for the sketch and he got it immediately, but he
too had his doubts over whether the FA would go for it. There
was one way to find out: I picked up the phone.

I guess it was a matter of timing, because Richard Curtis is
right: normally, it's an absolute no-no. But, as it turned out, just
as we were asking the Smithy question, the FA was trying to
think of ideas to reconnect the England team with the fans. They
felt the gap between the players and the average supporter had
been getting too big, and it wasn't healthy for the country as a
whole. So, amazingly, and without much prodding, they said
yes to the sketch idea and told us they'd guarantee us a minimum
of four players.

Richard, Ben and I were stunned: it was more in hope than
anticipation that I'd called them up. We had to strike while the
iron was hot. It's not often the England squad is together and,
when they are, their time is precious. Ben brought in the legend
that is his producing partner, Gabe Turner, who knew exactly
what to say when it came to speaking the fans' minds, and we
all worked together on trying to find the time to do it.

It was the perfect production team with the perfect opportunity
and all we had to do now was come up with the perfect sketch.
The truth is, we had plenty of ideas, but had nothing written
down, which was largely because we didn't know which players
were going to do it. We had to deal with the fact that it was
probably going to remain that way right up to the last minute,
so the different elements of the sketch would have to be fluid
and flexible.

The day got nearer and nearer and the guys from the FA were
being very supportive, but we still didn't know who the players

would be. We arrived at the hotel on the day of the shoot and the FA told us that the players would, at most, have twenty minutes to spare after a team meeting and before dinner. That was it, twenty minutes, which with the faffing around and sitting down when they got there, meant more like eighteen minutes if we were lucky.

We all took a sharp intake of breath: eighteen minutes is not a lot of time to shoot anything. With an episode of *Gavin & Stacey*, for example, it takes six days to shoot the twenty-eight minutes that end up on the TV. Still, that's what we had, so we sucked it up and got busy: we filmed the background stuff – Smithy arriving in the car, lying on his back fixing pipes in the corridor before hunting down the toilet – and, when that was done, Gabe, Ben and I worked on the lines we had about different players, hoping as many as possible would show up.

The big problem was we'd had no access to them beforehand. They were kept in a separate part of the hotel and nobody was allowed to see or speak to them. Fortunately, Rio Ferdinand had become a bit of a mate. A couple of years before that Comic Relief day, he'd got in touch with me to say he was a fan of *Gavin & Stacey* and we'd stayed in touch off and on. So I was texting him, trying to get an idea of who was going to show up, and he was texting back. He was totally instrumental in persuading lots of the players who eventually did come along. He told me that he'd be there, together with John Terry and Ashley Cole, and one other who he thought was going to be Shaun Wright-Phillips, but he couldn't say for sure. At least I knew who three of them would be, so I got working on the script. But I was desperately hoping Rio could come up with a few more because the sketch would be hard to do if there were only the four of them.

As the time drew closer, he sent me another text telling me that Peter Crouch was coming now as well. Then he mentioned that some of the players were coming down to reception where there were a stack of shirts to be signed. Bingo! That was my chance to grab a word with a few of them before the actual filming began and see if I couldn't persuade a couple more of the squad to join in.

The only problem was that we'd been told under no circumstances were we allowed to approach any of the players or even talk to them beforehand. This came down from the team management, and Franco Baldini (Capello's number two and the second scariest man I've ever met after Capello) was making sure that was how it was. You know Franco, the grey-haired, good-looking guy who sits next to Capello and looks like he might be a mob-enforcer – not the kind of man you want to cheese off.

But this was Comic Relief, so I put aside my fear of injury/death and hung around reception as the players came downstairs for the shirt signing. Franco was there, too, watching like an angry hawk. He didn't look happy. I kind of hoped that one or two of them would recognise me from *Gavin & Stacey* and maybe, just maybe, wander over to say hello. But no one really did. I was getting a little desperate when I saw Frank Lampard come down. Frank was a big name and I knew that if we got him, a couple of others might come along too. So, risking Franco's wrath, I walked over to where he was standing on the other side of the table. Franco moved in close – for the kill? – and was right there, breathing all over my left shoulder, but this was my chance and I just had to go for it.

'Frank,' I called. 'Frank!'

He looked up and smiled. Franco was there, hovering, but Frank didn't seem to notice.

'Hi Frank,' I said, shaking hands. 'I'm James.'

'Nice to meet you, James,' he said.

'Listen, have you heard about this sketch we're doing today?'

'Yeah,' he said, 'Rio's trying to get some of the lads down.'

'Great,' I said. 'Are you going to be in it then?'

'No,' he said. 'It's not my thing really. I'd feel a bit silly.'

'Frank,' I said, 'I promise you, mate, we're not going to make you look silly.'

Still he was shaking his head. 'It's not about you making me look silly. I'm no good at that kind of thing. I wouldn't be any good in a sketch.'

'Look,' I said, 'you don't have to worry about that. You don't have to do anything. You just need to sit there and listen.'

'I don't know,' he said.

'Frank,' I said, 'this sketch will save people's lives and your involvement will help us raise so much more money. People love you, Frank, they love you. It won't be the same without you.' It was real, savage emotional blackmail. I didn't want to go there, but this was Comic Relief. 'Frank,' I said, 'I promise you, if you come down, you won't be asked to do anything stupid.'

And then I shut up. I didn't say another word. I just kept on looking at Frank and he stood there with a kind of half-smile that told me he knew just how badly I was guilt-tripping him. 'OK,' he said finally, 'all right. If it's for Comic Relief, of course I'll come.'

'Thank you, Frank,' I said. 'That's great. And please do me a favour and just bring as many of the other players as you can.'

So we had Frank now, which was huge, but there was still the one name we wanted to get, the Big Kahuna: Beckham. Becks was in the squad, but he'd played for Milan the day before, flown in late and had been training all morning. We'd asked about him, of course, but they told us his schedule was really hectic and he needed that twenty minutes for a bit of downtime.

A bit of downtime we could understand, of course we could, but we still had a cunning plan to get him there. Ben Winston was – still is – really good friends with Simon Oliveira, David's agent. We'd been talking to him on the phone, begging him to get Becks in the sketch. He'd told us that David was keen to be involved but also how tired he was, so we would just have to wait and see when the time came whether he was up for it.

So we waited and waited and finally word came down that the players were on their way. One by one they arrived: John Terry followed by Frank and Rio. Peter Crouch and Shaun Wright-Phillips. Michael Carrick took a seat, as did David James. Ashley Cole came in and then last – and I couldn't believe it – the door opened and in walked David Beckham. Forgive the man-love here but the guy is so beautiful I didn't know whether to shake his hand or lick his face. As soon as they were all in, the clock started running. Twenty minutes and counting. Ben gave his instructions to the players and was about to call action but, just before he did, I stopped and said, 'Sorry, Ben, quickly, can I just talk to you for one moment?'

'What's up?' he said, rushing over and taking his headphones off. 'Is everything OK?'

'Nothing's up,' I said. 'Everything is fine. But listen, let's just enjoy this moment. I mean, you're the runner from *Teachers*, remember, and I'm Jeremy the geek, and this is the England team. Can you believe it?'

He smiled and patted me sweetly on the shoulder. 'Yeah, you're right,' he said, 'but, James, we really have to get on.'

So we got into it. The only bit that worried me came at the very end of the sketch when hopefully Smithy had the players all fired up. We hadn't told them about that bit, as we really needed them to be spontaneous and just go with it. But, hey, we were here and doing it, and if they didn't come with us, then what could we do? What I wasn't prepared for was how amused the other players were going to be when one of their team mates was getting laid into. It was so hard to concentrate with Ashley Cole trying not to crack up as I ripped David James about his hair.

Apart from that, the whole thing just flowed. Each and every player took whatever Smithy dished out on the chin, and then, at the end, when we really needed them to get up for it, all I can say is, God bless Peter Crouch. As I finished the rap, Crouchy went with it and was the first to shout, 'Go on, Smithy!' The others followed his lead, clapping, cheering and punching the air, and then one by one I patted them on the bum as they left the room, until it came to Rio. 'Ssshh,' I said, kissing him on the head. 'You do your talking on the pitch.'

CHAPTER 20

BEST MUSICAL ACCOMPANIMENT:
'Stop Crying Your Heart Out' by Oasis

BEST FILM TO WATCH ALONGSIDE:
any episode of *Lost*

BEST ENJOYED WITH:
toast and Marmite

The sketch went down brilliantly when it aired. I had been totally unprepared for the reaction to it. People were calling it the highlight of the night. I know, me making a good sketch. Who would have thought?

The next thing I had to do was write series three of *Gavin & Stacey* with Ruth. As the show had got more and more successful, writing time with Ruth became more and more precious. As before, we would often write in hotels so we could basically just lock ourselves away and concentrate. Being back in a room with Ruth was just what I needed at the time. It was good for the soul to be laughing with her again.

We knew before we started writing that this was going to be the last series we'd make and when it came to us writing the last ever line of our last ever script, it was around midnight in the Soho Hotel. We both stopped, stood up and hugged each other. That was it. This series that had meant so much to us, that had been such a big part of our lives – we'd finished it. Ruth and her husband, David, had been my only real constants over the last topsy-turvy couple of years. Ruth, in particular, had always been there for me, and was the first person I'd pick up the phone to speak to in times of triumph or despair. As I left her room that night, I couldn't help but wonder who, or what, would be my constant now that the show was finished.

After finishing writing, I shot *Gulliver's Travels* for seven weeks in the late spring of 2009, which was a fun experience. Working on something with such a huge budget was so different to anything I'd ever done before, and I had the added bonus of doing all of my scenes with Billy Connolly – a real dream come true. But however much I was enjoying the shoot, the turbulent relationship I was in still hampered my mood. In fact, it had gone way beyond hampering it – it dominated me. I was so preoccupied with myself that it can't have been fun to work with or be around me.

After *Gulliver's Travels* I went back to Cardiff to shoot the third and final series of *Gavin & Stacey*. As with the other two series, the shoot was wonderful and I loved every single minute of it. Well, almost every minute. During the last week of filming, my relationship with Sheridan finally ended, in a manner that meant there'd be no going back. Once and for all, after so many back and forths, it was over.

Only a couple of days after that came the final day of shooting. I was incredibly upset, both for the end of the relationship and for the loss of the show. The last scene we ever shot was the scene in the final episode when Smithy meets Nessa at a service station. It's a scene that has one of my favourite moments in all three series – it's Nessa's line when she says to Smithy, 'There's only one of you, isn't there?' Ruth delivers it perfectly and I think their relationship changes in some way during that scene. With everything that was happening personally, filming that last scene took it out of me. I cried my eyes out all day long. Everywhere I looked there were endings. I couldn't help but wonder what would be left of me after *Gavin & Stacey*. Where would I go from here? What would I do next?

I got back to London and within a few days Dominic and I

began renting a flat together in Primrose Hill. Dominic has always been an incredible friend to me and I remember our time together in that flat with great fondness. We had the top two floors of a five-storey house and to my shame I have to tell you that we were probably the worst neighbours you could ever wish for. That flat could have been lovely, but we never made it a home. I didn't bring any of my clothes or personal things from Beaconsfield to London, so it continually felt like somewhere I was just crashing in; on top of that, there was never any food in the house: no milk, no sugar, nothing useful. I remember at one point, for about two weeks, all Dom and I had in the fridge was some vodka, a bottle of pink vitamin water and a Lindt chocolate bunny.

We rented it furnished – which meant it had one tiny two-seater sofa in a corner, Dominic's black velour chaise longue (don't ask) in another room, the two beds and that was it. In a way, it was handy that we never really furnished it properly because it meant there was room for all the dancing that would regularly take place. I once got dropped in a cab four or five streets away from our place and, as I was paying the cab driver, I could hear this thud of a dull beating bass coming almost through the air. 'God, someone's having a party.' Said the cab driver.

'Yeah!' I said, taking my change. As I walked up and over the hill towards our flat, the bass just kept getting heavier and heavier. Until, as I arrived outside the front door, it was clear the party was in our flat and all of the windows were wide open. I climbed the stairs, passing people on every other stair and walked into the hallway. 'Where's Dominic?' I said to one guy who I'd never met before.

'Who?' He replied.

'DOM.IN.IC?' I shouted, trying to spell it out. He just looked at me blankly. I walked up the small staircase to the open plan top floor and there, in the middle of the room, was Dom, playing a drumkit. An electric drumkit that he'd threatened to buy for a long time. He was giving it all he could, like Animal from *The Muppets*, playing along to whatever music people were selecting on the iPod. There must've been twenty-five people in the flat that night.

Dominic looked up at me. 'LEVINE!' He shouted as he went round the tom-toms for the thirtieth time in as many seconds. I couldn't help but smile. I went over to him and said, 'Who are all these people?'

For some reason he chose to reply in an Australian accent. 'I've no idea mate, now grab ya'self a beer and loosen up, me old mucka!' So I did, and we went on to have a great night. I woke up in bed the next morning with someone I'd only just met. I wish I could tell you that nights like this were once in a blue moon but they were probably once or twice a week. They got so bad that one morning we woke to a note on the door from Camden Council saying that they'd been called out the night before but couldn't make themselves heard at the door. It also said that if they were called out again, they would fine us £25,000! This went on for a good couple of months, so I'd like to take this moment to apologise to our neighbours (although I'd be amazed if they're reading this book), who would regularly ask us to keep the noise down. Dom would blame me or I would blame Dom and that's how we'd get away with it. But, aside from the parties, there were plenty of other times when Dom would have to go to America for work, and it was at those moments, sitting in the barely furnished flat on my own, that the reality of my situation would start to hit home. I just wasn't moving on.

I'd been living there for a couple of months and Mum and Dad had been keen to visit. They'd never been to the flat and I'd not been in regular contact with them for a while. Then, one morning, Dad called out of the blue and told me that they were in Primrose Hill and they were coming over. Just like that. No warning or anything. I was hung-over and feeling really rough, but I knew I couldn't put them off any longer, especially when they were only round the corner. I tried my best to tidy the flat but within minutes the buzzer was sounding. When I saw Mum, though, I couldn't help but give a big smile; she came in and squeezed me so tight, just like she always had. I took them up to the room with the world's smallest sofa and the country's biggest electric drum kit, and we all sat down.

I've since spoken to Mum and Dad about this day and they remember it vividly. Mum said that they had been worried about me for some time and both felt compelled to come over that day.

We were in the flat – Mum and Dad on the sofa, me on the floor – drinking vitamin water together, and sadly, I had nothing to say to them. The conversation went from pause to even longer pause. Dad would ask about this thing or that, but I had no real answers, certainly none of any worth. I felt distant from them, so far away from the person they expected me to be, from the boy they had so lovingly raised. I hated them seeing me like this and I could barely lift my eyes to look them in the face. Then, all of a sudden, Dad came over to where I was sitting on the floor, knelt down and put his arms around me. I can't begin to tell you how it felt. I couldn't help but cry.

I felt so embarrassed at the way I'd been living my life, the arrogance and lack of respect I'd shown myself and my work. Every tear that left my eyes made me feel a little lighter. Dad said a prayer as he kissed my forehead and Mum came over and joined the hug. I've no idea how long we stayed there, but it felt like a lifetime. When they left later on, Dad turned to me and said, 'You've so much to be thankful for, James. I know it's been a tricky year, but you can't carry on like this.'

Mum told me only last week that after they'd left the house they drove the car round the corner and had to pull in because Dad had got so upset. They didn't know how to help me and were worried I wouldn't help myself. It's only now, after having a child of my own, that I can even begin to comprehend how hard it must've been for my parents. Journalists turning up on their doorstep asking about this and that, pictures of me falling out of clubs and bars, ringing my phone and me never answering. I knew that I was on a roller coaster, but it never crossed my mind to look behind me and realise that my family and some of my closest friends were riding it with me, hoping I would get off.

I needed a change of scenery. I got a call from Andrew, my American agent, about an audition for a film over in the US. It was the perfect opportunity to get away from everything. Normally, with early auditions like this, you would record yourself on video, send it via email, and if they liked what they saw, you'd go out and meet them in person. I made a snap decision – nothing was going to change as long as I stayed in this cycle of going out and feeling sorry for myself, so I told Andrew that if it was OK, I'd fly out the next day and do the audition there. I booked a flight and the next day I was in LA. Although the weather and new environment helped my disposition, I'm not sure LA's the best place to lick emotional wounds, and I only lasted a couple of days before I phoned home, spoke to my little sister Rudi and asked her if she wanted to come out and join me. I needed her, she knew I did, and she was on a plane just a couple of days later.

We had a wonderful time. Or I did anyway. That holiday mended me. I poured my heart out and Rudi just listened to it all and never once complained. During those few days she was much more than just my sister – she became one of my closest friends. I'd never have got through it all without her. There was a song she played for me over and over again. The lyrics were 'I am my brother's keeper and I will always be; as long as there's a need for him there'll be a need for me.' Daily, hourly, she told me I was going to get through the pain of Sheridan, of Shelley, and of everything else that had made me feel this way. She would talk about the fact that I was at a crossroads and that I had a choice: I could carry on the way I was going or I could go back to who I really was. It was all up to me.

Rudi reminded me of who I'd been before all the success and that, far from having arrived, I had only just got to the point where the real work began. We hired a car and drove to Las Vegas, talking all the way. We were so caught up in the conversation that we got stopped by the police for speeding. We tried to blag our way out of it, but state troopers aren't an easy touch and we ended up paying the fine. When we got there, though, we quickly worked out that Vegas isn't a great place to go as brother and sister, and so we stayed for one drunken night – where I wandered off and ended up in a completely different hotel – and drove back the next day. Let's put it like this: as a brother and sister in Vegas, it's highly unlikely that you'll be wanting to do the same type of things . . .

Home in London, I was beginning to get a little faith back. I was sick and tired of the way I'd cheapened everything. Don't get me wrong, I wasn't about to check myself into AA or NA, or for that matter a sex-addiction clinic; I just hadn't been as respectful to people as I could or should've been. I spoke on the phone to my older sister Andrea, who is a little sterner than Rudi but no less loving, and she told me there had been quite a few points where I'd been a dick and nearly squandered everything I'd strived so hard for. I listened and knew she was only saying it for my own good and had clearly been waiting for the right time to tell me – when I'd actually listen. Two days after that call, I received a card in the post from Andrea. This is what it said:

> It's never too late to be whoever you want to be.
> There's no time limit. Start whenever you want to.
> You can change or stay the same.
> There are no rules to this thing.

We can make the best or worst of it.
I hope you make the best of it.
I hope you see things that stop you.
I hope you feel things you've never felt before.
I hope you meet people with a different point of view.
I hope you live a life you're proud of and if you find that
you're not,
I hope you have the strength to start all over again.

The last two lines were the ones I kept reading and re-reading. It was good advice, coming from the people who knew me best. Andrea and Rudi will never know how much they helped me over this time.

I was determined to be the person I once was again. I knew I could get over the slump: the criticism I'd had in the papers had wounded me but had never really hurt; it was the emotional state I was in that had really dragged me down. I began to work on new ideas for stuff. I stopped going out so much and made a conscious effort to be a little more selective about who I brought home. I felt a difference in my mood almost instantly. I had a clearer head, a more positive outlook. I got together with old friends and, for the first time in my life (at the age of thirty-one), I even stayed in a few times on my own. Once you get over the initial fear, it actually becomes something you really enjoy. At first, it felt so strange to be going to sleep at ten o'clock in complete silence without a drink in my system or a stranger in my bed. But within a few days it became the most natural thing in the world.

On the professional front, there was a decision to be made about the future of the sketch show. The ratings had been so good that the BBC were keen for Mat and I to make another series. We understandably had been reticent after having such a wave of negativity come our way in the aftermath of series one. Some days we would think it was a good idea, and others we would be unsure. I was worried that we'd never be given a fair chance. The show felt tainted and was already being used by some as a byword for bad television. As though we were the only people around not making an amazing television show. There were lots of people telling us that we should do it, that we could have the last laugh, but I never saw it like that. It wasn't a battle or some kind of game; it was simply a question of whether we could make a show that was good enough and funny enough. In the end, after a lot of discussion, we decided not to carry on. It seemed like too big a risk to try again. It's still the biggest creative decision of my career. The way I see it, all that would've happened is the old reviews would've been rehashed and the pressure on the show to deliver would've been too great. What critic was suddenly now going to proclaim our show as the greatest show ever? Sketch shows by their very nature are always hit and miss. What one person loves, another person may hate.

Both Mat and I had offers to do other things, and it seemed like the right decision to try out different opportunities. We moved on. The strangest thing about us making this decision was that suddenly Mat and I weren't going to be spending as much time together. I loved every single second of working with him, though, and I hope that one day, in some form or another, we'll be able to do something together again. He is a wonderful friend, actor and writer, and will always have a special place in my heart.

As Christmas got nearer, the third series of *Gavin & Stacey* aired to some pretty amazing figures. On Christmas Day itself some 12 million people tuned in to watch the penultimate episode and even more watched the last show on New Year's Day. It was an incredible way to end the series. A month later we won Best Comedy at the National Television Awards and Ruth and I were named as the Writers' Guild Comedy Writers of the Year. Looking back on it, 2009 was a really strange year. I'd been as down as I'd ever been, become someone I barely even recognised and then ended the year on a huge professional high. Happily, as 2010 came round, things were finally looking up.

CHAPTER 21

BEST MUSICAL ACCOMPANIMENT:
'Give Me Strength' by Snow Patrol

BEST FILM TO WATCH ALONGSIDE:
Jerry Maguire

BEST ENJOYED WITH:
steak and chips

I was feeling so much more positive about myself and the future. I'm not sure I'll fully be able to realise what a knob I had been at various points. All I know is the huge relief I felt to be reconnecting with family and friends who I had taken for granted or abandoned somewhere over the last couple of years. I was still living in the flat, but was there mostly on my own as Dominic had been spending a lot of time working in the US. I had been staying in more, and finding time to work on a new television-show idea with Mathew Baynton – who played Deano in *Gavin & Stacey* – called *The Wrong Mans*. It was great getting back in the writing groove again after being away from it for a while.

When Dominic was in town, things weren't quite so quiet. I remember one day in particular – you'll see why in a minute – on which Dominic had flown in after a while away. He burst into the flat like a tornado. 'LEVINE!' he shouted up to me as he crashed through the door downstairs, once again, and for reasons still unknown, in an Australian accent. 'Get your best strides on, mate, 'cos we're going out. Got a big night planned and you'd be a dag to miss it.' I was thrilled to hear his voice echoing up the stairs. When he got upstairs, we hugged and he told me that we'd been invited to a Bvlgari party that night and that it was gonna be incredible. I sighed and told him I hadn't really been going out that much recently. He wasn't having it: 'All the more reason, then. This not going out is fair dinkum, mate, but you can't live like a monk. Let's get our glad rags on and have a bloody good time!' With or without the accent, Dom can be pretty persuasive and, much as I didn't feel like going out that night, part of me knew that it'd be fun. So he convinced me to go, and thank God he did, because that night was, is and always will be one of the most important nights of my life. It was the night I met Julia.

I didn't really know where this party was or what it was about; I just knew that we'd been invited by an old friend of Dominic's. We'd been there for about ten minutes – I was enjoying myself, it felt good to be out among people again after a while away – when Dom tapped me on my shoulder. 'Levine, I've got someone I want to introduce you to. This is Jules.' I turned round and in front of me stood Miss Julia Carey. She was smiling. 'Hi Jules,' I said before looking away at Dominic and staring at him open-mouthed, talking to him with my eyes in the way that only close friends can. We chatted for a while and she told me she worked for Save the Children and that the party was an event she had organised with the nice people at Bvlgari. After a while, she went off to carry on with her work and I immediately set about questioning Dom on who she was and, more importantly, whether she was single. Dominic giggled, 'Hmmmm, I thought you'd like Jules.'

They had known each other for about fifteen years and although I'd met many of Dom's old friends over the last few years, I'd never met her. Thank God! I mean, thank God I was meeting her *now*, at this moment, when I felt good about myself and positive about who I was and who I wanted to be. Another way of putting it is that, for the first time in a while, I felt ready to be in a proper relationship, one that mattered and had all the things that had been lacking before.

When Jules came back over, I decided I wasn't going to pussy-foot around. 'You're incredibly attractive,' I said matter-of-factly to her.

'Am I?' She giggled.

'Yes,' I said. 'This can't come as a shock. People must tell you this all the time.'

Jules seemed flattered and peeked up at me with the most beautiful eyes I'd ever seen.

'I don't see that it's up for debate. Everyone can see it. I can't believe for one minute that I'm the first to say such a thing.' I could see that Jules didn't really know what to say, so I suggested we go over to the bar together. After we'd picked up some drinks we found a seat in the corner of the room, in a quiet spot, and talked. And we talked and talked for the rest of the night. We spoke about our families, about her work and how much she was enjoying it; we laughed about the benefits of staying in and about how exhausting it was going out all the time. It felt like the most normal and natural thing in the world to be talking to her. I didn't feel on edge or as if I had to pretend to be anyone else – I was just being me.

Once Jules had got the last of her work done, Dom told us about an after-party near Berkeley Square. Jules came with us in the car and, again, we sat next to each other in the back and chatted the whole way there. It was during this conversation that Jules told me she had never seen *Gavin & Stacey*. She said she didn't watch a lot of television and didn't really know what it was. I was so happy. I remember thinking to myself, Wow, this really intelligent, beautiful, lovely lady wants to talk to me, just me. She's never seen *Gavin & Stacey* or anything. I had been so used to surrounding myself with the wrong types of people, and here was someone who was so genuine (though I'll admit I was less happy a few weeks later when Jules invited me round to her house and I discovered her *Inbetweeners* box set).

We got to the exclusive after-party, which seemed like the same party with the same people but just in a different venue, and we set about finding another quiet little corner to carry on our chat. We talked about places we'd been, things we wanted to see and do in the future; hour after hour ticked by. Dominic was off dancing and every so often would look over and smile. In just a few hours, Julia quickly became one of the best people I'd ever met. Her outlook and her views on life were so refreshing. She told me about the places she'd travelled with Save the Children, the array of things she'd seen and how it had given her a perspective on life. I listened, transfixed, wondering what the last two years would've been like had someone like Jules been around. Occasionally other people would come over and join us, but I couldn't take my eyes off Julia. She was perfect in every single way.

As sometimes you do in these situations, I got nervous. What if this was all in my head? What if I was feeling all of these things and she's thinking, God, Dom's friend is a bit intense. I hope someone comes over and rescues me?' Jules said she had to nip to the Ladies. This didn't help my worries – was that her polite way of trying to get away from me? – but just when the doubt was setting in, and it's when I worry or doubt myself that I normally become a bit of a dick, reassurance came in the strangest form. Natalie Imbruglia, who had been sitting a few feet away from us for most of the night, leant over and said, 'James, she's really into you. You two look great together.' At this point I didn't know her particularly well (I've since found out she is one of the loveliest people around), but I immediately shuffled over nearer to her.

'Really? Do you think?' I said in a rushed, hushed voice.

'Totally,' said Natalie confidently. 'Look at her. She's barely looked anywhere else. She's really great. Go for it.' At this moment

Dominic came over and shouted in a loud Australian accent, 'Where we going now, Levine? This place closes soon.'

Natalie Imbruglia, who is actually Australian, looked slightly taken aback, but replied in her genuine Australian accent, 'Why don't you come over to mine? Me and a few friends are coming back.'

Dominic now looked somewhat embarrassed. 'Yes, that'd be lovely,' he replied, using his normal voice. I wanted to go, but only if Julia was coming. 'Can Jules come?' I asked, and Dominic burst out laughing. He knew. He knew that I was falling for her. 'Play it cool, Trigger,' he said. 'Play it cool.'

We shared our first kiss in the car on the way to Natalie's house. And that night, as we were saying our goodbyes, I turned to Jules and said, 'You know how you said you were tired of going out and how exhausting it is? Well, I was wondering, would you like to stay in with me on Friday night? I'll cook and we'll do nothing. In fact, anytime you want to do nothing, I'd like to be there with you. That nothing could really turn into something.' We kissed again and it was perfect. And pretty much from that moment on, we've been inseparable. She did come over that Friday night and I cooked steak and chips. Still, to this day, Jules says it's the best steak she's ever eaten. In fact she thought it was so good she insisted on taking a picture of it so that we could remember quite how incredible the steak was.

I loved her instantly. London became a different place with her: the sun seemed to shine brighter, people were kinder, the air was lighter. The streets and bars around which I'd wandered at dusk and dawn felt so much calmer now. I felt more relaxed, stronger, happier in my skin. I introduced her to two of my closest friends, Ben and Gabe, who had been, shall we say, slightly worried about choices I'd made with girls in the past, and they immediately loved her. When we went to meet my family, within minutes it felt as if she had always been there. I was In Love. I had been in love before, but never like this. Never a love that felt so free, so honest. There is a wonderful song by Snow Patrol called 'Give Me Strenth' which sums up what I'm trying to say far better than I ever could. Give it a listen, I promise you'll enjoy it. It's impossible not to.

I felt that Jules allowed me to become the man I'd always wanted to be. A friend of mine told me the other day that Jules completed me, but I don't even think that's the half of it. It's hard to put into words quite how much I love her. Meeting her for the first time felt like the moment I started to find my own way out of the fog, or the forest or the labyrinth, or whatever analogy you'd like to use. She was there, waiting on the other side to make me whole again.

The only time we'd be apart was when Julia would have to go on trips with work. She went to Haiti and India within the first couple of months after we met, but from the minute she returned we would stay at each other's houses. We went on our first holiday together to the Maldives and it was the best time of my life. I came back so refreshed and no sooner had I landed than I got a call from Ben and Gabe, who said they had a new idea for something for us to do together.

When Ben and Gabe have an idea, it's always exciting. You never know quite when they're going to come, but when they do they're always worth listening to. They had two ideas that day. I went to meet them in a café near their offices of their company Fulwell 73, though it turned out it wasn't just them: Clyde Holcroft, a writer and producer, was there too. Clyde is one of the nicest guys you could ever wish to meet, and at the time he was working as a senior producer for *Sport Relief*, a BBC telethon that runs alternately with *Comic Relief*. I sat down and we all ordered coffee, except for Gabe, who ordered iced coffee, despite the fact it was snowing outside.

After the success of the last Smithy sketch, there had been lots of interest in doing another one for a different charity. In fact, there'd been offers for Smithy to do just about anything.

Most of them had been ridiculous: a TV series where Smithy travels round the world and tests lots of beers, endless adverts and – of course – football gaffes DVDs; offers were coming in pretty much every day. It didn't feel right to take the character away from the show. Ruth and I thought it could potentially cheapen the series to stop making the show but still cash in commercially on that character. I was interested to hear what the boys had come up with, though, as the idea of doing another charity sketch could be fun.

I could tell they thought they had something big. There was just that feeling in the room. Ben and Clyde both looked at Gabe and smiled. 'Tell him,' Ben said.

Gabe turned to me, took a sip of his iced latte and proceeded to show exactly why he's known to many as 'the ideas factory'. '*Sports Personality of the Year*. Smithy wins Coach of the Year,' he said with a smile. I thought about it for a second. *Yes!* This could be huge.

We immediately started talking about different ways we could do it; how he could talk about the changes in sport, say what true sports fans wanted to say themselves. As far as I was concerned, the only glitch was that *Sports Personality of the Year* was held in a quiet, controllable television studio, so how would we get the impact and the laughs we wanted? It had to be bigger. And then Clyde put me right: no, the studio, that was before – it was actually now held in an arena that would be full of 12,000 people. Ah.

Logistically, it was going to be a nightmare, but before we could even think about the speech, we had to work out exactly what form the sketch would take. We watched old videos of *Sports Personality* evenings and realised that, often, before giving the winner his or her award, they would show an edited summary of exactly why they were winning. We figured that this was as good a template as any to copy but, rather than Smithy just winning the award for the speech he'd given the England team, perhaps it would be funnier if he was shown being involved in all aspects of British sport. We immediately set about putting requests in with the biggest names: Jenson Button, Andy Murray, the Manchester United team, Tom Daley, David Beckham and Freddie Flintoff. Not one person we approached said no. All of them gave us their time and bought in to the idea.

We found time to film with them over the next few months and every single one of them was amazing: receiving a serve from Andy Murray, who is without question one of the warmest and funniest people I've had the pleasure to meet; jumping off a high board with Tom Daley – an unforgettable experience, though it's an odd feeling having your nerves calmed by a fifteen-year-old when you're both wearing Speedos; the fitness class with Man United – great fun, and Rio Ferdinand once again came through and made sure we got enough players to make it worthwhile. To film with Jenson Button, Ben and I had to fly out to Abu Dhabi. At first, when we got on the plane, we were told we'd have twenty minutes to film in the pit lane; when we landed, that had gone down to fifteen and, by the time we arrived at the racetrack, it was down to ten. The F1 officials were pretty strict about the time as the pit lane had to be opened for the practice laps to start. So we flew for eight hours, filmed for ten minutes and then turned round and had another eight-hour flight back.

So we'd got a few of the clips with the sportsmen in the bag, but everything was really hinging on the big speech. It is, without question, one of the most nerve-wracking things I've ever done. The BBC had been great about granting us access but because *Sports Personality* is filmed live, we were going to have to shoot our bit just before the actual show happened, when everyone was in their seats. Once the schedule had been finalised, it became clear we had eleven minutes – just eleven minutes! – to shoot what was looking like a ten-minute speech.

We got to the arena and all day my nerves were all over the place (not helped by the fact I'd been on my friend Jason's stag do with Gavin and Anthony the night before). I sat in my dressing room and kept running the speech over and over in my head. I had to start the speech at 6.45 p.m. and be finished by 6.56 p.m. and it was made very clear that I couldn't overrun by even half a minute. As the time ticked down, I called Jules to try and steady myself, then left the dressing room and stood by the stage, taking long, deep, nervous breaths. Then, in what seemed like no time, I was up on stage. As quickly as I could, I explained to the audience what we were doing, how it was for Sports Relief (Sports Relief was shown on TV a few months after this, so the speech wasn't broadcast live) and how if they felt like clapping, then to clap, and if they felt like standing, then they should stand. I basically asked them to imagine that Smithy had won this award and how amazing that would be. I went to take my seat and suddenly we were off.

Sue Barker started, then threw to Gary Lineker, who was standing with Sir Steve Redgrave. I, or rather Smithy, was sitting in the auditorium between Joe Calzaghe and Chris Eubank. Joe was great, but I'm not entirely convinced that Chris knew what was going on. I was so nervous and just trying to stay in character, but he kept trying to talk to me, asking me what was wrong. Why I was so nervous? I didn't have time to explain because in no time Sir Steve was calling Smithy's name.

Before, when we'd had our briefing, I'd been given strict instructions not to go near Capello. At this point in time, the BBC were so in awe of him that if he'd wanted to, they'd have let him host the *Nine O'Clock News*. Gabe and I had other ideas, however, and we decided that, if it felt right, then I had to go in for the hug on the way to the stage. I stood up, gave Chris Eubank a big kiss and strode down the aisle. Everybody was on their feet, applauding, and I was so fired up that I almost missed Capello. But I saw him, grabbed him and did the European double kiss on his cheeks. And then, when I got on stage, I shared another long and tender kiss (my third of the night) with

Sue Barker. A few people have since asked me what it was like to kiss Sue Barker and there's only one answer – exceptional. Mr Barker is one lucky man. The speech went better than I could ever have dreamt and was one of the best experiences I've ever had on stage. Something just clicked. I came off and felt elated. Ben gave me a look that told me we had it in the bag, so we decided to enjoy the night and indulge in a few drinks. The plan was just to have a couple of drinks as we had to be up early the next morning to film with Freddie Flintoff in the pedalo.

Freddie had been at the awards do, so we tracked him down and spent the night drinking together. Out of me, Ben, Gabe and Clyde, Gabe is without question the biggest cricket fan; for him, spending a night drinking with Fred was as good as it got. Gabe is a big presence and can match anyone for a drink and a party. Within the hour, Fred, Gabe and Fred's brother, Chris, all had horrendous red-wine lips and their speech was starting to slur. Fred was soon looking for the next party. Aware that we needed him fit and sober, we tried to persuade him that it was best to call it a night, so we bundled him into the back of a minibus, jumped in afterwards and told the driver to take us back to our hotels. I was so tired I started falling asleep in the cab but, just as I was slipping off, Freddie and Chris started bundling each other on the back seat. Gabe didn't need telling twice and, before long, a group of grown men were jumping all over one another in the back of the taxi. It was carnage. We got to our hotel first and, as we got out of the cab, Gabe leant in the door and said, 'Freddie, I cannot tell you what an honour it's been to drink with you tonight. It's been a real dream come true. You're a legend . . .' At that moment, Freddie moved towards Gabe as if he was going to hug him through the window, but instead he reached out a fist and smacked him right on the nose. A full-on punch! Ben and I stood there, open-mouthed, worried about how Gabe might react. He wiped the trickle of blood from his nose and then just burst into fits of laughter. Arms aloft, he shouted, 'Freddie Flintoff just punched me in the face. This is the best night of my life!' As the cab pulled away, we were all doubled over laughing. I've never felt more fortunate than the times when I've been able to work alongside my closest friends. It's not lost on me how lucky I've been to do such things. And the next trip we had planned showed just what a bunch of lucky bastards we were.

David Beckham had agreed to shoot something for the sketch, but we didn't know what or where or when. We found out the where was in Milan, the when was in a couple of weeks and we had to come up with a list of possible whats for David and his agent Simon to look at. Now, it's a tricky one to navigate when someone as big as David Beckham and his people ask you to offer suggestions. How do you play it? We only had an hour to film in his hotel suite so we decided that what we'd do is put a few outlandish suggestions at the top and then, by the time they'd said 'no' to a few things, the next batch would seem more realistic. So top of our list we put: share a bed with Smithy watching a film, have a bath together, have Smithy restyling David's hair and flower arranging. There was no way on earth they'd say 'yes' to them, so our next few ideas were: trying on clothes, having a romantic candlelit meal and spring cleaning together – much easier to sell . . .

We waited for the response, and an hour later Simon called to say he was happy to do everything we'd asked. (He also said David was looking forward to getting in the bath with me.) We couldn't believe it. Never in a million years did we think that they would go for all the crazy stuff we'd asked for. A week later we were on the plane to Milan.

When we got to David's hotel, Ben sent Simon a text telling him we had arrived and Simon said that he, David and the whole AC Milan team were having dinner in town and that we should come and join them. The team had played that day and the manager had given them the following day off training, which meant the squad could let their beautiful Italian hair down. And boy, were they letting their hair down. We got there and David welcomed us like long-lost friends and made us feel incredibly welcome. I was sitting opposite Paolo Maldini, who, like most of the squad, was drinking neat vodka. A guy called Ricky who took a particular liking to me started pouring me full tumblers of vodka and not letting me stop until I'd downed the whole glass. David told us that it was rare for the whole team to be out together, so this was probably going to turn into a big night. He wasn't wrong. Ambrosini and the other members of the team seemed intent on getting us really drunk. At one point the rapper Coolio came over and started speaking with a couple of players – I was so drunk I thought I was seeing things.

David left a bit earlier than us, probably when he saw Gabe dancing on a table with Flamini like they were best friends. By that point I was totally out of it too: I'd fallen asleep in the corner of the room twice and could barely speak. We eventually left out of the back of the bar and were heading home when Simon saw a bar that was open and said, 'I've heard this place is good. Look, I think they're still open. Let's have a nightcap.' We turned, looked, looked again and then fell about laughing – it was the place we'd just left.

The hotel was a ten-minute walk away, but it took us well over an hour. Thankfully, when we woke the next day, the shoot had been pushed back to the afternoon. If it had still been in the morning, I'd doubt we'd have ever got it done. We'd been told we could only shoot for an hour but, four hours after we started, the cameras were still rolling. David was incredible. He brought so much to the sketch. All of the dialogue in the sketch was improvised and I've got to say, his acting really surprised me. It was his idea that we both wear towels on our heads like women. For four hours we could barely keep a straight face. And then, the bath.

Now, getting in the bath with David Beckham is still up there as one of the most bizarre things I've ever done. We were both sitting there, just having a chat about anything and everything, and all the time I was thinking about the times I'd watched England play, how he'd made me jump out of my seat for joy: the free kick against Greece that took us to the Euros, the penalty against Argentina in the World Cup and all the other beautiful footballing moments. And here I was, in my pants, in the bath with him. If I'd moved my foot two inches to the left, it would have been stroking the golden balls of Goldenballs.

When filming had finished, David asked everyone to join him for dinner at his favourite restaurant in town. Not just us, the cameraman and soundman too. Being around him was a lesson in how to behave professionally and courteously. It made me think of my behaviour over the last couple of years and how being nice is so much easier than being arrogant or trying to be seen as one thing or another. When the sketch went out a few months later at Sports Relief, it was received better than any of us could've dared imagine. Ben, Gabe and I stood at the back of the studio at the BBC when they played it live to the audience, and hearing the roars of laughter was something I'll never forget.

Remember I said that at the café all those months ago there had been two ideas? Well, the other was just as exciting, and it came from Clyde. The 2010 World Cup was on the horizon and Clyde had been thinking about a TV show that could broadcast live post-match. He had talked to Suzi Aplin, who is one of the greatest producers in the country. She had some serious credentials, having been responsible for shows such as *TFI Friday* and *Friday Night with Jonathan Ross*, so we thought we had a good chance at getting something made. I've never really considered myself a TV presenter, but it's something I've always enjoyed doing, which is more than enough reason to do it.

So Ben and I went to the BBC with the idea of *James Corden's World Cup Live*, selling it to them on the basis that, although we couldn't guarantee access to the England team, since we'd worked with them before, we had a good shot at getting it. We told them it would be live, unpredictable, would have big guests and discuss all the big stories that happened at the World Cup. Unfortunately, the BBC turned it down. They liked the idea of the show but thought it would be expensive to make. Plus, they'd already decided they'd do all their post-show stuff from South Africa so they didn't have a slot for it. We were gutted. We'd been sure they would go for it. Actually, we'd been so confident that we'd set up a meeting with Adrian Bevington, the communications director of the FA, only an hour after our meeting with the BBC, to talk about access to the team.

We couldn't back out of the meeting with the FA so we sat in their offices pitching a show we knew wasn't going to happen. And here's the irony: they loved it. And as far as access to the players was concerned, they would help us as much as they could. Balls! If anything, the good news from the FA made us more depressed. We had access to film the players, but no TV show to put them on. But, then again, what we also had was an incredible executive producer in Suzi Aplin (I should say here that I love Suzi both professionally and personally, probably more than I should. I'd go so far as to say it's almost sexual. She is just brilliant at her job), and as Ben and I made our way out of the swanky offices of the FA, dejected and barely talking, Ben stopped and started reading an email on his phone. It was from Suzi and it simply said, 'I've told Peter Fincham at ITV about the show and he wants us to come in and pitch . . . tomorrow!'

Peter Fincham really got the idea and, once we'd calmed a few of his nerves about my lack of presenting experience, he told us he was up for it. We came up with an idea that we'd try and film an activity with each of the England team. It was a tricky one to navigate as we didn't know who was going to make the final squad, but we had to get as many in the can as possible. We cooked with Rio Ferdinand, golfed with Steven Gerrard, boxed with Jermain Defoe, bowled with Michael Carrick, practised Pilates with Rob Green, and did loads of other crazy things with the rest of the squad. The players were brilliant. They all wanted to be involved and the only demand they made was that their appearance fee would be donated to a charity of their choice.

They were all fantastic company, and really warm, genuine nice guys. I can't tell you how many times I would look around and see them helping members of the crew move filming equipment from one location to the next. They are often painted as money-grabbing mercenaries who couldn't care less about the game or the fans. But from where I've been standing, that couldn't be further from the truth.

CHAPTER 22

BEST MUSICAL ACCOMPANIMENT:
'Ooh La La' by the Faces

BEST FILM TO WATCH ALONGSIDE:
Back to the Future (not the third one)

BEST ENJOYED WITH:
rusks and milk

So this is it, the last chapter of the book. The publisher has just told me that I'm already 5,000 words over the required amount, which I can't quite believe. Imagine telling my teachers at school – like Mr Graham or Mr Hopkins – that I'd been set an essay and not only finished it, and handed it in, but had written more words than was contractually required!

This last chapter has come at just the right time. At this moment, as I'm sitting at my kitchen table typing, it's 7 a.m. and I'm all alone in the house. However, in two hours' time I shall be picking Jules and my newborn son up from the hospital to bring them home and, for the first time, we'll be here as a family. I'm so nervous about it. It does make me wonder about the future and quite how it's all going to change. It also makes me think of what may become of me professionally: I have responsibilities now, mouths to feed. The last year has been really good to me. As well as the things I've already told you about, I've shot another three series of *A League of Their Own*, which keeps getting bigger and better and remains the same brilliant fun. Oh yeah, and I've had a number one single in the charts with Dizzee Rascal – I know, ridiculous! Who would ever've thought?

Here's how it happened: at the National Television Awards, Simon Cowell came over and talked to me about the idea of doing a World Cup song. I'd been asked to do a few World Cup songs before and turned them down, but this was Simon and he is incredibly difficult to say no to. We talked some more on the phone and he told me he had a song that he'd like his A & R guy Nick Raymond to come over and play to me. I agreed, and a couple of days later I was in my kitchen listening to the song with Nick. It was a catchy little tune – a mix of samples from Blackstreet's 'No Diggity' with 'Shout' by Tears for Fears. In between there was this rap – nothing to do with football, just a rap laid down on the track.

'So what do you want me to do?' I asked him.

'The rap,' Nick said. 'We want you to do the rap.'

'You're joking. Are you mad? I can't rap.'

'Sure you can. We've seen you do it on *Gavin & Stacey*.'

'Yeah, but come on,' I said. 'That's a very different thing. I mean, a character rapping on a TV show is one thing, but releasing a record – I can't do that, I just can't.'

'James –' he was looking hard at me now – 'Simon told me I'm not allowed to leave here until you agree.'

At this point I got up to make a cup of tea. 'Nick,' I said, 'you have to understand, I know we're talking about Simon Cowell, but I will never rap on your record. It would be awful for you. It would be awful for me. It would be awful for music generally. I like Simon, I do, but it's just not going to happen.'

'OK,' he said, 'I can appreciate that, but what if I get a rapper to do it with you?'

'A rapper?'

He nodded.

'I'll tell you what,' I said. 'The only rapper you could get would be Dizzee Rascal. He's the only person with the right sense of humour, the only one who could pull it off and the only guy I'd do it with.' I'd met Dizzee a few times and really liked him.

'All right then,' Nick said, as I guided him to the door. 'So you're telling me that if we get Dizzee, you're in. I can tell Simon that, can I?'

'Yeah, you can tell him that,' I said, shaking his hand. 'Good luck, Nick. You'll never get him.'

Closing the door, I grinned at Jules and Ben, who had been there during the meeting. 'Well, we swerved that one, didn't we?' I said, confident that this was the last we'd hear of it.

Two weeks later I was in a studio with Dizzee Rascal, recording Simon's song for the World Cup. The power of the Cowell.

The record came out and, before I knew it, I was performing on *Britain's Got Talent* with Dizzee. It was the live final, with 20 million people tuning in. I remember scratching my head and thinking back to that moment in my flat when I managed to 'swerve' this moment so effectively. It was number one for two weeks. And I'm glad I did it. I had a brilliant time on *Britain's Got Talent*, and it was great fun working with Dizzee and Simon Cowell. I'd been reticent at first – with good reason: I ain't no rapper – but once we agreed to give the money to Great Ormond Street Hospital, it was a no-brainer.

After *World Cup Live* was finished, I went out to shoot another big-budget film, *The Three Musketeers*, which, at the time of writing, I've yet to see, but the trailer looks good and it was great filming it. I play the musketeers' servant, so I basically walked behind some really good-looking guys carrying their bags. I've no idea how my part will come out in the edit, but working with Paul W. S. Anderson, the director, was a great experience. I also filmed two episodes of *Doctor Who*, which is something I'm incredibly proud to have been part of. If I had my way, I'd work with Matt Smith every day of the week. He is the most splendid company. I hosted the Brits again and have been asked back to do it in 2012. I had a silly spat with Patrick Stewart at an awards do, which lots of people went crazy over, but we're all made up now. We are, we hugged and everything. And now, as I write this, I'm about to go back to the National Theatre to do a play for six months. It's called *One Man, Two Guvnors*, and Nicholas Hytner – who is now actually Sir Nicholas Hytner – is going to direct it. He called me whilst I was doing *World Cup Live* and the conversation went like this:

'Hi James,' he said.

'Hi Sir Nicholas,' I replied respectfully.

'Ha!' he laughed. 'Listen, would you like to do a play next year at the National Theatre?'

I thought for half a second. 'Are you directing it?'

'If you do it, then I most probably will—'

I didn't even wait for him to carry on speaking. 'YES,' I said.

'Do you not want to know what play it is?'

'I don't care. If it's with you at the National Theatre, then I would love to do it.'

Some people have said that I was mad to commit to something I'd not read or crazy to not take more time about the decision. But I think all eight of the history boys have a romantic attachment to Nick and that building, and would bite someone's arm off to be back there, working with him again. The play is a new adaptation of an Italian farce called *The Servant of Two Masters*. I hope it's going to be funny. It certainly feels so, but you never quite know how these things are going to pan out. I'm excited about doing it, though – and about being in a rehearsal room again.

People have asked me what I'd like to do in the future and I guess when I really sit down and think about it, the answer's quite boringly simple: I'm just hoping for more of the same. I feel so privileged to be able to do so many different things. Actually, I'm not sure if 'able' is the word here: many people are 'able' to do different things, but for one reason or another, they aren't allowed to do them. I feel incredibly fortunate that I'm in a position to do such varied things professionally. One of the questions I get asked most is whether we'll make any more *Gavin & Stacey*. I hope one day we'll find the time to make a one-off special. I don't think Ruth and I will ever make another series, but we do often talk about the characters and where we might find them if we did make a special. One day, we would definitely like to try and write something else together, whether that be a film or a new television series. The thought of being back in a room with her again makes me so excited. Ruth, me and a laptop, it doesn't get more fun than that.

In my personal life, I couldn't be happier. A few months ago, on a cold, icy Christmas Day morning, I asked Jules to marry me. It was a moment I will never forget. I knelt down, looking up at her, my eyes filling with tears, with a ring I'd designed myself shaking in my left hand. She said yes! I cannot wait to marry her. I already see her as my wife and it'll be lush to make it official.

Now, if you don't mind, if you have time, I'd just like to share one more story with you. It's something else I get asked about a lot, so it would feel odd not to include it in this book. A couple of months ago I made one more sketch for Comic Relief. Since the success of the previous two Smithy outings, Comic Relief asked if I'd be able to make another one. Ben, Gabe and I felt as though we'd possibly peaked with the last Sports Relief one, and to make another seemed risky. Clyde, however, felt we should definitely give it a try so, although we wouldn't fully commit to doing it, we said we'd certainly explore the possibilities of making one. We talked about maybe Smithy doing something in America, him being a life coach, or retiring from public life and going to live with Emma Watson. Clyde and Gabe wrote a script that required four full days filming with Tom Cruise. Ben and I agreed that this might be a touch ambitious. We got to a point where we were all having ideas that were totally unrealistic. We'd been so lucky before, because

Smithy had essentially walked into rooms that were full of the people we wanted to film with. All we had to do was turn up and switch the camera on. Now we wanted to do something where we had as impressive a cast list, but didn't know how we could get them all together at the same time. Whichever way we imagined it, we couldn't make it work, and I felt as though we should probably put it to bed. And then the genius that is Suzi Aplin had a brainwave.

She was producing Comic Relief this year, and she sent us over a video link of a sketch from an American TV show. It was Jimmy Kimmel's post-Oscar-night sketch called 'The Handsome Men's Club'. It featured a really impressive cast list – Ethan Hawke, Rob Lowe, Matt Damon, Sting and a few more – and was shot round a table where they had made it appear as if everyone was sitting together. This showed us how technically it was possible to shoot the biggest and best cast we could assemble and still make it work round everyone's schedules.

We set about trying to write a script and decided, as we had before, that we'd write it for the biggest people that we could think of, and if they said no, we'd adjust the script accordingly. The main premise for the script was a group of celebrities seated round a table at Comic Relief HQ, arguing about who they thought should go to Africa and shoot the appeal film. They all wanted to do it, but each time they put themselves forward, they'd be gazumped by the opinions of a more famous person sitting at the table with them. It would be a series of reveals, where the fame levels would just keep rising and rising, getting more and more ridiculous. We'd learnt from having done a couple of these before that we needed to start at the end – find one or two bona fide famous people to say yes and then everyone else would most likely fall into place. And we decided that the biggest and best person we could approach had to be Sir Paul McCartney.

We chose to ask him first as I had already been lucky enough to have some contact with him. When we were doing *World Cup*

Live the summer before, I'd got a phone call telling me that Paul McCartney wanted to speak to me. At first I thought it was a wind-up by one of the boys in the production office. A day earlier I'd thrown a bit of a tantrum, saying that the guests being booked for the show weren't big enough. I thought this was some sweet payback. I soon realised it was real when I got a call from one of his people telling me that Paul would be calling at 11.30 a.m. I had no idea what he wanted or why he would want to speak to me but, as you can imagine, I was incredibly excited. Maybe he'd got hold of a Twice Shy demo tape and wanted to talk about collaborating on some tracks.

At 11.10 a.m. the phone rang; it was another of Paul's people asking me if I was near the phone. 'Erm . . . yeah. I'm holding it in my hand now. That's how I'm able to speak to you,' I said to the polite young lady.

'No, I know,' she said. 'I know you're near it now. I just wanted to check that you're not about to go into any tunnels or lose signal.'

'No. I'll be right here. I'm looking forward to it.'

'Even if you need the toilet, you'll still take the phone with you, right?' she added.

'Yes,' I chuckled. 'In fact, I'm waiting till I get on the phone to the legend that is Sir Paul McCartney so that I can be sitting on the toilet when I speak to him.'

'Good. Well, that's great. Just wanted to check.' Not sure she got the gag.

I waited by the phone and, as it turned eleven thirty, it rang. 'Withheld number' flashed up on my phone.

'Hello?' I said tentatively.

'Hi, James, it's Paul,' said Paul McCartney in the soft Liverpudlian lilt you've heard a million times but never, ever expect to hear over the phone.

'Hello, sir, how are you?' I said, and then tried a little small talk. 'What have you been up to?'

Paul told me that he'd just flown home from Washington DC where he'd been honoured for his contribution to American arts and culture. The award had come from the Kennedy Center and had been bestowed on him by President Barack Obama. Sir Paul was the first non-American ever to receive the award and, after the ceremony, he had played a private gig at the White House. Jerry Seinfeld had compèred the evening and Paul said it was a really special night. It was followed by a personal tour of the West Wing from Obama himself. It had been one of the very best nights of his entire life, and he was telling me all about it on the phone. I was so amazed at how open he was. However, once he'd finished telling me about his week, he asked me what I'd been up to. I had no idea what to say. I mean, how do you follow the story he'd just told me? Flustered, but trying to sound cool, I said, 'Oh, er . . . I'm doing this World Cup show and we just came up with a game called "How many Peter Joneses?"'

'Oh right,' said Sir Paul, very politely sounding interested.

'Well, erm . . . you have to guess how many . . . well, Peter Joneses it would take to get from, say . . . Wembley to South Africa. That's pretty much what I've been doing.'

We talked about how lovely Peter Jones was in real life, and then I asked Paul what it was he wanted to speak to me about. He went on to tell me how much he'd enjoyed the Sports Relief sketch and had watched and liked various other things I'd done and that he wanted me, as Smithy, to introduce him on stage at the Isle of Wight Festival in a couple of weeks' time. He thought it would go down really well with the crowd and, if I was up for it, he'd love me to do it.

I couldn't believe what I was hearing. Paul McCartney wanted me to introduce him on stage? I told him I was blown away that he had even seen anything I had done and promised that I would do everything in my power to make it happen.

Once I was off the phone, I skipped straight into Ben's office and told him the news. He was as shocked as I was. While I was excitedly pacing around, Ben took a moment to look at the diary and delivered the bombshell. 'We've got a show that night, James. You can't do it. Sorry, dude.'

He was right, I couldn't do it. I even rang ITV and asked if we could do the show live from backstage at the festival, which, of course, they didn't even consider. I remember saying to anyone who would listen, 'But it's Paul McCartney! He was in the Beatles!' So, after a bit more whining, I called up Paul's people and delivered the news and told them how upset I was that I couldn't do it, but if Paul was still looking for an intro, I could film something that he could play on the screens. Paul said that would be great, so I filmed a big build-up for him. When I saw him at an event a week or so later, he thanked me and told me it had gone down well with the crowd.

So, with a favour in the bag, I thought we had a good shot at trying to get Sir Paul. We knew he liked the last Comic Relief sketch; plus we'd got on well when we met before. Clyde got in touch with his people, who told me I was to call Paul at midday. I jokingly asked Clyde if he'd call at 11.45 and ask Paul if he was by the phone, but he immediately told me to stop being a dick. This was big time, and I had to be prepared and know exactly what I was going to say. When midday came, I called Paul and explained the rough outline of the script. I told him the names of some of the people we were hoping would be involved, and then I launched into full charity-grovel mode. I told him that we would make the whole experience as fun and painless as possible, that we'd shoot it whenever was good for him and that, because now the sketches could be bought as digital downloads, it could make a decent chunk of money that would go towards people all over the world who desperately needed it. I then played the trump card: the simple fact of his involvement in the sketch would, without question, change people's lives. He paused and I could hear the smile come into his voice. 'Well,' he said, 'I've gotta tell you, James. I've heard some grovelling in my time, but that was the best yet. Have you got that written down?'

I laughed and told him that he hadn't heard anything yet. I told him that if he'd said no, I was going to offer to name my unborn child after him. Down the phone I could hear Paul burst out laughing. 'You're on. That's it. If you name your child after me, I'll do your sketch.' We both had a giggle and then, very graciously, he went on to say that – all joking aside – he would love to be involved. 'Count me in!' were his exact words.

I was chuffed to bits and so were the boys. But Paul was just the first domino to fall. The next person on our list of hopefuls was George Michael. I am, and always will be, a massive fan of George and his music; so many of his songs mean something to me. From the moment we started the script, I was sure that music would be the magic ingredient the sketch needed at the start and at the end to really lift it. Music would make the whole thing move with more pace, and the thought of Smithy and George acting like old mates in the same tracksuit tops was an image I couldn't – and didn't want to – shake. George was away in Australia but, after two or three 4 a.m. calls, he said he was up for doing the sketch. Just as we predicted, once we had those two, everyone else started wanting to be a part of it. Rupert Grint, Tom Felton, Lord Robert Winston, Tom Daley, Lord Sebastian Coe, Rio Ferdinand – who once again stepped up to the plate and gave the acting performance of his life – Keira Knightley, JLS, Dermot O'Leary, Clare Balding. Ringo Starr amazingly said yes as well, and filmed his stuff down the line from America; the former prime minister Gordon Brown even agreed to be in it and was the most fantastic sport, as did Davina McCall, Richard Madeley, Roger Lloyd-Pack, Justin Bieber, Lenny Henry and Richard Curtis. Phew. Think that's everyone.

It was the cast list we'd dreamt of, and over the next couple of months we filmed and filmed and filmed again. Technically it was a nightmare, and I take my hat off to Ben for making it happen so smoothly. Everyone was fantastic. For me the highlight of the whole experience was driving around in Smithy's Volvo with George Michael. He was such a good laugh and, in fact, the line about Smithy and Gavlar being closet bummers was all George. As co-incidence might have it, we were driving up and down the A40, the very road that years ago was the scene of my disappointment when Dad asked me if I wanted to knock the acting thing on the head. In just over twenty years, it was now witness to me and one of my heroes singing our hearts out to 'I'm Your Man'.

When the sketch finally aired, the response was bigger than for the other two sketches put together. The next day, people were calling it the greatest sketch ever made on a Comic Relief night. I'm not saying this is true, but it was nice that somebody thought it was. Immediately afterwards, the inevitable question came as to what we would do next year. I'm not sure we'll ever beat what we did in that sketch, but we've said that before, so who knows? I'm incredibly proud of it. I'm proud of Ben, Gabe and Clyde, and will for ever be thankful to all the people in front of and behind the scenes who made it happen.

I'm thankful for all of it really. All of the stuff that I've mentioned in this book – the ups and the downs. I'm grateful for every single moment. Just the fact that you, whoever you are, wherever you may be, are even reading this is enough to blow my mind. The truth is, often I'm not sure what I've done to deserve all this. To have so many great memories.

In just a few moments I will walk out of my front door and when I return I'll have my son and fiancée with me, all three of us together at home for the first time. We will, from now, start to become a family. My whole world is going to change, and I'm incredibly excited about it. And as I look back on the boy I wrote about at the start of this book, the boy who needed all that constant attention, who craved the limelight like oxygen, well, I realise I don't feel that any more – not as much, anyway. I still have ambi-tion, lots of it, and there are still plenty of things I dream of achieving. But 'attention' is perhaps not the right word for it any more. The flame is still there; it just doesn't burn quite as brightly. Now everything I need I get from Jules and my son. It's their love and their attention that's the most important thing to me now.

So, finally, it's time for me to go and bring him home. Here we go. Have I got everything Jules put on the list? Car seat? Yes. Thing to attach the car seat to the back seat of the car? Yes. Hat for the baby? Yes. Cardigan for the baby? Yes. Baby wipes? Yes. Bib? Yes. God, this is it now, isn't it? Endless lists of stuff. This is only going to intensify.

Here goes . . . Wish me luck!

Oh, and by the way, we've decided on a name for him. Oh yes. His name is . . . Max McCartney Kimberley Corden.

ACKNOWLEDGEMENTS

I've decided to use this opportunity to not just thank people connected to this book, but people to whom I owe so much.

There are so many people to thank for so many things. These are just the tip of the iceberg:

Firstly, I have to thank my publisher, friend and dance teacher, Jack Fogg. He has been a constant source of encouragement and this book would never have been written without him. He has been there on the end of the phone at every point, both good and bad. Thank you, Jack. Let's do some more fun things together.

Everyone else who is better looking than Jack at Century, which is basically everyone else at Century. Thanks for everything. You really are the best.

My agent, Ruth Young. For your wisdom, encouragement, and endless faith. I'd be lost without you.

Jess Alford, for your skills, groove and incredible loveliness.

Robert Kirkby. (Officially the writer's agent of the year). I now know why.

Clair Dobbs, for working so hard and guiding me in the in the right direction.

Gavin Early, Anthony Belcher and Jason Todd. My dearest friends, never will that change.

Ben Winston. My brother from another mother. My best friend. You shining light of friendship and loyalty. 'Thank you' isn't a big enough word.

Gabe Turner. The white Viera. There it is. In print. It's official.

Meri and Lauren. For being so incredible to your men, and the missus.

Leo Pearlman and Ben Turner. Fulwell 73. Let's do this.

Gary Lightbody. Never have I loved a man so fast. Thank you for the love, laughs and music.

Pam and Barry. For creating the greatest person on earth and immediately making me feel at home.

Louis Weymouth. So basically old bean it's blush, blush . . .

Ruth Jones. What a journey?! 'Friend' seems too small a word. I love you and I always will.

Dominic Cooper. Drop the pilot and paint my balloon. Where would I be without you, Levine.

Sir Nicholas Hytner. I will never be able to thank you enough. But I'll always try.

Mat Horne. What a rollercoaster, Cheeseman. Man Hugs now, tomorrow and after that.

Henry Normal, Linzi Hughes and Ted Dowd. The cow massive. Amazing.

Ben Cavey. You are so fit.

Danny Cohen. For your warmth, guidance and most importantly your forgiveness.

Russell Rook. My spiritual guru. Lunch?!

Peter Jones. The tallest lovely man in the world.

Take That. For being so damn good.

Richard Shed, Scott Rodgers, Greg Pearson and Kevin Wilkinson. Always.

Mathew Baynton and Jim Field Smith. The Right Mans.

James Gallimore. For knowing your stuff. Thank God!

Nick Jones and Kirsty. The kindest and most lovely people on the planet.

Richard Curtis, Kevin Cahill and everyone at Comic Relief and Sport Relief.

Clydo. Brighton's best kept secret.

Rankin. Quite simply the best photographer in the world.

Donald Mcinnes. The best in the business. I love you. Thanks for making me better looking!

Suzi Aplin. For your energy, warmth, encouragement, vision and beautiful face.

Stuart Murphy. For seeing things we didn't know were there. And still seeing more!

Marilyn Phillips. Thank you for believing.

Jacquie Drewe. For kickstarting all of this.

The other seven History Boys. I love and miss you all.

To anyone who classes me as a friend. I hope I'm a good one to you.

My mother and my father. My thanks to you is for everything. I love you both so much.

Joel and Ellen. You will never know how much you two coming along changed all of us.

Andrea and Ian. My big sister who sometimes knows me better than anyone and Ian, her wonderful husband and father.

Rudi. Reeyads, Ruth, my way buddy. Always. You saviour. We'll always have L.A. Marry him if he asks you.

My darling Julia. Thank you for putting up with so many things. For being so amazingly supportive all the time. For letting me be me. For laughing and smiling even when you know what jokes are coming. For being the greatest mum in the world. For making my heart smile again. I could be anywhere with you and I know I'd be happy.

And Max. You young man. Well, you've changed everything. And you don't even know it!

x

PICTURE ACKNOWLEDGEMENTS

The author and publishers would like to thank the following copyright-holders for permission to reproduce images in this book:

©Rex Features; ©Neil Bennett; ©*Radio Times* magazine; ©Nicky Johnston / *Heat* magazine; ©Steve Bagness / Matrixpictures.co.uk; ©The *Daily Telegraph* 2009; ©Guardian News & Media Ltd 2009; ©Sarah Dunn; ©Ted Dowd; ©Rachel Joseph; ©Des Willie; ©Comic Relief; ©Guy Levy; ©Dave Nelson; ©David Pullum; ©Stuart Wood; ©Hamish Brown; ©Toby Merritt.

All other images are care of the author.

The author and publishers have made all reasonable efforts to contact copyright-holders for permission, and apologise for any omissions or errors in the form of credits given. Corrections may be made to future printings.